This book is about fathers and
biological father, Marian disco........ ....
of faith leads her onto a treacherous road of self-discovery with
many surprises she did not expect. I was compelled to read
every page as Marian describes with painstaking detail the story
of her restoration that leads the reader into the very presence
of the God who gives each person saving grace who asks Him.
An inspirational and life-giving book for anyone whose life has
spiraled out of control.

—Tetsuo Peter Yoshida, MDiv,
Princeton Theological Seminary
American Theatre Wing Professional School
Professional Performer in film, TV, and theatre

Marian Poeppelmeyer has opened her life to all of us who have
the privilege to read her story. It is inspiring, heart-opening, and
compelling. As you follow her insightful journey, your own life
can be revealed for your healing.

—Lillian Zarzar, MA, CSP
Author, Interpersonal Coach, Professional Speaker
Adjunct Faculty Communication Studies, Ohio University

Marian has an amazing story of redemption and healing! It is a
great testimony to the power of forgiveness and that it's never
too late to forgive those who have hurt us and our loved ones.

—John Finch, Author, *The Father Effect*
Producer and Director, documentary film, *The Father Effect*
Founder of the Perfect Father Ministries, Inc.

In *Finding My Father*, Marian Poeppelmeyer brilliantly discusses
the impact of tragedies, trauma, and fatherlessness. Because of
events occurring since 9/11, her story is pertinent and timeless.

Well-researched and told with gut-wrenching transparency, her compelling story takes the reader through her journey of healing from the tragic death of her father. Responding to sobering questions that rock the soul, Marian offers answers of hope for a future fashioned out of the ashes of life. Throughout her healing quest, she shares her awareness of the character of God displayed through tumultuous times. Once you start reading her gripping drama, you will not be able to put this book down and may find yourself on your personal road to healing and lasting freedom.

—Lonnell E. Johnson, PhD
Retired Professor of English, Otterbein University
Author, Motivational, Speaker, Coach
Embracing Your Life Sentence: How to Turn Life's
Greatest Tragedies into Your Greatest Triumphs

I never knew you could grieve for a person you had never met. Then I followed Marian on her journey of profound loss in *Finding My Father*. Her desire to know her real dad and the trials she endured sent her on a riveting, soul-searching quest. This intricately woven path led her through many unexpected twists and turns and is guaranteed to touch every reader on many levels.

—Stacey Greene
Author, Life Coach and Speaker,
Letters to the Dead Men
and *Stronger Than Broken*

As a Trauma Counselor, Marian's story was of particular interest to me. Her life began with trauma, which she bore silently for many years until the day her emotions erupted. Like a caterpillar in its cocoon, God began wrapping her in His love, revealing truth to her, and transforming her through His amazing plan. Written with such rare depth of transparency, you will admire her hunger for wholeness and willingness to be real and honest about herself. You will be swept along her journey of healing and be amazed at how God released her from her struggles and what she discovered. But you will also marvel at the ways God brought her to total healing through His love for her. I find this book to be an excellent additional resource for counselors and for those who have faced trauma, grief, and loss in their lives.

—Millie McCarty, M.A., LPCC, Founder and Ex. Dir. Emeritus, Lighthouse Counseling Services; Founder & CEO, International Institute for Trauma Recovery, Trainer and Clinical Consultant; Author of *Pathways to Hope and Healing—Why We Can't "Just Get Over It," Identity Disorders and Trauma Recovery Workbook, RUTH: Secrets of the Silenced Voices, and A Guide to Working with People with Dissociative.*

Finding My Father

Finding My *Father*

Beyond Tragedy, Through Trauma, and Into Freedom

A True Story

Marian Poeppelmeyer

Printed in the United States of America

Published by Author Academy Elite
P.O. Box 43
Powell, OH 43065

www.authoracademyelite.com

Library of Congress Control Number: 2019937015

ISBN: 978-1-64085-629-5 (Paperback)
ISBN: 978-1-64085-630-1 (Hardback)
ISBN: 978-1-64085-631-8 (eBook)

Available in paperback, hardback, e-book, and audiobook.

All scriptures taken from the Modern English Version and marked (MEV). Copyright © 2014 by Military Bible Association. Used by permission. All rights reserved.

Psalm 68:5, Psalm 10:14, and John 14:18 quotations taken from The Holy Bible, New International Version® NIV®. Copyright© 1973 1978 1984 2011 by Biblica, Inc.™ Used by permission. All rights reserved nationwide. All marked (NIV).

Any internet addresses (websites, blogs, etc.) and telephone numbers printed in this book are offered as a resource. They are not intended in any way to be or imply an endorsement by the author and Author Academy Elite, nor does the author or Author Academy Elite vouch for the content of these sites and numbers for the life of this book.

Some names have been changed or omitted to protect confidentiality. The non-fictional narrative is based upon a true story, with the assistance of conversations with Marty H. Weber (1924-1998) and her letters. Other references sited in the notes. Sources of historic photos are indicated when possible; most are public domain. Recording of events are from the perspective of the author.

Cover design: Debbie O'Byrne, JetLaunch.net
Illustration: Rebecca Chambers and Colen Poeppelmeyer

Dedication

To my father, Marion Pierce Hobgood,
whom I never knew this side of heaven.
I will see you one day. Your life was never in vain.

To my mother, Martha M. Hobgood Weber,
who never showed any bitterness.
You taught me to love, show grace, and
extend mercy to others.

And to the surviving families of the many victims of
bombings, mass killings, shootings, and murders,
who, like me, are having to learn how to live
beyond tragedy, through trauma, and into freedom.

A father to the fatherless, a defender of widows,
is God in his holy dwelling.

—Psalm 68:5 (NIV)

Contents

Act III: Into Freedom

Contents

ACT IV

Epilogue

Appendices

Foreword

From my decade of teaching at the Christian Outreach School of Ministries, our faculty discovered in our Counseling I and II courses that many students confided, "Please slow the course down. *I need* to get *myself* together…to get healed in my *own* life first before I go out and minister to others!"

This is how Marian's book will help you and so many others. I have prayed for and counseled with many people over the years, and Marian's *Finding My Father* illuminates aspects of the healing process I had never seen. I have never before considered what it's like to be the one processing through spiritual and emotional healing until now.

Do you have any disconnect with your dad? Marian understands all too well and takes you through her journey to find her dad. She tells her own story as it unfolded in her life; yes, before she was born and on into her early 40s, she recounts it with relentless—even ruthless—honesty. At the same time, she has balanced her insights with the latest research.

Marian will tell you how she was delivered from incredible bondage, devilish sneak attacks, and fiery verbal arrows:

"You just need to grow up. Get over it!" is not the right thing to be told when searching for your father.

"You need counseling" was another good-intentioned remark Marian had to overcome.

"You need to forgive that person." Sure, but when it hurts so bad, how do you forgive?

Marian grasps the complexity of deep-rooted pain as she wrestled with this very question. Read the revelations she receives and how the joy of the Holy Spirit *first* opened and scrubbed out her corked-up bottle so her forgiveness could be pure and not contaminated with hurt and anger.

Marian's message invokes the questions: Did God give us our fathers, however imperfect, so we could better know His Father's heart toward us? Or, does He reveal His Fatherly goodness to fill in those father wounds we each have?

Marian shows us that God can work it for our best starting from *either* side: We can find Father God's tender love despite having a dad with faults and flaws; a dad who is completely missing in action; or a dad who is even criminally abusive. Though imperfect, the warmth and support of a very involved, loving, and godly earthly dad shows us a glimpse of God's love. God knew us before we were born, and indeed, He helps all of us in Finding Our Father.

This book is a gift to the orphan, the broken-hearted, counselors, and the church and must get into the hands of many.

May these pages release Heavenly Father's healing and confident spiritual footing in all aspects of your life!

—David J. Martin, MDiv, former Director and
Academic Dean Christian Outreach School of
Ministries; Pastoral Prayer-Counselor with
Cleansing Stream Ministry since 2006

Act I
Beyond Tragedy

Scene 1

Where Were You on 9/11?

It was September 11, 2001, New York City, NY. *THE* 9/11.

Each of us alive during that day will never forget. We can recall where we were and what we were doing at that exact moment. The whole world watched; nothing would ever be the same; and, I remember it all too well.

On staff at a megachurch, when the news broke, we hurried from our cramped cubicles and offices into a large atrium. TV screens and chairs had been set up by administrative staff. We stared at the repeating broadcasts. All the news networks pre-empted previously scheduled programming to cover the disaster.

Plane number one flew straight into the first tower. Smoke billowed. Eventually, the building began to crumble. Moments later, a second plane flew directly into the second tower. Most of the staff sat or stood, mouths dropped, and eyes opened with horror.

As the buildings imploded, the TV cameramen along with crowds of people were frantically running for their lives as massive clouds of smoke rolled behind them through the NYC streets.

As if this was not enough, a third plane hit the Pentagon, and a fourth plane crashed in Pennsylvania. If we hadn't known it was live footage, we might have thought it was another Hollywood catastrophe movie destroying NYC. But, no such good fortune. This was real. Our nation was indeed under attack.

In my shock, it never crossed my mind to check on my homeschooled children. I just wanted to scream and escape. Horrified, I looked for the only pastor who knew my family's tragic story, but he had not yet arrived at his office. No one else on staff knew that as those towers came crashing down, memories came roaring back into my mind, terrifying and suffocating me. I wanted to hide.

It wasn't long before someone opened the church café, and we gathered around the wooden tables. A gas, stone fireplace jutted from one of the walls with a stone bench wrapping around three of its sides. Couches surrounded the hearth, offering warmth and hospitality. Merely walking into that room would soothe anyone. The floor's beautiful wooden parquet and the rustic theme added to the cozy ambiance. On Saturday nights and Sunday mornings, this was the place to hang out. You would brush shoulders with many of the staff pastors. You'd bump into friends and make new ones sipping on the latest java or your favorite herbal tea.

I flung myself onto one of the couches. A lead pastor began to speak words of encouragement, calm, and peace. In time, we were led to pray for those trapped in the buildings, the rescuers, the families, the victims, the City of New York, and our entire nation.

For me, it was different. Internally, I felt and heard the crashes, the pain, the death, the screams of the victims, and the emotions of their families. Imagined or not, I fully identified with the terror unfolding before our very eyes. All I could do was bury myself into the pillows of the couch and scream without anyone hearing anything—how I wanted to leave despite being surrounded by a caring staff. To burst into tears and to have to explain my extreme reaction was too much to bear. That day was not about me. It was about the thousands trapped in the buildings, those who died in the hijacked planes, those who went down in PA, and those in the Pentagon. No, I had to repress how this news jolted me and remain calm.

By this time, our nation had already experienced the first World Trade Center bombing in 1993 and the Oklahoma City bombing in 1995. In 1996, TWA flight 800 exploded due to malfunction, not sabotage, and sank in the Atlantic Ocean, just off NYC.[1]

On Sept. 11, 2001, all I knew was that I could identify with the surviving families of everyone who lost their lives.

Ever since that fateful day, acts of terrorism through bombings and shootings have become routine in the USA and around the world. What should be our response? Once the media and people watch and view in horror what takes place, we gradually settle into our regular routines as if nothing ever happened. In shock and awe, we feel inadequate to assist the families of the victims and powerless to stop future attacks. Over time, we develop immunity from allowing the tragedies to touch us, as such violence seems to dominate the daily news. Our society becomes a conglomerate of subtly traumatized individuals, overwhelmed by the numerous calamities. Fear and mistrust clandestinely weave themselves throughout our culture.

It would be most unfortunate if we as a nation, fixated on both the crime and the criminal, become complacent, numb, and forgetful concerning what is truly important—the surviving families. Not knowing how to respond, we minimize the disaster by superficially thanking God that our families weren't there or touched by it. Without ignoring the severity of the losses, maintaining respect for the privacy of family members, how can we demonstrate genuine empathy? Exhausted in our personal daily lives for survival, we opt not to do anything. We press on, pushing aside the pain, and tend to our private affairs. On the other hand, by moving forward in life, we collectively send signals to the wicked, heartless killers that they can't and won't take away our American resolve and spirit.

While everyone travels this life differently, each person experiences tragedy, crisis, losses, hard times, and stressful events. Regardless of the severity of trials, pain is relative. Our pain is our pain. What you may consider painful, may not be painful to me. Your pain will not be mine, and my pain will not be yours. Suffering is suffering, and we never know when or how it may strike.

At the time of this writing, a small town in Alabama lost at least 23 persons when a raging tornado unexpectedly ripped through its rural setting. Two more mass killings occurred back to back on the same weekend. Without rhyme or reason, no satisfactory answer could be given for either the random strike of nature or the two evil shootings. The big "why" questions may never be resolved.

With every mass killing, it is most grievous to even conceive that innocent people could be so heartlessly and cruelly killed. Moreover, the story never ends with the victims or the pursuant investigation and trial. Through acts of pure wickedness, every surviving family remains instantly and forever shifted off its course. Loss of a loved one who can never return or be held again. The unbearable weight of the trauma and grief. The absence of that precious family member. No more kisses, no more hugs, no more traditional family movie nights, no more fill-in-the-blank. Their families must suddenly rebuild their lives economically and emotionally. With hearts full of sorrow and anger, they will forever long for a loved one who will never enter their front door again. Too many unanswered questions will remain for a lifetime, haunting them as they pick up their lives and try to forget.

You see, I know. I've been through this, for I am a member of such a family, one out of 43 others. It's not a comfortable journey to take but promises to provide an eye-witness account of triumph over evil. I invite you to come along with me. It's a chronicle of how tragedy does not need to define you; hope, freedom, and new life are possible. With so many traumatic crises occurring today, I figure it's time I pull my head out of that pillow, take you back in time to November 1, 1955, and unfold my story.

May it bring healing and hope for the future when both seem impossible to grasp.

Scene 2

Leaving on a DC-6B

"Don't know when I'll be back again. Oh, babe, I hate to go."

—John Denver, *Leaving on a Jet Plane*

Tuesday, November 1, 1955
Hatfield, a suburb of Philadelphia, Pennsylvania

"**H**obby, do you really have to go?" Marty pleaded.

"You know I have to, darlin'," said Hobby, her husband. He stopped packing for a moment, wrapped his arms around Marty, and pecked her on the cheek. Toddler Nancy held onto her mother's leg, begging to be picked up and pulling her skirt.

"I know," Marty said as she sighed. Her thoughts drifted for a moment.

With Nancy at her feet, Marty recollected their first and only argument had been over what carriage to buy for their first baby. Right before Hobby would be leaving for several weeks, Marty certainly did not want a heated argument over his trip. Hobby had no control or say-so in the matter. Their conversation that morning wasn't a get-in-your-face argument, like the one over the carriage, but a sincere plea from a wife who had an uncanny sense of things.

Whenever Hobby's corporation would send him on an electrical engineering job, the company would fly him to the factory location. Hobby would remain until the completion of the electrical project and could be gone three to six weeks at a time. Hobby furthermore had re-entered University to gain his masters so that he could gain professional advancement to take care of his family. Thus, another reason he could not refuse his company's wishes.

"Mmm… I have always managed when he is away on a business trip. Nothing's ever happened, and he writes to me almost daily. He always comes back safely. Why do I have this strange feeling inside?" Marty thought to herself. "There's no reason for this hesitation. After all, I'm used to him going on these trips. I ought not to argue with him. He can't help that his company chose to send him instead of the other man."

Her trail of thoughts continued, keeping them to herself while Hobby kept packing. "We recently settled into our new home, and the company had just sent him on a trip a few weeks before we moved. So, why now? Don't they know I'm in my last months of having a baby?"

Marty's mind wandered to her mother-in-law. She recalled that Hobby's mother always questioned his flying. But, then again, Marty reasoned,

"His mother dotes on him, almost suffocating him at times. To her, he can do nothing wrong." To Marty, it was no surprise that Hobby's mother continually worried about her favorite son traveling on airplanes.

"I still can't figure out why his mother favored him over his only brother, L.G.," Marty thought. She recognized that this favoritism was a burden L.G. bore throughout his life, but as a wife and daughter-in-law, there was nothing she could do about this either.

Marty had placed her faith in God for everything and did not fear Hobby flying. Her hesitations on his taking this business trip came from within her, not a fear of his flying. Substantial reasons existed for Marty to understand why her mother-in-law feared for her son. After WWII, the passenger airline industry broke ground and made great strides since 1938 when the government established the Civil Aeronautics Board (CAB).[1] Although the mighty American fighter planes helped win the victory in WWII, the commercial and passenger airplanes required continued innovation. The nightly news periodically reported crashes due to malfunctions of some sort. Undoubtedly, passengers flew at their own risk.

Marty stood still and recollected Hobby's past conversations with his mother. She paused. With a strange kind of peace, she could imagine Hobby with his deep South Carolinian drawl grinning and always reassuring his mother with the same answer,

"Ma, I know who my Maker is and when it's my time, I'm ready."

"Why am I remembering this now?" Marty questioned herself.

Martha Pearl McNeer (Marty) and Marion Pierce Hobgood (Hobby) were happily married slightly over four years. At a youthful age of 19, Hobby fought in WWII for the US and the world's freedom in the European arena. He returned having witnessed atrocities of war and earning Bronze and Silver Stars. Although he gained a smoking habit, these experiences did not seem to dampen his optimistic personality.

Like many young WWII veterans who were fortunate enough to return, Hobby picked up life where he had left off before the war. In his wartime role, he repaired radar communications equipment; he took the next logical step and obtained a degree in electrical engineering. His career led him up north to Philadelphia where he worked for a premiere producer of electronics such as TV's, record players, and other up-and-coming products in a post-WWII era. In the summer of 1955, he began a master program in engineering to advance professionally to provide for his family.

The economic post-WWII boom benefited the entire nation. This generation became known as one of the greatest generations in history. A happy-go-lucky attitude permeated the atmosphere.

Victory and hope for a prosperous future ensured the achievement of the American dream. All of life was before them—could Hobby and Marty ask for more?

Marty graduated from Madison College (now Madison University) with a B.S. Degree in chemistry and gained employment in a chemistry lab located in the Philadelphia area. She too, born in the southern Blue Ridge Mountains, had been transported from the south to the north. At one time, she fell in love, but when the young suitor proposed, she realized he was not the one, so she turned him down. Divine coincidences later orchestrated the crossing of her path with that of Hobby in Philadelphia.

As she watched Hobby get ready for his flight across the country, their courtship flashed through her mind, "To think, if we had never met at the young adult fellowship at church, I would not be here, in this house, with Nancy and one more on the way. I couldn't be happier. But why does he have to go?"

Little did Marty know how vital this young adult group would be to her. The group had become family to each other over the years. Each pursued their lives with zest while doing life together. The young adult group did everything together: parties, Bible study, mountain climbing, skiing, picnics. It was only after a double date, in which they were paired with different partners, did she realize her attraction for Hobby, and he reciprocated.

Standing years later in their new house, that Nov. 1, 1955, she smiled and said to herself,

"To think Hobby and I had doubled dated that one night, only I was the date of another fellow, and Hobby's date was this other girl. Well, I won the prize. Oh, how I love him, and…" She paused, looking toward him. "Oh, why do I have this gnawing feeling about his going on this trip?"

Marty remembered the exact day weeks after the double date when they walked downtown Philadelphia window shopping; December snowflakes softly fell that brisk wintery day. She said that Hobby asked her to help him shop for a present for his mother. Bundled in winter coats, they strolled past Wanamaker and Gimbel, popular department stores, and stared into the windows of jewelry shops. With signs of Christmas cheer everywhere, they laughed and enjoyed each other's company. Like a movie scene from a romantic love story, Hobby placed his arm around Marty's petite waist and pulled her in close to him. Fitting perfectly next to his tall physique, Marty leaned into his warmth and felt his amorous strength. Marty vividly reminisced that was when they both knew they loved each other more than as friends.

To her, it seemed that within two years, many within that close-knit young adult group paired off and eventually married. They followed suit. By June 17, 1950, Hobby officially proposed and on August 25, 1951, they said the big "I do."

Abruptly, Marty snapped out of her meandering recollection. Hobby, standing almost six feet tall, leaned over and tenderly held Marty, his ever-loving wife, as he called her, at a petite five feet. He said, "I'll be home before you know it. You know I don't want to leave you for weeks. You know that it was between another co-worker and me to go out to Oregon for this job. For some reason, they chose me even though they know that we have little Nancy and one on the way. You never say 'no' to the one who pays your bread and butter. You know how it is."

"But, couldn't you have said anything to them? How am I going to manage the little one with another one on the way? I'm so physically uncomfortable now, and my feet hurt all the time. The baby isn't due until sometime in January, but we never know when the company will bring you home. I have days full of stamina and other days when it's all I can do to keep up with Nancy—she sure is a tiny fireball with boundless energy! She is constantly under my feet. I really need you now."

"I know, Honey. As I said, please know how much I don't want to go this time. But I can't stay home, and you know that. I wanted to, but when a boss says 'go,' you go…don't worry one bit, darlin'," Hobby said, tenderly stroking Marty's hair and looking in her eyes which communicated a love more profound than any words "I love you" could.

"I'll write every day because you an' Nancy an' the itty-bitty wee one in your cooker will always be on my mind and in my heart. I'll be home before the cock crows cockle!"

Marty just stood there, gazing back into his eyes, grasping to hold onto his love, and wanting desperately to believe that he would be back soon. Hobby saw her concern and held his arms tighter around her. She sensed great comfort from him. She marveled, "He can still reach around me! Oh, I don't want to let go and this moment to end."

She hoped silently in her heart that he would complete the job faster than usual, and that he would be right. However, her inner being, her heart, and her gut were telling her different. She didn't know why she had this feeling. She instinctively didn't want him to go. Within her, she continued to question why the company picked him out of the two men. It was only two months before Christmas, and the baby was due several weeks after Christmas. Tossing back and forth over his departure, she repeated over and over to herself, "Oh, it's going to be all right. I'll be OK. I can do this. He'll be home before I know it."

"I love you with all my heart. You know that."

"Yes, dear, I know. I love you so much," said Marty while she held back her tears, choosing to be strong for him. She could not be enthused but mustered up a good spirit for him.

Hobby stood dressed in his finest traveling suit and wore his famous grin on his face, which always cheered up a room. The gleam in his eyes, combined with his ears that stuck slightly out, finished the touch.

"Well, I'm all packed; this sure is becoming routine," said Hobby. "It's like I just got back from the trip in August. Why, I've barely been able to enjoy our new home with you. But, don't worry, I'll be back in a blink of an eye. Promise."

He picked up his suitcase, fully packed with paper, stamps, and envelopes to write her often, an alarm clock to wake him up, and clothes for at least three weeks with no specific return date. Looking down, he noticed little Nancy playing at his feet. A smile broke out as he put down the suitcase, bent down, and in one fell swoop he lifted his baby girl into the air. Nancy giggled in delight, her little legs kicking. Giving her an airplane ride, he landed her right back onto the floor and picked up his luggage again.

"He is so stunningly handsome," thought Marty. "I pray he'll be back in time for Thanksgiving."

She looked around the house and sighed. It was only three months since they had moved into their new home. "What a celebration!" she thought.

She stared into space for a moment and replayed the moving party their friends held on that hot day in August. Marty could not wait for Hobby and herself to re-situate themselves in this beautiful two-story home on a corner lot. Purchasing a home completed one of Hobby's and Marty's family goals.

When they were first married, Marty worked hard as a chemist for over three years to save up enough for a sizeable down payment on their first home. As was the practice in the 1950s, when her pregnancy progressed with her first baby, she left her profession to be a mother. To her, the new home meant stability, space for their growing family, and no more being cramped in an apartment. They could have room to breathe, relax, and enjoy each other. With the second baby, their move into the house made perfect timing with their ideal life—rapturously in love and living their American dream.

That morning, November 1, 1955, marked the beginning of their third month in their new home in the suburb outside of Philadelphia. Small town America made the perfect place for raising a family.

From the street, situated on a slight hill, their two-story house stood greeting the entire neighborhood as a welcoming watchtower. Another road banked their corner lot. Halfway up from the ground, hewn stone adorned the outside, and white stucco carried the eyes to the rooftop. This combination added to the house's character. A long, curvy sidewalk wound from the main road with large mature oak trees paralleling it. One of the trees grew as a double tree, like a double portion. Years later, the two young children would enjoy many hours sitting between the two tree trunks. In the fall, jumping in enormous piles of leaves brought much delight.

In the back, grapevines lined the back yard and created a natural fence. The garage was attached off the side of the house and opened to a gravel alley. On top of the garage, off a third bedroom, a flat sunroof begged for sunbathers or tired workers to relax with glasses of iced tea. A modest front porch welcomed guests, while a side-roofed porch facing the other street provided plenty of room for children to play on while entertaining guests.

Inside the home, the front door opened into a vestibule, a grand entranceway fit for a princess. It reminded Marty of a small version of a mansion in Germantown. Those Germantown mansions had grand entrance hallways with three stories and wood banisters that curved from top to bottom, making an excellent slide for children. In Marty and Hobby's smaller version, the stairs in the hall led up to the second story.

On the main floor, to the right of the front door, a formal dining room could seat large parties. Off the dining room, an extended narrow kitchen connected to an eating nook. In line with the 1950s décor, a diner-style red, vinyl booth with metallic silver accents made it seem like a restaurant.

Arched doorways between the rooms added character and charm. To the left of the front door, the all-in-one family living room stretched from the front of the house to the rear. Two side doors on either side of a fireplace led to the side porch. Giving a very cozy, nostalgic setting, a fireplace with built-in bookcases on either side would warm the room.

Once upstairs, to the right, a guest bedroom was always ready for anyone visiting from a distance. A door opened to the sunroof. To the left, down the hallway, the master bedroom lined the back of the house, and the second bedroom, facing the front, housed Nancy. It would not be long before another little one would fill the room.

"I cannot wait to decorate for Christmas," Marty thought while Hobby double-checked his bags and played with Nancy.

"I can see my homemade stockings hung on the mantle. The tree can stand in the corner left of the fireplace. Hobby will be carving a Christmas card design on an ink stamp block to commemorate another Christmas together. Five Christmases—two children—and a new home! Yes, it's all perfect! We are home at last!"

"Vicky is coming over to watch Nancy while we go to the airport. Once she arrives, we can take off," Marty told Hobby. "I'm so thankful for her! Her babysitting for Nancy saves me from chasing Nancy around at the airport. What good friends! We've truly been blessed with all of our friends—the move, the housewarming gifts, the parties."

"Yes, we sure are," said Hobby who reached down to pick up Nancy, gave her a big hug, and continued to carry her around. She squealed and laughed, her blonde curly hair tossing against his cheeks. Her little legs kicked back and forth as she threw her arms around his neck.

Hobby remarked, "My, my—how you love your daddy! You're my pride and joy, my lit'l sunshine!"

"Now Nancy, I want you to help your mama there. You have another new bitty friend coming soon, and your mama could use your help. Be a good girl, and I'll be home before you know it." He clutched her close as if he never wanted to let her go.

The fifteen-month-old wasn't yet talking but loved her daddy. Every time he came home, Marty enjoyed watching their ritual. Nancy would greet him as if it would be the last time she'd ever see him, giggling with glee and jumping at his feet, with her little arms flinging with excitement. He would swoop her up and throw her into the air, catch her, and then twirl her around. Putting down his briefcase, he would hug Marty and peck her on her cheek. This daily routine reinforced their love for each other and added to their family traditions.

Once Vicky arrived, and goodbyes were said, Marty and Hobby pulled out of the garage in their sleek, grey Oldsmobile with its roof and trunk sloped back toward the rear fender. On the way to the airport, Marty remained silent, deep in thought. Once inside the airport complex, before Hobby could board his flight, the couple stopped short in front of an unusual kiosk at the airport.

"Do we get any?" Hobby wondered, looking at Marty.

"What do you think? It seems like we'd be asking for something bad to happen," said Marty.

"Yeh, let's not toy with fate," said Hobby as they both walked on past the vending machine selling life insurance policies on the spot.

"Honey, I love you and will be back before you know it. You go on home, I'll be fine, and I'll write—I got the paper and stamps all right here. I'll miss you," said Hobby, slapping his brown leather briefcase. He bent down and gave Marty a loving embrace and one last kiss.

"I'll stand and wave to you from the observation deck. I'll be able to see your flight take off. Just know that I'll be there. If you can, look out your window. I love you Hobby, so you come back soon, OK?"

"Sure thing. Take care now. I'll think of you every day. Love you always!" He walked down the ramp and out of sight.

To board a plane in the 1950s, most travelers had to walk outside the airport lobby at the gate that then opened to the tarmac. After being weighed, airport personnel would load their luggage underneath the plane, with no baggage inspections or checkpoints, and no TSA. Once outside, the passengers would then walk over to the steep steps and up into the DC-6B airplane. While Hobby took off to board his flight, Marty found her way to the airport's observation deck and waited.

"Oh, my feet hurt; this walk to the observation deck was long, but I want to see Hobby's flight take off and wave to him. It will be a miracle if he sees me. I need to put our argument behind me, so I hope he does—my, I love him and am going to miss him. Standing here, I can sense his love for me. I hope he gets to see me," thought Marty.

Catching her breath, she told herself, "I'm thankful that Nancy is safe with Vicky and not squirming and tugging on me." She soon saw Hobby on the tarmac and watched him board the plane.

"Maybe he will turn, see me, and wave back," she hoped. "Oh dear, it looks like he has to keep in step with the other passengers. I'll just keep waiting."

Once the plane door closed, it was a matter of minutes before it taxied down the runway. Marty could not tear herself away and kept waving while the airplane climbed into the sky. She said to herself,

"My, I must be a sight! It's November. It's cold, and here I am six-and-half months pregnant, standing outside and waving!"

With her short and petite frame, she ballooned early with both babies, and her feet and back continually ached. Despite this inconvenience, she stood and waited until the plane was in the air and out of sight. She waved the whole time, throwing kisses to the love of her life, while a lingering, foreboding cloud swirled about her.

United Air Lines DC-6B in flight, Source: Postcard: United Airlines DC-6, Enell, Inc.; www.facebook.com/afacwa/posts

Marty and Hobby's wedding photo – August 25, 1951

Cutting the wedding cake – August 25, 1951

Marty and Hobby on honeymoon

Marty and Hobby dancing

Hobby (Dad) holding newborn Nancy - 1954

Easter 1955 – Dad with Nancy on a picnic blanket

Marty and Hobby's first home-Hatfield

Moving Day Party August 1955 – Hobby is on left

Dad playing with Nancy at new home, summer 1955

Portrait of Marion Pierce Hobgood

Scene 3

The Night the World Changed

I saw three men standing under my bedroom window.

—Marty

"Hello, Vicky! I'm home! Thank you so much for watching Nancy for us. I decided to stay longer to wave Hobby off."

"Nancy and I had fun—what a high-spirited young lady she is! I got her fed, and she is now taking a little nap. If you need anything while Hobby is gone, please give me a call anytime, OK?"

"OK. Thanks again so much. I may just take you up on your offer. Nancy is so squirmy and never stops. I can barely get off my feet to rest. I might need or want an extra hand, so I appreciate your willingness to help out."

"You two sure have a sweetie pie! Bye now. We'll talk later."

After Vicky left, Marty sank onto their couch to catch her breath and relax.

"I wonder how long Nancy will sleep?" she said, looking at her watch. "I hope at least twenty minutes. I want to rest, put my feet up, and get a second wind before Nancy wakes up."

Her remaining day went as planned. Once up from her nap, Nancy's enthusiasm for playing kept Marty busy chasing her around the house.

"At least Nancy is keeping my mind off of this uneasy feeling inside," she thought.

Throughout the day, she kept checking her watch.

"Where is he now? Is he eating well? Did he get any catnaps? Does he have a nice seatmate?"

"Oh, stop being silly," she said to herself. "Why shouldn't Hobby be alright?"

Accustomed to his traveling, Marty kept pace with the usual daily routines. By 6:30 PM ET, she put Nancy down to sleep in her crib. Nancy had outgrown the oversized wooden cradle that her daddy had made. Hobby crafted the cradle from strong, thick wood, held by bolts, which could be gently rocked. He stained the wood a brownish blonde to match the furniture. To ensure the cradle would endure many more children, he coated the wood with a clear shellac, layering it several times.

"Hobby's plane should have arrived in Denver. My, what a long day he must be having."

"I'm calling it a night. I'm too exhausted even to watch the evening news or to listen to it on the radio." She said and crawled into bed, snuggling under the blankets.

"I sure wish Hobby was here with me and not in an airplane halfway across the country. How I hope Nancy will sleep all night. I must get some rest. I love you, Hobby. Goodnight, my love, wherever you are."

Marty's head hit the pillow, and her long-awaited sleep arrived. Promptly at 11 PM that evening, she abruptly woke up. Startled, she heard pebbles thrown at her bedroom window at the back of the house. Simultaneously, as the sound of the ping—ping—ping of little rocks hit the windowpane, the phone rang.

She scrambled out of bed as fast as she could and hurried to the window. Below her in the moonlight, three men were shouting and waving their arms. One of their best friends, her OBGYN, and their pastor were urgently trying to get her attention.

"What is going on? Oh no, this cannot be good," she said while everything in her filled with fear.

The phone kept ringing. Marty grabbed a robe and ran down the stairs, hoping the baby would stay asleep. By now the three men rushed to the front of the house and knocked fervently. As she opened the door to let the men in, she picked up the phone.

"Marty! Marty! Marty!" cried the men.

On the phone, her only sister, Francis, in Oakridge, Tennessee, was crying in shock.

"Marty, did you hear the news? Hobby's airplane went down and crashed within minutes after take-off from Denver, just before flying over the Rockies—the news says there were no survivors—there were no survivors, Marty, no survivors."

"Francis, are you sure? Are you sure?" Marty managed to force the words out between sobs, as the terrible news bounced in her head.

"Yes, Marty, we checked. It was Hobby's flight. United Airlines Flight 629 heading to Portland."

"It just can't be! It just can't be! NO—NO—NO," Marty screamed into the phone without thinking. The shock overwhelmed her, and she sloppily laid down the phone off the hook.

All Marty could hear was "No survivors…no survivors…It looks like it exploded midair, outside of Longmont, Colorado… all 44 passengers declared dead." The words "Everyone died—no survivors—explosion—no survivors—plane blew up—all dead" riveted nonstop through her entire being as if she were in an echo chamber. Her body trembled from head to toe with shock and horror.

Everything happened within moments. Before the men could say anything more, Marty darted as fast as she could back up those stairs into Nancy's room. She scooped up her baby girl, held her tight against her chest, and screamed and screamed and screamed. Not just a short scream, but with loud wailing, long and hard as if her very life was being sucked out. Grief, fear, and panic screeched uncontrollably.

Within hours from the time she waved Hobby goodbye, their world changed forever. Her life and her children's lives would never be the same. Gone were her hopes and dreams. Gone were the comfort of Hobby's voice and the warmth of his arms embracing her. Gone was his smile. Gone was the endearing look in his eyes that Marty loved. Gone was his laughter, his strength, and stability. All gone. She and Hobby were forever separated. The once happy, peaceful home was shattered by her earth-rattling screams of horror.

"It just can't be—it has to be a dream!" screamed Marty.

The three men stood there and reached out to comfort Marty, trying to calm her down as best they could.

"Marty, we're so sorry, so sorry," they repeatedly said, lost for words.

She kept gasping for air as tears flooded. She was thankful they planned to come together to be with her. She could tell in their eyes, their voice, and body language that they were equally distressed. No words could bring any comfort. Their presence meant everything.

As a friend, doctor, and pastor, they managed to contact each other to arrive at the same time to deliver the hard news and be there for Marty. Jim lost his best friend. The OBGYN was concerned for Marty's state of well-being and her emotional toll. The pastor knew Hobby quite well and lost a friend, too. He was there to provide any spiritual help, although he knew there were no words enough to tell her it would be all right. Life wouldn't be and couldn't be ever the same.

None of these men could change the course of events. In their shock, they placed their strong arms around Marty's short, quite pregnant frame, hugged her with Nancy, and wept with her. Marty vaguely remembered anything they were saying.

"We will help you in every way we can. We'll be there for you. Hobby would want it that way," Jim said as comfortingly as he could.

"Vicky told me to stay as long as needed tonight. I will stay down here on the couch if you'd like. She's organizing the other ladies from our church group to come tomorrow morning. Is that all right with you?"

"I know you will, all of you. And, yes, please stay, Jim. And, yes, on the ladies coming over tomorrow. I don't know what I'm going to do. I'm falling apart," said Marty through her gasps for air in between sobs and each word. Her lungs had tightened, her stomach churned, and her body numbed.

To Marty, time was quite a blur that night. The men stayed into the wee hours of the night and made sure that Marty calmed down enough. She remained downstairs hugging Nancy, knowing she could not just return to sleep. She wondered if she dared to sleep, or if she even could settle down.

Sometime after midnight, the phone rang again.

"Hello," Marty hesitantly said.

"Hello, is this Mrs. Marion Pierce Hobgood?"

"Yes. Who is this?"

"I am from United Air Lines, Stapleton Airport, in Denver Colorado.[1] We have been searching for anyone who might have survived the plane crash. On behalf of United Airlines, we regret to report to you that Mr. Marion Pierce Hobgood, a passenger on United Airlines Flight #629, which crashed earlier, did not survive. You will be notified by the FBI once identification is official. We are so sorry and are doing all we can. I have some instructions to pass onto you..."

Marty tried to remain alert to hear what more he would say and struggled to listen. Going through the motions, she grabbed a pen and paper and responded, "uh hmm... uh... oh...I see... can you repeat that? ...OK..."

After hanging up, she told the three men,

"Thank you, gentlemen, for being here when that call came and for coming out in the middle of the night. What would I have done without the three of you? I was wondering when I would officially hear that Hobby is not coming back. That was United Air Lines. They waited until the search party accounted for him. They confirmed there were no survivors. I will be hearing from them again as to what to do next. They said the FBI would be in touch with me also. Oh my, oh my—God, what am I going to do?"

Both the pastor and the doctor reassured Marty of their support and help before heading out. The doctor handed Marty a very mild sedative that would be safe for her and the baby, in case she needed it. Jim stayed on the couch until morning to remain with Marty.

The women would be coming midmorning. As much as Marty needed time alone to grasp all that just happened, she said to herself, in between sobs and moans,

"Hobby, we sure do have great friends, don't we? I'll be all right; I must be. Don't you worry one bit. You married a resilient southern gal, didn't you? I can't believe you are gone. I miss you terribly—so, so much. I love you."

After the worst day in her entire life, Marty gathered Nancy in her arms, laid down to try to sleep with Nancy in bed with her, and hoped beyond hope that this was just a nightmare—that she would wake up to discover that Hobby, her beloved, would be coming home.

Scene 4

Meanwhile Back in Denver

Amidst the worst human character exhibited,
the best in humanity and the American spirit displayed its
courage, love, and compassion.

—Taken from my journal

Tuesday evening, November 1, 1955
Denver, Colorado

While Marty's three friends comforted her on the night of Tuesday, November 1, hundreds labored throughout the night, just north of Denver, Colorado, until 4 AM the next day before calling it a day. Local farmers, the first responders, police, fire departments, United Air Lines, the FBI, numerous agencies, and the entire community in Platteville, Colorado investigated the crash scene scattered over a large tract of beet fields.

Earlier, the evening seemed to be business as usual at Stapleton Airport, later known as Stapleton International Airport. Denver had been chosen to be the mainline stopover between the East Coast and the West Coast. United Air Lines (UA) named their planes flying through Denver, *Mainliner Denver*. Travelers filled the airport, waiting to board their flights. Airport staff bustled to and fro. People were dining in the airport's restaurant facing the runway so that they could watch the flights arrive and depart. Pilots and airline flight attendants hurried to their gates. United Air Lines Flight #629, Hobby's flight, sat on the tarmac on the runway to wait for presidential dignitary to board.[1]

The airline industry entered its golden years, and airlines rolled out the royal treatment for their passengers. The travelers dressed their best for the flying event. The stewardesses (flight attendants) made sure every passenger enjoyed their share of abundant food, drinks, and snacks. Certainly, Hobby would have taken full advantage of this luxury as did the others on board while they waited for the plane to leave the ground.

Delayed, UA Flight #629 left the runway by 6:52 PM MT. Soon the pilot reported to the air traffic controllers that they were safely in the air. Four minutes later, the pilot reported clearance of the Denver Omni. Abruptly, communication stopped. Flight #629 exploded approximately 7:03 PM MT, eleven minutes after take-off. The air traffic controllers saw two white lights falling with approximately the same speed. Radio calls were made to all aircraft within the Denver Airport air responsibility and all except Flight 620 responded. A gigantic ball of fire appeared in the atmosphere. Later, witnesses reported seeing it as far as twenty miles away. Back in Philadelphia, the time was 9:03 PM, and Marty had already crawled into bed without listening to any news.

Eyewitness accounts from farmers surrounding the area reported seeing a ball of flame lasting two to four minutes before crashing; others witnessed the loud explosive noise and saw the plane streak through the air and plummet. The collective reports confirmed that there were two explosions. One farmer's wife thought she was looking at the moon coming up. Their house shook, and she ran outside to see what happened. Upon hearing a second massive boom, she reported seeing a mushroomed ball of fire and smoke in the sky.[2]

A railway worker who stood on the back of a train caboose passing through the area witnessed an object burning across the sky that looked like fireworks falling from it. In seconds, he saw a big mushroom of oily smoke like an atom bomb and sixty-foot flames that were so bright "it was like four or five haystacks burning all at one time."[3] Others described it as a space rocket and feared falling fragments would land on their houses or barns.

Farmhouses nestled next to the borders of the fields which were divided into 160-acre parcels for each family to farm. Fortunately, most of the wreckage landed smack in the middle of an extensive tract of beet fields and not homes. Recently settled in for the evening, these farmers and their families came out from their homes and stood on the grounds in total bewilderment. It was shocking enough that they would see such mayhem on their beet fields which were almost ready to be harvested. More appalling, they discovered that it was a commercial passenger plane with people on board. Assessing the seriousness, in addition to calling their local fire stations and police, they were the first on the scene and eventually met each other in the fields. They found parts of the plane, bodies, luggage, seats, and everything on board scattered over the six square miles, throughout hundreds of acres. Some debris landed as far as twelve square miles away which no one would discover until the search continued through the night.

The phone lines to the local police stations became overloaded as multitudes of eyewitnesses reported the explosion. In response, Western Union reopened its office to augment communication needs. Also, the phone company sent out teams to put up telephone poles with wires within the field itself to facilitate communication among the rescuers.

Three farmers, two from one side of the field and another from across the acreage, approached the site with fire and smoke still coming from the plane debris. They were genuine heroes—first in the fields and first to find bodies. Before all the EMT personnel could arrive, they covered up bodies where they discovered them with any article of clothing or blankets scattered nearby.

The impact was so hard that the wreckage made two craters. The southern crater, in which was found the plane's left wing and other engine parts, measured 20 feet wide, 25 feet long, and 6 feet deep. The investigators found two other engines and the right wing in the longer and deeper northern pit. According to the CAB's Accident Investigation Report, released May 14, 1956, the distance between these two craters indicated that the separation of the tail assembly occurred before the wings separated from the fuselage prior to impact. An aerial view in the photos provides a look at this phenomenon, Other evidence indicated that parts of the plane struck the ground with tremendous force in a vertical descent. The widespread dispersal of pieces of the DC-6B and its fragmentation pointed to an extremely violent shattering of the airplane.

By 7 AM, 12 hours later, as the search was nearing a close, some rescuers thought they found a burnt baby doll, only to discover it was the body of a 13-month old infant. They tenderly wrapped this lifeless figure. Due to the high impact, the bodies and debris landed at minimum 12 inches deep. In the next planting season, crops grew around in shapes of these bodies and plane parts, a terrible reminder of this heinous crime.[4]

Not long after 7:03 PM, traffic jammed the road leading up to this area for miles as media spread the word of a fiery plane crash. People drove from all directions to see whatever they could. Photographers and press quickly gathered, adding to the circus scene. The real heroes were working in the fields checking for bodies and examining what probable cause could have torn a DC-6B to pieces with such force. The tail and the head had landed a mile and a half apart from each other. Finally, the authorities blocked the traffic to stop this sensational gazing and to clear room for emergency vehicles and all responders needed on the scene.

Worse than the sightseers, a few onlookers were seen stealing watches, jewelry, and valuables from the dismembered bodies.

Counted among the irritating bystanders, some photographers, perhaps eager to make history or to climb their career ladders, took pictures of the disfigured victims against the will of the authorities. Regardless of motives, it seemed to the first responders that these profiteering journalists demonstrated lack of conscience and grave disrespect for the dead and their families. Against the urgent order from the authorities, some news outlets even sent photographers in low flying helicopters to film the mayhem. Media, photographers, and gawkers had no place hampering the way of the rescue mission.

However, amidst the worst display of human character, the best in humanity and the American spirit showed its courage, love, and compassion. Looking for survivors dominated search efforts, then gathering the deceased. Both happened concurrently. Many heroes walked the rubble and fires that night—too many to name, and others remain unknown.

Among the most touching scene, two Catholic priests took it upon themselves to walk into the field. While searching, they covered and prayed over each person found, disregarding any religious preference, at a period in time when religious differences mattered.[5] I, the author, cannot possibly imagine doing what these two priests did, or, what any of the farmers and first responders did. Each one displayed the American heroism and compassion, which constitutes the spirit and fiber of America.

Even though the evidence seemed to indicate otherwise, the experts still considered this crash to be an accident due to some plane malfunction. The carnage and mass destruction, though, exceeded what any authority had previously experienced. In other airline crashes, the planes remained intact. This episode proved entirely different, puzzled all the authorities on the scene, and eventually stirred suspicion of sabotage.

After WW2, the commercial airline industry developed but not without much trial and error. Airplane crashes had become almost routine due to some engineering failure or defect. Just weeks prior, a United Air Lines flight experienced such an accident in which 60 plus passengers and crew perished.

Seizing an opportunity to profit, insurance companies placed insurance vending machines inside airports. For 25 cents, a person could purchase almost $7,000 of insurance before board-ing. Several passengers of Flight #629 did just that, including John Graham on behalf of his mother, Daisy King. He also took out several policies in Daisy's name, with him as a beneficiary. Remember, even Marty and Hobby toyed with the idea as they waited for Hobby to board his flight but thought they had better not play with fate.

Of course, the news media on TV and radio had soon announced the downing of Flight #629. Using the passenger list, UA staff members were given the difficult task of calling the families of the victims. From reports, United Air Lines had not yet been able to contact all the families of the victims for several hours or until the next day. Logistics such as identification of the bodies and a final count of victims slowed the process. The human spirit always hopes for the best, that survivors might be found, and the entire team on the fields would not stop give up searching until the following morning. As individuals were identified, employees of UA called the surviving families to advise them of their loss. Other reports indicated that the FBI also placed calls to the families, officially con-firming their identification through fingerprints or other evidence.

The long delay by the UA staff to communicate with the vic-tims' families plus the two hour time zone difference, explained why Marty received the tragic news first by her friends and her sister. Marty usually watched or listened to the nightly TV or radio broadcasts, but that night she did not. Looking back, this was most likely for the best. She would have been alone in the house with no one to catch her upon hearing the news. She shared years later that she was thankful for the loving support of those three men as she faced the shock, horror, and panic. In the arms of loved ones, she collapsed.

In Denver, the top priority that first night was to look for sur-vivors to provide medical attention; second priority, to transport with care and respect the bodies to Greeley Armory which had a sufficiently large facility to accommodate the victims. For years, Greeley Armory had become a theatre, never expecting that 44 body bags would fill its floor with real-life drama.

Using the registered passenger list, UA staff members painstakingly called the families of the victims, but this did not happen immediately. Gathering from reports, various logistics such as identification of the bodies and a final count delayed notification. The human spirit always hopes for the best, and, the entire team on the field was no exception. Laboriously sifting through the debris, each rescuer hoped to find a survivor. Responders could only readily identify nine victims whose personal effects remained close to them or whose fingerprints had already been on file. Since Hobby had been in the military, he might have been among the first nine reported deceased. Thirty-five required their prints or other identifiable means to match records, which took until the following mid-morning and a few into the next day, November 3.

As soon as they could, UA staff had already begun calling the families of the passengers on the plane. When Marty Hobgood received her call, she never talked about it. However, it had to have been after midnight ET (10 PM MT, 3 hours past the actual explosion), and after the three men came to her window at 11 PM ET, and the phone call from her sister.

That first night, tirelessly working, the Longmont American Legion kept hot coffee running for all workers while two local grocery stores supplied sandwiches. Once the bodies were found and accounted for, teams worked diligently without breaks until 4 AM. In the middle of smoldering fires, they cleaned up the debris and retrieved as many personal effects as they could. Even the postal service arrived on the scene because the plane was carrying mail across the country which now laid scattered, torn, and burned throughout the hundreds of acres.

While fires burned over a few days, United Air Lines provided the proper cargo caskets and shipped the rightfully identified bodies to their families. Surprisingly, for Marion Pierce Hobgood, this occurred by Sunday, Nov. 6, 1955.

Another multitude of teams, including the FBI, Civil Aeronautics Board (CAB) and other agencies, began to explore what could have caused such a mid-air explosion. Throughout the following days, teams initially salvaged all that they could throughout the six square miles. Plane parts were brought into a warehouse at the airport and investigators meticulously examined everything. The FBI physically reconstructed the plane from the debris to scientifically and forensically discover the cause of this devastating explosion. The November 28, 1955, issue of Life Magazine documents the first weeks of the forensics with photographs. The tail of the plane landed in one corner of the large beet field, while the nose of the aircraft was found a mile and a half away. The mid-section was found embedded and flattened into the ground in other locations. Seats, dining equipment, compartments, food, and other items lodged themselves throughout that field. From beginning to end, teams continued to find fragments of the plane and its contents covering as far as twelve square miles.

Jack Parshall, the investigator with the Civil Aeronautics Board (CAB), stated that he had never encountered anything like this in his fifteen-year career with the agency. If the plane had merely crashed, then it would have fallen in one piece. He became suspicious that an explosion occurred instead of a malfunction but had not yet considered deliberate sabotage.

Because debris covered such an expanse, people worked around the clock to locate, label, retrieve, and transport every fragment to a secret warehouse. The Department of Justice, the FBI, the CAB, The Aeronautics Branch of the Department of Commerce, United Air Lines, the Army Ordnance Department, the Colorado National Guard, and the Airforce worked together to complete the rescue mission and to solve this baffling catastrophe. Possibilities of various kinds of fire or explosions caused by a malfunction in the plane were being eliminated based upon the forensics.

By November 7, Parshall and James Peyton of CAB notified the FBI that they suspected sabotage. Between these agencies, all evidence, based upon the discoveries from the clean-up and reconstruction of the plane, pointed to a dynamite bomb purposely placed on the plane. The crash of Flight Number #629 now became a sabotage case. The FBI's duty was to find, charge, and arrest the culprit.

This bombing was the first and the worst mass murder in Denver history. It was also the first airplane sabotage in US history. The entire nation was captivated by the unfolding events, like on 9/11. Every news media, including radio, TV, every magazine, national and local newspapers, continually covered the aftermath and investigation.

Even President Eisenhower held high interest not just because it became a famous FBI case, but he knew two persons who lost their lives on that flight: Dr. Harold Sandstead, Pres. Eisenhower's Deputy Secretary of U.S. Public Health Service, and John Des Jardins, related by marriage to Pres. Eisenhower's Chief of Staff, Sherman Adams.[6] Ironically, President Eisenhower received medical treatment in Denver when the UA flight took off that night. Waiting for Dr. Sandstead to arrive from Washington, DC, UA #629 delayed its takeoff. This delay caused the explosion to occur before the DC-6B reached the Rocky Mountains. Had the bomb exploded over the Rockies, any rescue endeavor for the bodies and wreckage could not proceed until spring after the cold, snowy, winter months.[7]

To eliminate all possible suspects, the FBI began an inquiry with all families whose loved ones had been on that flight. In the beginning, the FBI interviewed families of everyone who had purchased a life insurance policy through those vending machines before taking off. They did not overlook a single lead.

For example, a simple alarm clock had been used to set the timer on the bomb. Even Marty reported the FBI questioned her on account of a travel alarm clock found in what was left of Hobby's luggage. Four decades later, by the look on her face, as Marty told the story, she seemed still disturbed that the FBI could even consider her committing such an evil act. Nevertheless, she understood why.

Seven days later, Monday, Nov. 14, after the FBI investigated every possible suspect by following all leads and tips, John Gilbert Graham, Daisy King's son, age 23, was arrested and signed a confession. People in Denver had stepped forward with testimony which confirmed Mr. Graham to be the top suspect. He was committed to the United States Marshall in place of any bond. On November 17, 1955, the court charged him with one count of murder of his mother, Daisy King. It was easier to prosecute on this one count than to prove that he purposely planned to kill all the other 43 people on board and that he knew them by name. The case would have been tied up for years.

The State of Colorado handled the case, not the Federal Government. The death penalty existed under Colorado statutes, and this decision by the Federal government moved the court proceedings quicker and kept the death penalty option wide open. By January 11, 1957, he breathed his last in the gas chamber. All reports indicated that he never showed any remorse and didn't care about the other passengers. Calloused and hardened, when questioned by doctors as to why this crime, he said,

"…(I) realized that there were about fifty or sixty people carried on a DC6B, but the number of people to be killed made no difference to me; it could have been a thousand. When their time comes, there is nothing they can do about it."[8]

While all the media focused on every move of the trial for the following fifteen months, the families of the victims were coping with their loss and grief. They had to pick up their devastated lives. Each had to attend to all legal matters concerning funerals, life insurance policies, inheritance issues, and pure economic survival.

For Marty, instead of enjoying the last two and half months of her pregnancy, the excruciating pain and sorrow drained her. Her dreams of living in the new house with Hobby and their two children died the night of November 1, 1955.

In place of Marty's and Hobby's future together, mounds of paperwork and legal procedures combined with overwhelming grief buried her. Her friends made sure to take care of Nancy and gave Marty space to work through the maze and shock. For her and the other families of the victims, Thanksgiving and Christmas certainly would never be the same.

Detroit News headlines on crash

Airline Trip Insurance Vending Machine,
Life Magazine Nov. 28, 1955

Headlines of John Graham's
confession, Rocky
Mountain News

Aerial view of nose and tail in the beet field, note the tail at bottom right corner, the crater formed, and the plane debris top left, FBI.gov

Tail on the field with Mainliner on the side of plane and investigators, no identifiable source

Investigators looking at the plane debris, Denverpost.com

Wreckage with man pointing to place of possible explosion,
nydailynews.com – photographer, Edward O. Eisenhand/AP

Plane reassembled in non-disclosed warehouse, FBI.gov

LIFE
Vol. 39, No. 22   Nov. 28, 1955

IN A DENVER WAREHOUSE SOME OF THE SEATS THAT HELD 44 ILL-STARRED TRAVELERS IN THEIR LAST MOMENTS ARE RANGED FOR STUDY BY CRASH EXPERTS

SUCCESS FOR SMART, PAINSTAKING DETECTIVE WORK IN . . .

A CASE OF 44 MID-AIR MURDERS

Four days after a DC-6B airliner exploded in the darkening sky over north central Colorado in a wild glare of light, its every findable part had been numbered, sorted and grouped in a guarded, supersecret Denver warehouse. That was a tremendous undertaking, for while most of the metal, luggage and flesh fragments had been found in a 6-square-mile area, some tatters were scattered miles away on rolling ranch-and farm-land, which had to be mapped by surveyors so the location of every piece could be diagrammed. This had been supervised by an army of inspectors, agents and experts, for

what was under investigation was possible murder—which if proven would be the biggest, most hideous mass murder in U.S. history.

At 6:52 p.m. on Nov. 1, United Airlines Flight 629, New York to Seattle by way of Chicago and Denver, took off from Denver's Stapleton airport. It was 22 minutes late starting on its 1,075-mile last leg, mostly because it had waited for a late arriving passenger. Aboard were 39 passengers and a crew of five, joined briefly by the chance fellowship of travel like the five who once started across Thornton Wilder's *Bridge of San Luis Rey*. Flight conditions

were good (34°, clear), the four engines purred thunder, and in 11 minutes the plane had reached 11,000 feet. Then in one blazing instant of hopelessness 44 people were plunged into eternity.

Only a few hours later the questions began. The modern airplane conceivably may catch fire or break up in the air, but it does not explode. Had explosives been carried onto this one? By innocent accident or lethal design? And if the latter, then which of the passengers it carried (*see next page*) had—unsuspectingly—brought death to all 44 on Flight 629?

Passenger seats reassembled in warehouse, FBI.gov/Life Magazine,
November 28, 1955

THE 44 WHO HAD A RENDEZVOUS ABOARD

JAMES, SARAH DOREY
A factory inspector from Whitman, Mass., Dorey was taking his wife on their first flight, to see a married son in Portland.

LEE H. HALL
The pilot of United Flight 629, Captain Hall had been with the line for 15 years. He had married a stewardess and lived in Seattle.

DONALD A. WHITE
The copilot on the plane, Don White at 26 had been flying for 10 years, joined United in 1951. Married, White lived in Seattle.

SAMUEL F. ARTHUR
He was the plane's flight engineer, had had nine years with United. His wife June and two children were waiting in Seattle.

JACQUELINE HINDS
The senior stewardess for the flight, which she boarded at Denver, Miss Hinds of Eugene, Ore., had been with United 4½ years.

HELEN FITZPATRICK, SON
She was flying to join her husband, an Army officer, who left for Okinawa a day after James II, now 14 months old, was born.

BROR H. BECKSTROM
The owner of three electric contracting firms in Seattle and Fairbanks, Beckstrom had been visiting New Mexico with his wife.

IRENE BECKSTROM
A native of Nova Scotia, Mrs. Beckstrom and her husband had been visiting their son Howard on Army duty in Albuquerque.

JOHN P. BOMELYN
Superintendent of the county humane society in Seattle, he was heading home from a national convention in Grand Rapids.

FRANK M. BRENNAN
A Seattle builder and an officer of Associated General Contractors, Brennan had taken part in an A.G.C. conference in Denver.

GURNEY EDWARDS
A leading Providence, R.I. attorney and a trustee of Brown University, Edwards was beginning a lengthy vacation with his wife.

ELIZABETH EDWARDS
With her husband, Mrs. Edwards was flying to visit her sister in Seattle and then their son, who is on Navy duty at Pearl Harbor.

VIRGIL HERMAN
Operator of a used-oil reclaiming business in Vancouver, Wash., Herman was returning from a trip to St. Louis with his wife.

GOLDIE HERMAN
After years with no vacation, Mrs. Herman and her husband had flown (for the first time) to visit his sister in St. Louis, Mo.

ELTON B. HICKOK
Manager of the Seattle chapter of Associated General Contractors, Hickok was returning from the A.G.C. meeting in Denver.

LELA McCLAIN
The oldest passenger, Mrs. McClain, 81, was returning to her home in Portland after seeing a stepson in Glastonbury, Conn.

JAMES W. PURVIS
A Tacoma contractor, Purvis was one of four on the plane—Brennan, Todd, Hickok—returning from a Denver A.G.C. meeting.

HERBERT G. ROBERTSON
A marine engineer for the New York firm of Gibbs & Cox, Robertson was going to inspect a ship repair project at Portland.

HAROLD R. SANDSTEAD
A nutrition expert with the U.S. Public Health Service in Washington, Dr. Sandstead was flying to speak at Oregon State College.

JESSE SIZEMORE
An airman second class, Sizemore was heading from leave at his home in Jenifer, Ala. to duty at an Air Force base in Alaska.

Passengers and crew on Flight #629, Life Magazine, November 28, 1955

FLIGHT 629 AND WHY THEY WERE THERE

PEGGY ANN PEDDICORD
The second stewardess serving the flight, Miss Peddicord joined United after college, had been a stewardess for only 10 months.

BARBARA J. CRUSE
A United stewardess on vacation, Miss Cruse had left Denver, where she was stationed, to have some time at home in Seattle.

SALLY ANN SCOFIELD
Another vacationing stewardess, she had planned to visit Barbara Cruse in Seattle, was to marry a United pilot in late November.

F. E. AMBROSE
"Jack" Ambrose, a United sales agent, was returning to Seattle after checking a new job the airline had offered him in Denver.

STEWART, ANNE MORGAN
Mrs. Morgan was with her husband, a consulting engineer, on a business trip from Chicago to Vancouver, their former home.

LOUISE BUNCH
The widow of a minister, Mrs. Bunch was returning to her Forest Grove, Ore., home from a church convention in Colorado.

THOMAS L. CROUCH
A carpenter's apprentice from Wichita, Crouch was heading to Seattle to take a new job with a Washington construction firm.

CARL F. DEIST
A regional Oldsmobile sales manager, Deist, from Burlingame, Calif., was en route from a Denver meeting to one in Portland.

JOHN P. DES JARDINS
General manager of a chain of department store beauty shops, Des Jardins, from Overland Park, Kan., was on an inspection trip.

BRAD, CAROL BYNUM
Bynum, a geologist for Sinclair Oil, was returning to Sherwood, Ore, with his pregnant wife, after visiting his parents in Amarillo.

MARION P. HOBGOOD
An electrical engineer for Philco, Hobgood was en route from his Philadelphia home to oversee an installation in Portland.

J. W. JUNGELS
A heating engineer from Aurora, Ill., Jungels was on his way to inspect a heating system his firm had installed in Portland.

DAISIE KING
The owner of a drive-in diner in West Denver, she lived with her son and his wife, was going to see a daughter in Alaska.

GERALD G. LIPKE
A division sales manager for a Pittsburgh engineering company, Lipke was flying with his wife to visit her sister in Portland.

PATRICIA LIPKE
The vacation trip to Portland with her husband (left) was the first plane ride for Mrs. Lipke. Their three sons stayed at home.

JAMES E. STRAUD
An assistant general sales manager for Oldsmobile, Straud, of Okemos, Mich., was bound for Portland along with Carl Deist.

CLARENCE TODD
The manager of the Associated General Contractors' chapter in Tacoma, Todd was heading back home from the Denver meeting.

RALPH W. VAN VALIN
A retired dentist from Newberg, Ore., Dr. Van Valin had been on a visit to his Unionville, Pa. birthplace with Mrs. Van Valin.

MINNIE VAN VALIN
A genealogy expert, Mrs. Van Valin made a side trip to check records in Washington, D.C. on her visit east with her husband.

ALMA WINSOR
A housewife from Newfoundland, Mrs. Winsor was flying to Tacoma to see a daughter whose husband had contracted polio.

CONTINUED 37

Marion Pierce Hobgood (Hobby) on 3rd row down, far left;
Daisy King (killer's mother) on 3rd row, center

Scene 5

True Friendship

A real friend is one who walks in when the rest of the world walks out.

—Walter Winchell

Wednesday, November 2, 1955
Hatfield, Pennsylvania

After having a restless night with Nancy by her side, Marty woke up early the next day, November 2, having scarcely slept. She had opted not to use the sedative left by the OBGYN. The men had stayed for a couple of hours, and Jim's spending the night on the couch gave her reassurance.

"I have to have my wits about me. Nancy needs me. How I wish my brain would stop swirling with questions," thought Marty.

"Is this happening? Am I dreaming?" She pinched herself. Shocked, she had a difficult time accepting her new reality—that her beloved would no longer be there with her and the children. Bombarded by thoughts which ambushed her mind in rapid fire, she kept thinking,

"I'll never see Hobby again. The love of my life will not return as he promised. Thanksgiving will not be the same this year. Christmas will be empty without Hobby. Every moment will never be the same. I won't see him walk through the front door saying, 'Darlin', I'm home!' Nancy won't ever be able to run into his arms giggling. I'm all on my own to raise two children by myself. Something inside told me that something wasn't right with Hobby's leaving. And, we didn't purchase life insurance at the airport. It seems like fate got us anyway. All my family lives far away in Virginia and Tennessee. The world has come to a stop as I know it. I've got a lot to do."

Besides anticipating the birth of her second child, Marty knew her days and weeks ahead would be occupied with surviving and her next steps. She wanted to hide and never come out, but she couldn't. Despite her emotionally frozen state, she sat at her dining room table and began to keep a list of everything that came to her mind. Intermittently, in between sobs, she would stop, stare into space, and gaze her eyes on their wedding picture which sat on a shelf across the room.

"Doing this will keep me focused," she thought. Her analytical, scientific mind kicked into action, as questions swirled in her mind:

How am I going to hold up and be strong for Nancy?
What about the baby that's coming?
How can I be both father and mother to our children?
How can I survive this?
How do I plan a funeral?
What dress am I to wear?
I'm fully pregnant; who carries black maternity dresses?
How am I going to pay the bills?
When would our life insurance money come?
Would it be enough?
Did Hobby ever change his WW2 Insurance beneficiary
    from his mother to me as I had asked?
What about the mortgage?

How can I even contact relatives, and what about our
    friends?
What do I do with Philco, the company Hobby
    worked for?
What about delivering the baby without Hobby's support?
Where's God in all of this?
Who's going to hold me?

More questions flurried about her, and her list grew. Besides
Hobby's loss, her first concern was keeping the house and a roof
over their heads.

The news the night before did not announce what caused the
explosion of the plane. It was all too fresh, and the cause did not
matter to her. She could only concentrate on her present and
her long-term situation. Instantly widowed, two children and
no job. While the families of the victims were all hearing their
news and facing such devastating new realities, the authorities
in Colorado were set into motion to solve this national disaster.
Marty only knew she was not alone—all 44 passengers died with
no survivors, each one with their surviving families picking up
their broken pieces like herself.

"I have to snap out of this," she told herself as she was getting Nancy ready for the day. "The questions are too many, and
it won't do Nancy or me any good to dwell on them. I have to
trust in God."

"I have a reason to live. There's Nancy, then the new baby.
Stay focused, Marty," she told herself. "Stay focused."

By 8 AM the phone rang.

"Hello."

"Hello, Marty! This is Vicky. I have called our friends, and we
are coming over this morning. We'll help see you through this.
We are all so sorry, so sorry. Would 9:30 AM be soon enough?
Will you be OK until then?" Vicky asked.

"Yes," Marty said, crying. "I didn't sleep well, and I have
Nancy's wiggly little body to occupy me. She has no way of
knowing what's just happened. I don't know what I'll do; I don't

know where to start, or how to make it through. Everything seems blurred—like this can't be true. Having Jim here through the night helped me settle down. Thank you for lending him. He just left a half hour ago."

"We will all get through this and help you, too. We are so sorry, so, so sorry, Marty. We don't know what to say. Nothing's making sense. We're here for you and will do all we can to help you and Nancy."

Marty was thankful for Vicky. It seemed to her that of all the people in their group, Vicky was always the self-confident one, the one who took charge and enjoyed helping others. Marty knew she could lean on and trust Vicky. Vicky stood tall at about 5 feet 8 inches, her black wavy hair flowed over her shoulders, and her countenance mirrored her positive outlook. A woman of action, she rarely sat still.

"Hobby would like this," Marty thought to herself. Then, she kept sobbing silently inside, trying to maintain herself for Nancy and her friends. "My heart feels like a 100-pound weight on my chest with all my life sucked out."

By 9:30 AM, five other girlfriends drove out from the city and knocked on her door.

"Come on in," Marty said as she opened the door. "My, what a welcome sight to see. Come on in Ruth, Patsy, Donna, Jean, and Sue. Vicky said you were coming. She is already here."

The women gathered around her, and they cried together.

In her mind, she said, "What words could they possibly say? They are all shell-shocked, in disbelief, sorrow, sadness, and bewilderment just as I am. Hobby had been their beloved friend, too."

In a flash, Marty looked back into time. They each knew Hobby when both she and he were single and dating others. As if they could have heard her thoughts inside her head, she said out loud,

"I remember we'd rotate parties from house to house and play games together. We even made progressive dinners. Remember when Hobby brought the dessert, only it didn't turn out and fell apart? We laughed so hard and pitied him. We saw movies and went to the theatre together. We climbed mountains, skied in the Pocono Mountains, and stayed in lodges together. We attended church together, ate together, hung out together, and studied the Bible together. Do you remember?"

"Yes, Marty, we do, and nothing is going to change that," said Patsy while the other women nodded.

"You were all a part of our wedding, too."

"You two were so in love; we could hardly separate you two! No doubt you were meant to be. Hobby dearly loved you, Marty," Ruth reassured her.

Never in a blue moon, did any of them, especially Marty, ever think she'd lose him so soon. All were young in their late twenties and early thirties. Life was great. Nothing would ever make sense to any of them.

"Poor little Nancy, she doesn't know what's going on," Sue said. "Don't you mind, Marty, we will take care of her for you."

The ladies took turns attending to Nancy, who was toddling around, falling, then getting back up again, giggling. But having Nancy underfoot broke the sadness many times that morning, giving the continual signal that life goes on.

"Hey there, baby girl, come to your Aunt Donna!" Donna reached out and placed Nancy on her lap. Nancy enjoyed the attention and laughed, without a care in the world.

Sometime that morning, Marty received the call from the FBI, officially confirming that Hobby had deceased. Hobby might have been among the first identified because his WW2 fingerprints remained on file which the FBI, once they arrived, could match. Others had been severely mutilated, burned, or marred, and only family members could identify them. The identification of all the bodies did not finish until Thursday, November 3.

By the end of the morning, after having brunch that Sue brought, the ladies had a plan set in place. Each one would rotate staying overnight with Marty and Nancy, at least until Marty could manage to be alone at night or needed time alone.

Donna and Jean sewed all their clothes, so they took measurements of Marty's well-rounded body. Their charge was to make a black maternity dress for Marty. The authorities notified Marty that Hobby's body would be sent to the funeral home in Winnsboro, SC. The service could then be held on November 7, 1955, at Bethel United Methodist Church, the Hobgood family's church.

Vicky and the rest would rotate taking care of Nancy for a couple of weeks or as long as necessary to relieve Marty. Instead of changing homes every day for Nancy, the women wisely chose chunks of days at a time, hoping to give Nancy a sense of security and stability. Their thoughtfulness alleviated Marty so that she could focus on all the funeral arrangements, insurance paperwork, and other details to ensure safety and provision for her, Nancy, and the new one to arrive.

The strength of her friends demonstrated through their shower of love-in-action carried Marty through this nightmare. Whatever help Marty needed, between their husbands and themselves, they would do all they could to assist Marty at this crucial, traumatic time.

Marty's quiet faith kept her looking up—although, she walked through very dark nights of the soul.

Marion P. Hobgood – Funeral Flowers, November 6-7, 1955

Scene 6

In the Garden

I'll never stop loving you.

—Marty

Monday, November 7, 1955
Winnsboro, South Carolina

On the exact day the CAB and the FBI determined sabotage caused the plane to explode, November 7, 1955, Marion Pierce Hobgood was laid to rest in the Hobgood family plot at Bethel United Methodist Church, Winnsboro, SC. From the country highway, a gravel driveway looped around the property and led guests up a slight hill to the entrance. The funeral service took place in the small, charming, non-assuming grey, granite block church with a white steeple. Hewn at a local quarry where Hobby's father worked, the granite blocks added a southern, quaint touch to the church. The Hobgood family history seemed etched into the church's very foundation. Old stained-glass windows, wooden pews, and a carved wooden altar with a choir loft added simplicity to the worship décor.

Only a week passed since Hobby vanished forever. Marty had only six days to prepare for the funeral and burial services. A memorial service had previously been held at their United Methodist Church in Germantown, PA. By Sunday, November 6, Hobby's body arrived at Dunbar Funeral Home, Winnsboro, SC.

Whirlwind of activity kept people busy in Philadelphia and Winnsboro. Both sets of friends and family, shocked and in great mourning, managed to remain strong for Marty. The news of Hobby being on the flight hit home for the Columbia, SC area where he lived most of his life. Local news covered the disaster, along with the rest of the nation. Many came to pay their respects; cards filled baskets and colorful floral arrangements spread a sweet fragrance in the country church and later circled the gravesite.

All the family surrounded the graveside while Marty held up the best she could, holding Nancy by her hand.

"I want to cry, but I can't. I'm just so numb I keep pinching myself hoping I'll wake up and its just a dream. It's all too surreal. This can't be happening!" Marty thought. "I have no one to lean on, except you, God. You know all and see all. Will this ever make sense?"

A hush settled, and each one stared at the casket with profound sorrow. Francis, Marty's sister, put her arms around her and stood in solemn silence with Marty. Chap, her sister's husband, positioned himself nearby. He of all people knew the horrible state of Hobby's body, and it had to have taken his willpower not to have that image stuck in his mind. Because of the condition of Hobby's body, her OBGYN prohibited Marty from viewing and identifying him. Instead, Chap and L.G., Hobby's only brother, went together to identify the body before the funeral. Both men agreed that Marty must not ever know the final condition of his body. He had not been buried whole.

"What a shame—what a shame—what a shame." While not spoken, Marty could see it upon each face and expression of each one gathered. She said to herself,

"I'm thinking the same thing. What a shame. My children will grow up without their dad. It's real; I'm now a widow. I'm only 31. Hobby was only 31. I wish I could have said one last goodbye to him, but Dr. Williams said I should not be the one to identify him. Oh my, I'm so thankful for Chap and L.G."

She looked around and was comforted by the presence of her dad, mother, her brother Rembert, and his wife, Lottie. Her father, Rembert McNeer, Sr., who had been a circuit rider pastor in the Methodist Church in Virginia, was already a strong tower for her. Her thoughts continued,

"Seeing Daddy gives me strength. He'll have the right words for me. He always does."

"What am I thinking? There are no words; what can anyone say?" Marty understood their silence and their hugs.

There was L.G., his wife Doris, and all seven of their children. Doris was also expecting in the new year, making that eight. Hobby's and L.G.'s mother, Mrs. Bertha Hobgood, managed to keep herself together, despite losing her most favored son (she always made this known). L.G., too, stood watching his mother and readied himself to support her if needed.

In flash moments, Marty began to review Hobby's life. Hobby was dearly loved by all who saw him grow up. His father moved the family to a typical stone house provided by a stone quarry company along a country road nearby, not far from the church. The house still stands today, but the quarry office and plant now resemble ancient Roman ruins.

Outside the house, on a curve in the road, marks the location when Hobby, as a curious young boy, had carried the family's only radio outside. He had dismantled it in the middle of the road, oblivious to any occasional traffic that might come barreling around the corner. It is told his father caught him red-handed and gave him quite the southern-fatherly discipline known as "a lickin'."

Deep in thought, Marty kept talking to herself. "This is too ironic. He came back from WW11 alive! Who would have ever thought that Hobby's life would end as if in a war zone? Wasn't he supposed to live long, forever in love with me? We had our whole lives ahead."

Others reported their happiness was contagious. Hobby and Marty together brought joy to everyone. Now, it was up to Marty to carry the weight of both father and mother to Nancy and the one to come.

More memories flooded Marty's mind, and flashes of their lives together like still-life photos zipped through her—their courtship, their honeymoon, the times they spent at the lake, Nancy's arrival, and the many picnics they shared. She recalled them dancing together and looking into each other's eyes—loving each other.

"You always made me laugh," she said to herself hoping he could hear her from above. "Darling, I'm sure going to miss you. I'll always be your ever-loving, and you'll always be mine; you know that, right?"

Suddenly, she felt a tug on her skirt which brought her back to reality. Glancing down at Nancy, Marty bent down and picked her up, telling little Nancy,

"I'll be strong for you; we will make it. With God's help, we will."

Faced with the harsh truth of Hobby's absence, worry, panic, and mourning plagued Marty. Settling Hobby's estate and affairs, paying the bills, and saving the house weighed her down, but the most significant concern remained in her heart as she thought, looking down at Nancy and the baby inside,

"How am I going to be both mother and father to you both?"

Deep in thought, crying, sobbing, trying to hold back the tears, Hobby's favorite hymn ran in the background inside her head, reassuring her that Hobby was now in the arms of His Savior.

1. I come to the garden alone,
   While the dew is still on the roses,
   And the voice I hear falling on my ear
   The Son of God discloses.

   Refrain:
   And He walks with me, and He talks with me,
   And He tells me I am His own;

And the joy we share as we tarry there,
None other has ever known.

2. He speaks, and the sound of His voice
   Is so sweet the birds hush their singing
   And the melody that He gave to me
   Within my heart is ringing.

3. I'd stay in the garden with Him,
   Though the night around me be falling,
   But He bids me go; through the voice of woe
   His voice to me is calling.

"In the Garden" by Charles A. Miles, 1913, Public Domain

Saying goodbye, as she walked away, she said softly,

"I'll never stop loving you. I'll see you one day in the garden."

Scene 7

Taking Care of Widows

*Religion that is pure and undefiled before God, the Father, is this:
to visit the fatherless and widows in their affliction
and to keep oneself unstained by the world.*

—James 1:27 (MEV)

Wednesday, November 9, 1955
Hatfield, Pennsylvania

Once back in Hatfield, Marty had little time to grieve, mourn, or take care of herself. Even though she was exhausted, she had to adjust quickly to her new world. Within the next weeks, her brother, Rembert D. McNeer, Jr., would be traveling north from Virginia to bring her to Philco to sort out Hobby's affairs, Worker's Compensation, and Social Security benefits. Her sister, Francis, would be traveling from Oak Ridge, Tennessee, to spend time with Marty and Nancy for a while.

"This mound of paperwork is impossible to go through. Nancy is constantly needing my attention. I had no idea how much there is to do," Marty sighed on her first day back from the funeral.

"I never bargained for this. Why, Hobby, why?"

Knock. Knock. Knock.

"Come on in!" said Marty as she opened the door.

"Marty, I came first thing to see what I can do to help."

"Vicky, how can I ever thank you? Come on in and sit. Have some coffee. My, I'm sure needing company right now. I miss him so much."

"I know you do. We all do. We're all crushed. It's much worse for you. I can't imagine what you are going through. But we're are here to walk with you through this, " said Vicky. In one breath, she continued, "Here, let me get the coffee. Is the coffee in the percolator and ready, or do I need to make a fresh pot?"

"Yes, thanks. It's freshly made." Marty went into the dining room and stared at the chair where Hobby would sit. Vicky helped herself into the kitchen and poured two cups of coffee.

"Do you take cream and sugar, Marty?"

"Just cream."

Vicky walked back in and sat down, facing Marty. Marty noticed Vicky was her usual upbeat self.

"She must be my angel," Marty thought.

"I have good news! All of us women are lined up to watch Nancy to give you time to yourself. We have as many days as possible already assigned. Now that we know that your sister Francis plans to stay with you a while, we will readjust our schedule, so don't you worry," said Vicky. She noticed squirmy cute Nancy tugging at her mother's lap. Marty picked up Nancy and balanced her baby girl on her shrinking lap.

"My, how do you do it, Marty?" Vicky asked.

"Do what?"

"Keep your eyes on Nancy all the time. She sure is a fast, little rug rat!"

"In the evenings and weekends, it took both of us—Hobby and me—to keep up with her. Many nights we had no sleep. But she seems to be sleeping much longer and better now. Whew, if this didn't change, without Hobby, I have no idea, if it weren't for God's help, how I could manage."

"How are you doing, Marty? How are you holding up?"

"Oh, Vicky, I'm not holding up very well. What has helped me so far is this sixth sense that Hobby is near. I have felt Hobby's presence around me ever since; the sensing that he is near, comes and goes. I feel his love upholding me, I can hear his voice, and I look everywhere to see him, but I can't. I long to feel his arms around me, but I can't. Yet, it's his love for me that keeps me going. It's a strange, but comforting feeling."

"My, Marty, what can I say? I love you and Nancy so much, you know that, don't you? I am here for you. So are all the others from our group," Vicky said.

"If you'd like, I am prepared to take Nancy for a few days. Our family is looking forward to her being with us. My kids are eager to play with her. Would this help you?"

"Oh my, I know she needs her mama now, but that would be super. She's always responded well with you and your family. My sister, Francis, plans to come for about a week. I can let you know when she arrives. Will this work for you?"

"Yes. Perfect. The rest of us have coordinated several weeks as I shared earlier and we can adjust the schedule when Francis arrives. I am so thankful to hear that she can be with you."

"Me, too. My brother is coming from Virginia to help walk me through the legal paperwork. Sometime after this week. But, that is when I could use help, too."

"No need to worry—we will take care of anything you need. I can give you a written schedule of the days and times. Would you rather have me bring Nancy here again or have the next person come and get her from me?"

"I'd want to see her, but, maybe…can I let you know later?"

"Of course! Also, we thought your house will need cleaning at least once a week. Since Sue can't take Nancy, she has offered to clean for you."

"I can certainly clean!"

"Oh no, we insist. You mustn't have anything more on your plate but taking care of necessary affairs and giving yourself time to rest. After all, you have two—you and the new baby—to take care of," said Vicky.

"The church women are bringing meals for you, too. You'll be getting calls. Speaking of meals, would you be our guest after church on Sunday?"

"Oh, yes, I'd love to. Being at church without Hobby will be difficult, but I should go. So many have already called me, brought flowers, sent cards. It'll be good for me."

"And, don't you worry one cent about Thanksgiving or Christmas. We are all planning something for you and Nancy. Oh yes, be thinking about a baby shower, also. We thought of holding it before Christmas before any bad Philadelphia winter weather hits us."

"You are all so incredible. Simply remarkable. I love you all so much," Marty said as tears streamed down her face.

"My, my, my. Don't get all mushy on me now. You can make it, Marty. We're all praying for you. We're all here for you. You're not alone." Vicky got up and hugged Marty.

"I know. Hobby must be looking down and so proud of all of you. All of this is just mighty kind of you," said Marty as she wiped her tears and got up.

Taking charge, Vicky left the table, picked up Nancy, and began to go upstairs.

"Want to come with me? You can help me pack a bag for Nancy—her clothes, any special toys, diapers. It's a good thing Nancy was with you and Hobby at most every gathering. All the faces should be familiar. She shouldn't have any problems adapting. She'll be just fine."

"I'm coming!"

Marty got up from the table. Her eyes glanced at a hutch she and Hobby had bought which held their wedding china and crystal. Other memorabilia from their honeymoon and four years of marriage sat on different shelves. On one shelf, coffee mugs sat which she and Hobby painted and portrayed scenes from their skiing trips. On another, sat a green round tray with tole painted flowers that Hobby had given her as a gift. Popular in the 1950s, this form of decorative folk art depicted floral designs hand-painted with single brush strokes on metal and wood. On that same shelf, stood a myrtlewood plate Hobby had just brought back from a business trip to Portland in August, the very same month they had moved into the house. The beautiful wood grain, coated with a clear finish, reflected both the beauty of the wood and the light. A buffet lined the other side of the room and displayed their wedding photos.

"We were a beautiful couple, weren't we?" Marty smiled to herself as she turned to walk up the stairs.

"Vicky, I feel so overwhelmed. I can't say 'thank you' enough for what everyone is doing."

"Now, Marty, quit saying 'Thank You' at every turn. It's what friends do. There's more coming, Marty, but I can't say anything. You, Nancy, and the new one coming are family to all of us. We are not going to let you go."

"Thank you."

"See, you did it again!"

"Oops!" Marty laughed.

"There's that smile back. With us and God's help, you will make it, OK?"

"OK. God's the only one who can see me through. And, of course, you are all just so wonderful to Nancy and me."

Once Nancy's overnight and diaper bags were all packed, Vicky loaded her arms.

Marty held Nancy close then took her little hands to walk her down the stairs. She talked to the tiny girl as if Nancy could understand her.

"You're going to have a fun time with Aunt Vicky, Uncle Jim, and their kids. Now don't go driving them nuts and running throughout their home, OK? Go to sleep when they put you down. No need to worry, you'll be back with Mommy before you know it. Mommy loves you, and Daddy, too. Oops, you almost missed a step there, but you're OK, sweetie. You're OK. Everything's going to be all right."

At the bottom of the stairs, Vicky once again took command.

"Now, Marty, don't worry! Just call me anytime. I'll call to let you know how Nancy is doing. Today's Wednesday. How about I bring her back Saturday? Remember lunch after church at our house. Don't bring a thing; we'll have everything. Come Monday morning the schedule with the other ladies will take over. If you ever need a full week, or full two weeks of reprieve, please don't hesitate to ask. I don't know when the church meals will start, but they will."

Vicky paused, turned, and looked directly into Marty's eyes.

"Don't worry; Nancy will always be in good hands."

Marty stood there and shrugged her shoulders as her hands went up in the air then flopped down at her sides, a typical Marty expression. Looking up at Vicky, she smiled—that contagious smile that only Marty could make. Her eyes appeared to twinkle for the first time in days. With renewed hope, she said,

"OK. I got it. I love you, Nancy! Be good! And see you soon!"

Vicky's tall, athletic build enabled her to carry both Nancy and her bags to her car. Marty stood at the front door waving and watched Nancy's blond curls bobbed over Vicky's shoulder. Marty could swear Nancy's little hand waved at her.

After goodbyes, she closed the door. Inside, with her back to the door, she breathed a sigh of relief, her hands placed on top of her belly, as if to reassure the baby inside that everything would be fine.

"I think I'll take a nap."

The silence felt good.

Scene 8

Encouragement in the Maze

A word fitly spoken is like apples of gold in settings of silver.

—Proverbs 25:11 (MEV)

"Well, it's just you and me now for a few days," Marty spoke to the baby kicking inside her.

"I'm thankful for you and Nancy. You both remind me that life does go on, and there is a reason for me to live. But where do I even begin?"

Because her friends watched Nancy, cleaned her house, and checked in on her, Marty began to breathe, rest, and regroup herself. So, during the next three weeks, Marty handled as much as she could to settle Hobby's affairs and to figure out plans for provision.

Marty sorted the mounds of paper which consisted of mail, cards, crucial letters, insurance policies, bills, and junk mail. First and most comfortable to focus on would have been the thank you letters to everyone who gave condolences, sent cards, and helped her directly. However, paying the bills was a top priority. Creditors wanted their money on time no matter the reason for the delay in payment.

She continually thought to herself,

"Making sure my children have a roof over their heads is my greatest concern. I can't lose this house. I poured all my earnings into it. Hobby would want me to stay here. Where would I go? I have no job. My job is my children."

She opened a letter from her childhood friend, Nancy T. Nancy could not attend either of the funeral services because of the distance to travel, and her words to Marty reflected her regret and sorrow. "I am so sorry that I cannot travel to Hatfield to be with you at this time." She mentioned this over five times, indicating her deep sorrow for Marty and the loss of Hobby. In her shock and grief, Nancy had no other words adequate enough to comfort Marty. Better it be sent, than not. The letter warmed Marty's spirits, a welcomed gift of love amidst the hardship she faced.

In another pile of mail, she came upon a letter sent to her by the Philco Corporation's Supervisor in Microwave Systems Engineering, dated November 2, 1955. It was sent out to field representatives around the world: France, Japan, Spain, French Morocco, New York, Rome, and Washington, DC. She paused and read it out loud,

> *You have no doubt read of the United Air Lines plane explosion and crash in Colorado on November 1. Marion Hobgood was on that plane and died with 43 others on board. Hobby was on his way to Portland to assist the other boys there on the Bonneville System.*

Her eyes welled up in tears, and her voice wavered as she read on,

> *Hobby was a great inspiration to all who worked with him. He had attained a position of admiration and respect with all who knew him and was one who we all confidently consulted with a feeling of competence and sincerity.*

She passed through the part about him graduating from the University of South Carolina in 1950, and then his joining Philco. And, about his wife and 15-month-old daughter Nancy with one on the way. His Supervisor in the letter continued,

> *He had very often proudly expressed his happiness with his new set up.*

From this statement, she learned something she didn't know about Hobby, which brought a smile to her face. He was so happy with their marriage, their daughter, the new home, and the new upcoming baby that he often expressed this with his co-workers.

She said to herself, with tears in her eyes,

"I knew you loved Nancy and me. I miss you, Hobby."

Her eyes then fell on the last sentences,

> *I know that you were shocked by this news as we are here in the lab. Hobby will long be remembered not only from our professional association but as a true, sincere, and loved friend.*

Mulling over these words, Marty said,

"A true, sincere, and loved friend. That you were. You were my best friend. I love you, sweetheart, and always will."

Since November 1, in secret, she had cried gallons of tears, often sobbing herself to sleep. During waking hours, she remained unwavering for Nancy and for herself to maneuver through the maze of crucial tasks that had deadlines. Among the mound of documents and letters demanding her attention, these words from the Philco Company brought joy to her heart. Marty folded the letter, put it back in its envelope, and placed it in a special keepsake box.

The Philco Company, a thriving, cutting-edge technology company, had been of great assistance to Marty throughout the first years. According to Marty, Philco hired the best lawyers in

Philadelphia to investigate the possibility of issuing a lawsuit against United Air Lines for their probable negligence. Philco also, through another letter, took the pressure from her by obtaining all of Hobby's certificates (birth and death), and any other documents she needed. She had access to Philco executives, too. Philco furthermore walked her through the process to obtain worker's compensation.

A collection was taken up for her throughout the multi-building Philco complex. In one building, a Quality Control Manager heard about it, and although he said he met Hobby only one time, he had so much compassion for this widow left with two children and raised double the average amount for such a gift offering. Little did he know, years later, he and Marty would meet.

Not only did Marty need to make many phone calls as she continually fought her way through the bureaucracy, but she also had funeral expenses, investments, and insurance policies to track. In the days before computers, she painstakingly drafted well-thought, handwritten letters, reviewed them, and then typed each correspondence on onion paper with carbon copies. Perfection with typing saved time and many headaches. She also had to work with United Air Lines to retrieve what remained of Hobby's personal effects.

"With all this, I just can't even think or focus on the holidays," she said.

Marty's eyes wandered over to the living room. From where she was sitting in the dining room, she caught a glimpse of the fireplace.

"Without him, the fireplace won't be the same at Christmas time. It will always be one stocking short. Our traditional Christmas card print block, carved by Hobby, won't be ever be made again."

Scene 9

Two Letters, Hope, and a Reason

Valleys of trouble will become doors of hope.

—Hosea 2:15

Among all the tasks to complete, Marty tackled filing the claims on Hobby's insurance policies. He had one from work and the VA insurance he kept after the war. As for worker's compensation insurance, the Philco Corporation processed the claims, once her brother and she would take any required documents to the company. All she had to do was wait. She desperately needed money for bills, the mortgage, food, and the baby.

She found both insurance policies. "OK, I know what to do with this one from work."

Looking at his VA insurance, Marty's heart sunk.

"Oh dear, he never changed his beneficiary from his mother to me like I kept asking him to do! We've been married over four years! I can't believe he didn't do it!"

What unfolded was a nightmare she wished she never had to confront. She should never have suffered it. She placed a call to Hobby's mother, Mrs. Hobgood, in South Carolina. During the conversation, his mother made it clear she did not intend to hand over her rights to the insurance money to Marty and Nancy. Her mother-in-law accused Marty of being snobby, uppity, and worse. Their voices raised; Marty was furious and mad. After Marty relentlessly pleaded, Hobby's mother still stubbornly refused to relinquish her portion of the claim. This conflict arose because Hobby never finished the process to change his beneficiary over to Marty's name.

Marty pondered this very hurtful and hateful action by her mother-in-law for several weeks. She did not know what to do. She consulted the lawyer, her sister Francis, and her husband Chap as sounding boards. Apparently, in consultation with the lawyer that Philco provided, there was nothing legally Marty could do.

Letter One

Not taking this sitting down, Marty decided to make a written appeal to Mrs. Hobgood. She kept writing drafts of what to say, crumpling the handwritten pages and throwing them on the floor. All her emotions poured through the ink and onto the paper. After running a final draft letter by Francis and Chap, November 26, 1955, she sat down and typed the following words of a broken-hearted, angry, distraught, and grieving widow and mother:

> *Dear Mrs. Hobgood,*
> *I just can't believe it—that Hobby knowingly left his insurance so that I would be left with two children, a $10,800 mortgage, and that I'd receive only about 2/3 of his insurance—$16,500 for me and the children (from other sources) and $10,000 (from the VA insurance) for you alone surely seems unreasonable. I find on discussing it with our insurance man and with Philco officials that the insurance left me will provide an income of little more than $50 a month for about 20 years. Then, it will be all used up. This with the social security and workman's compensation is only a bare living, and of course, the social security benefit ends if I go back to work even before the children are*

18. Workman's compensation lasts only about six to seven years. I'll still have the more expensive years to take care of out of the meager insurance, as well as needing something for myself after the children are through school.

I'm utterly heartbroken over it; it practically destroys all my love, the faith in Hobby, and his love, which has been keeping me going these last few weeks. To think that he didn't really love Nancy, the baby to come, and me is more than I can stand. As much as he wanted to help you make your constant dream of a house come true, I can't believe he'd take his children's home away from them just to give you a house, or, destroy the dreams I thought we shared. Our house does not have an insured mortgage. The G.I. mortgage does nothing but insures the lender of the mortgage money that he'll [the lender] receive $7,500 no matter what happens.

While we both scrimped and did without to save my pay-checks—it was my money I had earned while working under strain most of the time at Wyeth which made it possible for us to buy this house that I am proud to own. It was also my money which had been given to L.G. and which repaid the $400 Hobby somehow owed you. I never did understand why he owed it to you. If I had known he was in debt to you when we married, I'd have postponed our wedding until it was all paid. But loving Hobby, I paid for it. All these sums of money were paid from my salary, not from Hobby's.

Marty's anger rose as she continued. In her state of grief, sorrow, and mourning, together with her pregnancy and hormones charging, she was not a woman with which to be reckoned. People considered Marty very easygoing and peace-making, so this fury marked a fiery side of Marty. To provide for her family, Marty had to confront this selfishness and greediness on the part of her mother-in-law. Unashamed and outraged, she continued:

Neither would I have written the checks to the Veteran's Administration had I known he had never changed the beneficiary on his insurance. I didn't realize it had not been done. It seems incredible that Hobby would discuss all his affairs with you and leave me not knowing what he told you. When we were first married, I agreed to his not immediately changing his beneficiary on the policy as I knew there was an overly strong attachment between you. I did not want to be demanding. Then he planned to change it when you married Steve. I was not sure then whether he did it or not, but I know positively he intended to do it again after I quit work and Nancy was born. At the time the change of beneficiary form was left at Hobby's own request, we were getting no peace or rest with Nancy, and Hobby was trying to do school work, too, so I can see how the actual change was neglected.

Marty then sarcastically reminded her mother-in-law that while she paid for the payments for the insurance coverage as well as the bills for the house, she could not have changed the beneficiary over to herself.

I could always write the checks and pay the bills, but of course, I couldn't sign the papers.

To know that Hobby knew it had not been changed leaves me completely lost, with a big emptiness where I treasured Hobby's love. (My insurance was made over to him very soon after our marriage, my father or mother or other relatives receiving nothing as is proper and usual.)

The pain of losing Hobby and the fear of losing the house, with no possible income in sight, took over her already fragile state. Exasperated and infuriated, Marty began to question Hobby's love for her and the children over his not changing his beneficiary from his mother's name to her name.

After all, you still have L.G. to care for you—I have <u>two</u> babies to <u>take care of</u>, and I can't possibly do outside *work for a number of years. I do want the children to have advantages above bare existence and a home. I love them if Hobby did not.*

Marty's heart and emotions dripped onto the paper as she continued venting and presenting her position:

I am glad Mr. J could give you an accurate picture of my financial condition. While at first, I thought my financial situation would be reasonably good, I find that it is very poor indeed. Hobby must have been having delusions of grandeur when he talked to you. I am surely sorry I missed that conversation; we would not be in this deplorable situation now if I had. When I wrote last week, I was expecting to receive the VA insurance and was hoping for additional settlements. Now I am distraught. As Mr. J no doubt told you, I cannot anticipate any sizeable financial aid from any source and have only the $16,500 insurance, social security, and workman's compensation to count on since the plane was blown up by criminal activity and not caused by the negligence of the airline.

Her heart-wrenching thoughts turned to question her mother-in-law's love for herself as a daughter-in-law and for her grandchildren. She had been offered to move in with either of her siblings and pointed out their generosity. Marty wrestled, in these first few weeks, with how she could keep a roof over her children's heads without Hobby and his income.

"Though you have professed your love and affection for me as a daughter-in-law and for Nancy as your grand-daughter, if this tragedy had happened to L.G. I don't believe you would have been so eager to take the house away from his children as you seem to be to take it away from Hobby's children. I had hoped I might be able to have a home for the children even if I decide to sell this one on

account of its location. While my relatives are generous in their offers, two families in one house are not very satisfactory and can be only a temporary measure. I surely can afford to pay neither high mortgage interest nor the high rents necessary to live in a decent apartment. Without Hobby's VA insurance, I'll have to sell the house. I'll lose agent fees and taxes which will prevent me from getting the down payment back in full.

Marty's mother-in-law expressed no sympathy for Marty when she had told Marty in a phone conversation that Marty could always go to work. Marty struck back hard, stood her ground, and did not take any low blow. She bore her heart.

I understand that you told Mr. J that I could go to work as you did when Mr. Hobgood, Sr. died. Well, your children were grown at that time. Hobby must have been at least 21. Both boys had been in the service, therefore having a chance to earn and save money of their own, and to go to school under the GI Bill. In other words, they were self-supporting, and you had only yourself left to support. So far as my working goes, there's quite a difference between us as I have babies to care for during all their formative years. Three to support completely, and I must be both a mother and a father to them.

Marty spared no words and did not hold back her feelings toward Mrs. Hobgood. She decided to make her appeal as one mother to another.

Most mothers want to make things easier, if possible, for their children and grandchildren, so I really cannot understand your attitude in retaining your claim on Hobby's insurance. It doesn't seem morally right that Hobby's own children should be denied educational opportunities and other advantages which Hobby had dreamed of for them, while this windfall builds your dream cottage. $5,000 of *the insurance I'll receive was ear-marked for educational purposes but now will have to be used for living expenses.*

Also, my income is now fixed, and as the insurance policies are used up, it will gradually decrease. At the same time, economists expect the cost of living to rise indefinitely, thus reducing the purchasing power of this income. $300 per month now may be worth only $200 - 250 five years from now. In that case, my fixed income will barely provide for the necessities of life. Your earned income will rise with the cost of living.

Marty's great concern was that her children would now be raised without a father and made every attempt to appeal to her mother-in-law's sense of compassion for her fatherless grandchildren.

It's going to be extremely hard to raise the children with no father—they need a daddy—without having the additional financial problems caused by my not having the extra income the VA policy would provide. That amount would not provide luxuries, but it would ensure freedom from want and perhaps offer a little leeway for the children's education and a house.

Not desiring to give up the fight, Marty made a final effort to appeal to her mother-in-law's conscience.

I think that you should prayerfully consider what use you make of Hobby's insurance and see if you can accept it with a good conscience. It will especially be difficult for the children for now, and I am sure you will want to see that Hobby's children and your grandchildren will have something above a bare living.

As Hobby's wife and your daughter-in-law, I have no recourse, but to ask you to release your claim on Hobby's VA insurance.

Sincerely,
Marty

Satisfied, Marty signed the letter, placed it in an envelope, and put a stamp on it. Less than four weeks had passed since Hobby's death. Instead of being able to grieve reasonably, she had to contend with her narcissistic mother-in-law and fight for her future. Once mailed, she would have to be patient for a phone call or a written response from Mrs. Hobgood. It became a waiting game.

Hanging on by a thread, Marty recorded that Hobby's love for her held her up during these dark days and weeks. She felt his love around her ever since his departure. His love sustained her and enabled her to keep going. This grievous situation with his mother not wanting to hand over her claim was like a seething sore as if someone repeatedly stabbed Marty in her heart. The shock of her mother-in-law behaving this way just increased Marty's dismay and frustration. She felt helpless. Sent from someone who should be consoling Marty, poison dart arrows targeted Marty's integrity and character and endlessly penetrated her soul. Placing the stamped envelope in her purse, Marty said to herself,

"There, I've done it. How could a grandmother do this? What kind of woman does this? Oh, Hobby, why didn't you do it? Why did you keep postponing changing your beneficiary? You loved me more than your mom, didn't you?"

Letter Two

Within weeks of Hobby's funeral, Hobby's mother still refused to hand over her claim on the insurance policy. The word battles had become heated and brought additional levels of hardship upon an already delicate, frail, and distraught widow. On top of her loss, the undeserved stress and agony heavily burdened Marty's wellbeing. The entire situation of Hobby being so close to his mother that he did not change that beneficiary nor talk with Marty about conversations he had with his mother stirred up deep questioning in her own heart about Hobby's love for her. She knew deep inside that Hobby loved her, yet her feelings floundered when she wrote L.G. early in December and begged him to talk to his mother:

> *L.G., I agree wholeheartedly with you. I know that Hobby loved us, and many friends have mentioned to me how an intensely devoted a couple we were. He must have loved us to be as a wonderful husband and a father. But his not putting us first and from what your mother says, doing this knowingly, makes it seem that Nancy and I were of less importance to him than I'd always believed we were. That makes it so hard to reconcile the principle involved (Hobby placing his mother above his family) with Hobby's deep and abiding love as I knew and treasured and believed in it. One does not say 'I love you' in one breath and take your home away from you with the next.*

Marty continued defending Hobby's character.

> *Hobby's action in this insurance arrangement, if indeed intentional, does not jibe with the complete love and faith we shared, which I've felt sustaining me. I just can't believe he meant it to be so. It is not in character with his nature to do so irresponsible a thing.*
>
> *As for Hobby, he was as modest and unassuming a person as I've known.*

Having been accused of being haughty by her mother-in-law, Marty refused to take such assault on her character sitting down.

> *I greatly resent being called overbearing, selfish, and domineering. If I had any of these characteristics, I would surely have seen to it that Hobby's insurance policy was made over to me immediately after we were married. This situation then would have been avoided. I am sure no one has ever used those terms in describing me. And as for being money hungry, I'd not have married a Junior Engineer*

if I were, I'd have hunted for a man in a more lucrative business.

Marty's words fell onto the page, one after another, as she defended herself and Hobby. In one paragraph, she discussed how her father, a pastor, earned only $3,000 a year; she even grew up in homes with outhouses. She expressed the value of family when she wrote these pointed phrases:

> *I surely know what it is to do without and know that there has to be real love to pinch and sacrifice as our family has done. True love, within a family or otherwise, is unselfish, a giving kind of love—with no demands or strings attached, either financially or emotionally.*

Whenever people grieve—as was in the case of L.G., Hobby's mother, and Marty—people can say cruel things; and, misunderstandings can proliferate, adding to the anguish. Marty recognized this and intended to set the record straight to avoid confusion over words. She reassured L.G. of her utmost respect and love for him, his wife Doris, and their family.

Since Marty had been accused of thinking she was more intelligent than Hobby, Marty, standing up for herself, relayed she always believed Hobby to be smarter than herself, although both had degrees. She continued to clarify what she meant by sharing one time how Hobby matured so much in the five years they were together, including the one year they dated. According to her letters, Hobby's family took great offense at this observation.

Whether Marty knew it or not, in the course of defending herself, she wrote words of wisdom, worthy of passing on. On maturity, she wrote:

> *Maturing does not mean that our basic natures or personalities change, or that our love for our families and the family ties are changed in any way by this process. It is*

merely a growing up process—one of learning to be independent, of planning one's life, and of shouldering responsibility for it.

The significant part of this letter outlined the reasons why she needed the mother's claim to the VA insurance policy. Compelled to justify her stance, she disclosed all her financials in the letter. When she crunched all the numbers, she would not have any income beyond 20 years, and some funds would drop off before then. Besides, no one could have lived even in the 1950s on just $50 a month. With Hobby's income abruptly robbed from her, she needed all the financial help she could get.

L.G. seemed unable to assist Marty in convincing his mother to turn over her claim on the insurance policy. Instead, Marty had been questioned at every turn. For example, she responded to questions such as why she doesn't return to work, why she needed Philco executives to help, and why didn't they stay in L.G.'s house with an outhouse when they last visited that fall. In a polite way as possible, Marty's letter reflected her need to protect herself, defend Hobby, and justify her every decision.

In her plea, she suggested a compromise that Mrs. Hobgood's portion of the GI VA insurance could be placed into a special education fund for Hobby's children to be able to go onto college. Having their children go to college was a mutual goal and dream of theirs as young parents. She wrote,

I know Hobby would want his children and me provided for as well as possible, to have a home and be independent.

By December 8, just one month after Hobby's funeral, she received news that United Air Lines disclaimed all responsibility and liability. There was little chance of any settlement from the plane bombing, except receipt of Hobby's personal effects which were not yet released. She made sure that L.G. knew this fact.

She finished this letter with a few thoughts, desiring to persuade L.G. to do all he could to change his mother's mind. She also reinforced her love for his family. She wanted no bitterness to set in from either side. She also left a hint about how difficult it was for her to be without Hobby by her side.

> *I do hope you see my need and that it seems only morally right and fair that I should have the VA insurance money. Please think about this, talk it over with Mom, and pray that you'll decide on the right and fair thing. I know you want to do as Hobby would have you do.*
> *Love,*
> *Marty*
>
> *PS. It is a terrible big thing to contemplate—this job of raising two children alone. I can only pray for the strength of mind and body to do it. And, there is always this loneliness and need for Hobby. It gets harder every day.*

⬥⬥⬥

Mrs. Hobgood never gave over the money.

Years later, the author had been told that L.G. and his family left for a long-term electric job out west. When they came home, they discovered their two-story home had an unexpected renovation job: an entirely newly upgraded and expensive/top-of-the-line siding job. Another story passed down said that a full-size single apartment had been built upstairs. It took over half of the second floor and had a kitchen, full bath, bedroom, and living room. L.G. could do nothing about that permanent surprise. Whether it was the siding or the added apartment (an older cousin is entirely convinced it was the siding), he knew that it surely would be up to him to take care of his mother, who proved to be quite a character.

⬥⬥⬥

With the help of her friends in Philadelphia, Marty and Nancy spent a good Christmas. Then, on December 28, 1955, another daughter decided to arrive ahead of time. Instead of naming her Patricia as she and Hobby were going to do, Marty honored Hobby by naming this newest addition, Marian Patricia Hobgood, the author of this book.

By mid-January 1956, L.G.'s wife, Doris, had a baby boy, named him Marion Pierce Hobgood and gave him Hobby's family nickname, "Perry." Hobby had been so well-liked, that one of their daughters had also been named Marian years before Hobby ever died. The three Marians proudly carry forth his name to this day.

Six years later, Marty had to contemplate getting a job or get married again. When her youngest, Marian, approached six years old, she did indeed remarry. The two daughters finally had someone to call "Daddy." Coincidentally, this new Daddy was the Quality Control Manager at Philco whose heart went out to the widow and her children and collected double the customary funds.

It was not until the youngest child, Marian, turned 11 years old that the two children ever met the Hobgood side of the family. They worked and saved their money for a year. Marty, their mother, put them on a Greyhound Bus, a 21-hour bus ride, from Cleveland, Ohio to Columbia, SC to spend six weeks with the family they never knew. Nancy and Marian were so excited when they heard about their eight cousins and especially the youngest, a boy close to their age. These visits continued for two more summers.

Although Nancy and Marian knew about the VA insurance issue, they never knew how great the contention had been. Marty was not one to hold grudges and walked in forgiveness. The introduction to long-lost relatives filled a gap for the children and gave them a tangible link with their biological father. L.G. and Doris loved and embraced the two girls with opened arms, as if the girls were their own.

Life has its way. We never know times or seasons, how long we have on this earth. One crisis happens, and before you know it, another one comes. Tragedy and trauma know no bounds. The two travel together, arm in arm. Without any faith, most people do not seem to cope very well. Faith, trust in God, and a loving family community become a refuge in which an individual can hide and find comfort when storms come.

Marty was not exempt. Not even three months after saying goodbye to her first love, another significant death happened. Suddenly in January, Marty's mother, Pearl McNeer, passed away. Sorrow upon sorrow. Two grievous losses back to back. With her two baby girls, she flew from Philadelphia to Newport, Virginia to attend the funeral services. Being the youngest on the flight, the airlines awarded baby Marian a Sky Cradle Club Certificate.

Once back in Hatfield, PA, Marty decided it best to spend a year with her mourning father. She and her father always kept a close relationship. The two together would walk through the grief process together. Marty rented out the house she and Hobby had just bought. She had only lived in the dream house for less than six months. With the help of a friend, she moved everything to Newport, Virginia. With her father, Marty would be able to continue wrestling with all the emotions and paperwork. In less than four short months from Hobby's death, the three had been uprooted from their community and the loving support of Marty and Hobby's longtime friends who had been her pillars to lean on.

As a surprise to Marty, their faithful friends in Philadelphia worked diligently throughout 1956 to establish a Marion Pierce Hobgood Memorial Fund. Hundreds of people, from Philco, church, and strangers donated to the fund. As a way for me, Marian, the author, to say thank you and honor them, you may read the list of all the donors located in the Appendix. The fund was set up for Nancy and Marian to have Christmas, with a set sum released to Marty each holiday season. Her friends surprised Marty with a special dinner in her honor later in 1956 and presented her with the memorial fund. Their closest friends from that young adult group never wanted Marty to go without and knew her new life would be difficult. They honored Hobby, blessed Marty, and took care of the girls. They knew how to be family.

Not everything worked out immediately for Marty and the children's survival, but Marty's unwavering faith in God kept them living in that house. The two daughters sustained Marty through the years. She shared many decades later,

"You two gave me hope and a reason to live. Without you, I could not have made it."

Marty with 4-week-old Marian

Marty with baby Marian and Pastor who came to the window the night of November 1, 1955

First Christmas 1956 with the MHP Memorial Fund

Life Goes On – Marty with the girls 4 years later, 1959

ACT II
Through Trauma

Scene 10

When Past Meets Present

Our past may explain why we're suffering,
but we must not use it as an excuse to stay in bondage.

—Joyce Meyer

Before we continue with the story, we must consider: When does our past influence our present and affect our future? Can we forget every painful memory, every wrong turn? Do our present behaviors—both worthy and questionable—reflect our past? Which in turn either block successful living or allow us to merely sail through life, often treading with our heads slightly above water?

Most of us have heard that you should never look back. If you do, you won't be able to move forward in life. Don't have any regrets; keep your eyes ahead. Haven't many of us been taught to stay focused, envision our goals, and pursue them? These are essential steps toward achieving anything in life, and many books have been written on this subject.

When contemplating either the importance or irrelevance of our past, two Biblical principles confirm what the success gurus teach. (1) Jesus taught that anyone who puts his hand to the plow and looks back is unfit for the Kingdom of God (Luke 9:62). (2) Paul exhorted people to forget what is behind and to press on toward the goal of Jesus Christ (Philippians 3:14).

Without opening an in-depth theological discussion or creating any new theology, let's briefly examine these verses. Jesus teaches we must live a life committed to Him with our whole heart, not part. Using a farming analogy, a person plowing the fields cannot dig a straight row while looking backward. Paul encourages people to persevere and not to allow past sins, obstacles, and behaviors to hinder their walk with Jesus.

Could it be that Jesus knew our past would hold us back? Should we press forward in life toward our destiny, purposes, and callings while our hand is still on the plow? Could it be that the plow represents our entire past, including negative responses and thought patterns, and Jesus is calling us to be free from them? Could it be that ignoring our history and living from behaviors cultivated from our past can cause us not to break through barriers blocking us from our dreams? Without addressing them, how will we know if we have been set free from them or recognize that we need freedom in areas of our lives?

While he calls us to forget what is behind and press toward our prize, could it be that the Apostle Paul, too, recognized our past influences our ability to live up to our potential as God intended? Paul's admonition that we let go of everything that hinders, including the sins that easily entangle us, calls us to address our past so that we can move forward in freedom (Hebrews 12:1).

How do we know what to let go if we don't take a look at our present behaviors in light of our past?

No one enjoys being with someone who is always regurgitating the past. Their memory loop keeps replaying on overdrive, and they relive their past to the extent that relationships, both work and friendships, deteriorate. When we meet with that person at our favorite coffee shop, we eventually hear the same saga and woes. Until that individual can address his past, he remains frozen in development, unable to enjoy life.

When I was growing up listening to 33 rpm vinyl albums, the worst sound I heard was a record skipping. One scratch on a vinyl record could cause the diamond-tipped needle to either jump or slide across the grooves. I'd be bee-bopping around in the house when suddenly, the music would be abruptly interrupted. It would play a few bars, then, jump back to what I just sang. The same stanza would repeatedly play as if stuck in a roundabout without any escape. It was called a broken record. Little could be done to fix those scratches.

In time, the tape cassettes took over the record album industry. Once anyone got their first tape recorder, they knew they were *in* and *cool*. The tape recorders had a remarkable feature: The Rewind Button. No more did we need to reset any album to play again by lifting the needle and placing it back to the beginning. All we needed to do was push the rewind button and watch the tape automatically rewind to the beginning. In more sophisticated tape players, it could be directed to rewind and repeat itself. The player could be set to play all night long.

Since I was an avid John Denver fan, this technology in the 1970s was heaven—well, next to West Virginia, of course. Until the tape itself would twist, jam, or break. If the tape didn't break, I'd pull out a pen, place it through one of the tape-cassette holes and re-wind the tape by hand, smoothing out the jammed and folded portions of the tape, hoping that the tape would still play. Like these tapes, our minds and memories can become jammed, twisted, and broken.

Our brains store memory and log events, conversations, and behavior, including touch, sight, sound, and smell. Like those albums and tapes, once triggered, we find ourselves repeating patterns of reactions—some harmful, some healthy, and others neutral. They become second nature, and we do them without thinking. We forget that with every action there is a reaction, and subconsciously we respond in ways which cause a situation or thought pattern to become even worse. Blinded by ourselves, we wonder why the same thing keeps happening, why we either explode in anger or cower in fear, and why we can't handle failure or success, among many other "why's" in life.

We live life unaware that we have become stuck in a pattern of harmful repeats.

When is it appropriate to revisit the past?

We never know when our wounded past will collide with our present by infecting relationships, work, and life; its pain crescendos until we cannot tolerate it any longer.

I had fallen into the trap of the broken record cycle and replayed tapes over and over, rehashing everything. These mind loops reminded me often of my insecurities, fears, and shortcomings. I walked with a sense of shame and insignificance. Authority figures could convince me, in my vulnerability, I had done something wrong even when I had not. I aimed to please and tried harder in life to overcome negative thought patterns.

One of my greatest fears was never having enough, including losing our home and being abandoned. Notice I said, "one" as I had many others. Never believing I had to look back into my past to become free, I grew to be the Great Stuffer of my emotions. I didn't recognize I had repressed any feelings or memories. I remained clueless with what laid in the depths of my heart and wholly unaware of any correlation between my past and present. Until one day, my past finally met my present in a head-on collision.

Once I reached a breaking point, with my back against a wall, my buried inferno burst through years of lying dormant. I could no longer keep it at bay. All my past boiled to the surface in such disarray.

I had been uncorked to feel.

Yes, that was me. I was like a bottle of champagne whose bubbles remained contained. The champagne inside a corked bottle lies peaceful, enticing someone to open and taste it. With one sudden yank on the cork, the cork flies, the sparkling bubbles burst out and spray the delicious fruit of the vine over everything within reach. The bottle resembles a fountain shooting off streams of expensive champagne at least several feet, pouring like foam down the outside. To some, it's chaos; to others, it's beautiful and celebratory.

For me, when the unavoidable release happened, chaos invaded my world, and I turned into one complete emotional mess. Like Ms. Humpty-Dumpty, no one on earth could put me back together, except one.

An Invitation to a Journey

Through these pages, I am not providing a clinical or a typical approach on how to overcome trauma because each person lives a different story and travels a custom-made Road to Freedom. Through a peek at my soul-searching journey, you will learn principles, frameworks, and guidelines, but no quick-fix formulas and no magic wands.

All my healing occurred between God and myself. I had no counselor to guide me. Although, nothing is wrong with professional counselors should you find yourself traumatized, walking through difficult times, or stuck in life. For me, I determined to go to the One with the answers. My counselor was the Almighty Counselor Himself. Only He knew my most innermost parts and secrets, and through His Son, He made a way out.

You will be invited into my darkest struggles, my walk out of denial, and the ugliness in my own heart. As I tear back the curtain, for the first time, profound divine encounters weave a message of victory, hope, and freedom. Since God does not play favorites, I know that what He did for me, He will do for anyone. He fashioned and formed you; He knows all that you have been through and never took it lightly. No two of us are alike, and He loves us each with such reckless love, that He does not dole out cookie-cutter solutions or guided group tours to wholeness. Instead, He promises that those who diligently seek will find absolute freedom.

My journey has been one of dysfunction to function, disorder to order, and from high anxiety to peace. It took me beyond tragedy through trauma into lasting freedom. It's a wild, painful passage toward healing from the brutal killing of my father and his resulting absence in my life. In the search to find my natural dad, I was led down an unexpected path, full of surprises.

Once thrust onto this road, there was no turning back. My past finally crashed into my present. I was desperate. It's a path I did not initiate. I didn't know when or if healing would ever come. I had no recognition I needed to embark on such a spiritual road trip with God. But, then again, none of us do when we find ourselves on His journey.

What led up to that fateful day when everything exploded within me? That can only be answered by looking back and moving forward to the day of my Great Uncorking.

Scene 11

Fast Forward Forty Years

Whether we admit it or not, or are aware of it or not, we all have a deep longing inside to know who we are, what we are made of, why we are here, and where we are going in life. We're all searching.

—taken from my journal

I was no exception.

Oh, before I continue, let me formally introduce myself—I am Marian Patricia Hobgood Poeppelmeyer—the second daughter of Marty and Hobby, the guide through this narrative. I wish I could write that after my mother had remarried that life was a breeze and we lived happily ever after. But that was not the case. To understand the immense, insidious impact the loss of my dad had on my development, let's venture back to my past to fast forward forty years.

Life Influencers

Growing up fatherless left a gaping hole in my soul and fostered a fascination with family roots. I wanted to know who my father was and what he was like. Did I carry any of his traits? What other family characteristics did I possess? In trying to define myself at an early age, I adopted a core value that everyone mattered and that every person brought across my path would somehow fashion me as a person.

I know it sounds a little quirky for a young girl, but I got this idea from a friend from a youth group I attended. I thought it made plain sense. I lived life to the fullest, made great use of my time, and welcomed new adventures. I gleaned values, attributes, and wisdom from others I met throughout my life. This practice instilled a greater awareness of others, their value, and worth, and developed an ability to learn from most any person or situation.

I call these persons, Life Influencers. Key individuals, events, or periods in a life span can make lasting impressions, for good or bad, on our values and character development. Positive company, people with morally upright lives, bears good fruit. Bad company, people with habitually destructive lifestyles, bears rotten fruit. These Life Influencers either impart positive or contrary attributes and wisdom. Life Influencers may be parents, siblings, and extended family; or, a teacher, mentor, boss, friend, sports coach, or even a co-worker.

Like ingredients in a cake, I opted to absorb characteristics I admired, incorporate the better qualities in others into my personality and chose how to live out my life. Together when mixed and allowed to bake through time, I figured I would develop as a contributing member of society, with a little bit of everyone who touched my life.

For example, my closest friend growing up in those formative years, lived up to her name, Joy. Her father taught her not to be anxious over any trouble or crisis by laughing at it. She lived a comfortable, happy life with a loving father and mother and eventually gave her life entirely to Jesus before I did. I loved being around her because she taught me not to get upset over little things. Because of her influence, our daughter's middle name is her namesake. While I have not perfected her reaction, I can still see her laughing at an unwanted situation, reminding me to lighten up. Without ever meeting her, my daughter portrays this positive attribute.

On the other hand, negative Life Influencers may also leave their marks on our lives, but most often stealthily. We are often unaware of any such negative Life Influencers until we each take time to ponder how in the world when our lives are falling apart, did we get ourselves into such a predicament? The river of denial loves to keep us in the dark and underwater, oblivious to the snares laid by our past.

By the time we reach this juncture, if ever, we become forced to inspect the good, the bad, and the ugly. Often a closer look forces us to take one of three roads:

- The same path we have been on—we know we have problems, but ignore them;

- The smoothly paved street—we don't know we have issues or do not want to know them; or,

- The wilderness road, less traveled and laden with bumps and adventure, which leads us to freedom—we acknowledge we have problems and choose to face them.

Many prefer the fast, easy, painless way out and either stay on the same path or elect to live blindly on the smooth street known as denial. Exceptionally few choose the road less traveled.

I was aware of healthy people influencing my character but never considered that negative people and traumatic events also shaped my thinking and behavior. Negative patterns of behavior incorporate themselves subtly into our personalities, like mold growing inside a home. These unhealthy beliefs become a part of us and affect our decisions and actions. We end up living the Big Lie. Years can pass before we tire of tripping over them. They expose themselves through self-proclaimed, often subconscious statements, such as:

"It's just like me to be ignored or overlooked."

"It's just like me to feel like I don't belong; I'm not accepted."

"My dad or mom was like this or did this, so I guess I am just like him or her and will do what they did."

Besides key personalities in our lives, Life Influencers could be significant events where life did not go as planned: a birthday party or a school function to which a parent did not attend, a firing from a job, long-term unemployment, or a difficult marriage. Loss of a business, sickness, an accident, or loss of a pet. Life changing events can be moving and changing schools for children. The most tragic include death of a loved one, with the loss of a child among the most grievous. Abuse in any form compiles the deep sense of loss—loss of identity, self-worth, and in the cases of sexual abuse, the loss of virginity and innocence that can never be brought back. These unexpected traumatic events can shock us physically, emotionally, and spiritually.

The death of my dad before I was born certainly changed the course of my beginnings and whole life trajectory. However, until I reached the age of forty, I had shoved my dad's death behind an iron wall, living as if his absence and murder had no lasting effect.

Unbeknownst to me, my negative Life Influencers piled on top of each other, compounding damaging emotions and not so perfect reactions to situations, which led to my eventual major life crisis. Years of repressing and believing lies overwhelmed my circuitry and ability to cope.

A New Daddy

A man who I could call "Daddy" entered into my world when my Mom remarried; I was almost six years old. Ecstatic to finally have a daddy, our family life was somewhat ordinary, at least for a few years. While Mom dated him, we knew him as Uncle George. After he and our mother married, he became Daddy. This new father figure became a huge Life Influencer, for better and for worse.

Little girls need a daddy and greet Uncle George before marriage to Marty in 1961.

He played with us, sang to us, and tucked us into bed. I still can see him standing in our bedroom doorway, with his guitar strapped over his shoulders, and hearing him sing his favorite lullaby:

"What will we do with a drunken sailor, what will we do with a drunken sailor..."

While not a typical bedtime song, my sister and I giggled during his bedtime serenades and then fell asleep.

We played one of my favorite games called "Sleeping Giant." He would lie on the floor pretending to be asleep, and we girls would sneak up on him. He would lovingly grab us and tickle us, just like a dad.

Our new Daddy took us to International Folkdance Festivals, which cultivated a passion for missions and foreign cultures. Mom supported and led a world missions group at church. At eight years old, their influence produced in me a desire to major in French in college and to live a year in France.

Later, Daddy lost his position at the Philco Company, and we moved out of our home in Hatfield, Pennsylvania to Youngstown, Ohio. When the steel industry began to tank, we moved to rural Novelty, Ohio, outside of Chagrin Falls northeast of Cleveland.

That fall, I entered the sixth grade and my sister the seventh grade. Pre-teen years can be a stressful time with changing hormones running wild. Add moving and changing schools during a critical time for that age group, and you have a recipe for disaster. Making friends had become difficult in this new setting. Nancy and I were having trouble adjusting to living in the country and attending our new schools.

My sister stumbled from one crisis to the next, and all hell broke out. Arguments frequented our once happy family life. Daddy turned into an unpredictable rage-alcoholic. He didn't drink but thrived on rage. I can still hear him continually shout,

"Marty, they're your girls!"

When arguments flared, I escaped three houses up to the neighbors. This family offered me refuge and a loving environment. At night, I often cried myself to sleep. Not wanting to disturb the Sleeping Giant and suffer his wrath, I focused on my studies and activities. To counter the hostilities, I adopted the role of peacemaker in the house. I did all I could to please him. What could I do, helpless and without a voice, but adopt a "Good Girl" persona so as not to ruffle the feathers?

Making things worse, for some unexplainable reason, this new Daddy did not want Mom ever to discuss our real dad. Silence about our biological dad contributed to a massive void in my life. Eleven years after my real dad's death, mail would still come addressed to him. One of those days etched a permanent memory in my mind. Daddy yelled at Mom so much, as if it were her fault. Her meek frame crumbled and cowered in fear as she took the brunt of his verbal blows and put-downs. She did not deserve this treatment, and I was powerless to stop him. Fear of his rage gripped me.

Since I repressed all my questions about my real dad and had no voice to stop the yelling, my Great Emotional Stuffing began in my childhood.

Teenage Years

Hiding in my studies and feeling emotionally insecure, my last expectation was winning a popularity contest. I simply wanted to be accepted and included. At four feet and eleven inches, mousy and shy, I could be found either at the beginning of every line or the end of every line, depending upon how we were told to stand. In gym class, no none wanted this runt on their team, especially volleyball. I certainly could run fast but could not jump the hurdles in track. When I joined the girls' Powder Puff Football team, the girls' coach did not select me to run the ball even though I excelled in running and getting through crowds. Instead, they placed scrawny me as linebacker. I didn't even know what a linebacker did. In the last quarter, the coach sent me into play. My three minutes of fame resulted in my jock teammates running over me.

Feeling rejected most of the time, I adapted and decided to make friends with everyone: the hippie crowd, the 1950s greaser crowd, the rowdy bunch, the misfits, and other students, except the jocks and cheerleaders.

Something transpired, though, between my junior and senior year. I became accepted into a social group: the academically advanced students. I cannot explain this transformation. Perhaps it was the summer trip to the United Nations that I won by an essay competition. Because I was out from underneath the stereotypical labels, I blossomed on this trip with students from three states. I could be who I wanted to be, not who others thought I was.

My new high school friends belonged to the Honor Society group, as I did. In our senior year, we could opt out of study hall and volunteer to tutor students in a backroom in the library. With three full lunch periods without any scheduled classes, I joined this tutoring group. However, we did no tutoring. Instead, we did what a bunch of nerds would do. We covered for each other when we skipped out to lunch, we read the Ohio Revised Code's sexuality laws, and we pranked the librarian. We took what we learned from an advanced history class and formed a political interest group against the prom. We put together a slate of candidates who were least likely to be King, Queen, or members on the court. We passed out the slate of Prom candidates, on which my name was listed, to our senior class. The block voting worked. The class voted the entire slate of least likely to sit on the prom court. Making a mockery of the senior prom caused an uproar from the administration. Because we were honor students, we got away with it. However, the administration forced another election.

Acceptance. Finally.

During this time, I never talked about my biological dad with anyone. In a history class during a discussion about abolishing the death penalty, I remained silent. No one knew my story, and no one would understand my convictions on the matter. Tears welled up, but I kept them at bay. Not wanting to share my perspective or background, my thoughts and emotions stayed internalized and corked.

Despite the turbulence on the home front, walking on eggshells, and my struggles with rejection, my senior year ended quite well. I was ready for college.

University Years and France

I put my past behind me and looked forward to my future.

Upon graduation from high school, I entered Otterbein College (now Otterbein University), located in Westerville, Ohio, and decided to do a double major in French and Political Science. I studied diligently, became involved in a Christian student organization, volunteered with juvenile delinquents in a Detention Center, and played piccolo in the marching band. I flourished in the academic setting. By attending a Christian group, my faith grew, and I quickly gathered new friends. I could be who I wanted to be, not what others thought I should be.

Following my lifelong dream, I studied French at the University of Dijon, France, 1975-1976. With a Eurail train pass in hand, Europe and France beckoned me to travel as much as I could. I made French friends and experienced French culture with zeal. I spread my wings, reached for the stars, and lived every moment to its fullness. I went a tea drinker, came back an espresso lover. I went a teetotaler, came back a wine snob. I returned bolder, more confident, and self-reliant. France was good!

Identity Crisis

When I returned to the United States in 1976, I had an identity crisis: I loved France so much that I did not want to come back to the US. Torn, I wondered, do I stay in France or return to the US? I had to return to earn money to finish my last year and needed to complete my BA Degree. Slowly I fell into a year-long, deep depression. I struggled with reconciling that I was American and not French.

"Why was I born as an American?"

"Why couldn't I have been born French?"

"What am I doing here when my heart is there?"

As the year continued, the depression lifted but only when I reached out to God[1] for help. A group of students loved me back to life and introduced me to a closer walk with God through the power of the Holy Spirit as is written about in the book of Acts. My prior theology (my view of God and understanding of the Bible) had not allowed for this newer experience of faith. I wasn't quite sure what I was asking for when, according to the scripture John 20:22, I prayed only one thing one night in a group setting:

"Jesus, I want to receive Your Holy Spirit."

Once I asked, an unexplainable power—which felt like fire—descended upon me, engulfed me, and the depression lifted immediately. The next day, my closeness with God took a significant step forward. Others remarked my countenance had changed, and joy replaced the heaviness I had been feeling the entire academic year. Emboldened, with unspeakable empowerment, I finished my senior year well—winning a scholarship based on a research paper I had written—and graduating with a group of friends so close and tight that most of us remain in touch to this day.

After graduating in 1977, I landed my first job as a Management Analyst with a state agency. I had my own office with a door, a window, and a secretary. Still corresponding with one of my French friends, I longed for the day to return to France.

By 1978, I returned to France for three weeks to seek out if I should live in France, only to discover that America was my home.

Love

Two months before my self-discovery vacation back to France, I met an American young man, nicknamed Pep. We dated every day for two months. When I returned, he threw me a surprise curveball—he proposed to me! God sent me home to the United States because He had other plans for me. Months later, we were happily married on June 16, 1979. I went from being a Hobgood to Mrs. Marian H. Poeppelmeyer.

Following Our Passion

Knowing that Pep felt called to the ministry, a local pastor recommended we attend Christian Outreach School of Ministry (COSM). We took no time to leave our good state government jobs and spent three years in the hills of the Ozarks south of St. Louis, Missouri. Situated on 110 acres of rolling land, the school for pastoral and missionary training boasted having cabins, a swimming pool, an outdoor round-shaped chapel, and a campground fellowship hall. Students flocked from around the world and abandoned well-paying jobs to follow their passion and calling to serve the Lord wherever and whenever. The Jesus movement, in which thousands came to know Him, was at its peak, and many adopted a life of being sold out one hundred percent to Jesus. Most students arrived the same as us: no jobs, but the sure call of God on their lives.

These three years built a strong foundation for ministry which exemplified the love, grace, and mercy of God. We grew in faith, the Word, and in understanding how to build Christian community. Since most who moved there did not have two coins to rub together, it seemed as if the same dollar bill kept passing among the congregation. No one in that church went without; we took care of each other, just as in the first church in the second chapter of the book of Acts. Every Sunday, we would read the church bulletin, not for the order of service, but for who had a need, for who had something to give away or something to sell. People generously gave washing machines, TVs, bags of groceries, or even rides to the city. We have yet to ever belong to another church who exemplified this level of caring for one another.

We forged lasting friendships, as was the case with Dave and Beth. Dave, not much older than us, served as a professor at the school. Standing tall, he had black hair and blue eyes that radiated the love of Jesus, Dave and Pep shared a special brotherly bond. He and Beth had five children. Beth made everything from scratch and knew how to stretch every bit of food. When I was a young newlywed, Beth served as an example for me, unaware she was used by God to mentor me. Once we returned to Ohio, we kept in touch over the years. At one time, the men discussed ministering together, and Dave loudly hinted he would like us to purchase a plot of land next to their house.

Life is Not a Rose Garden

We moved back to Ohio after Pep's ordination in 1983, determined to make an impact for the Kingdom of God in the Columbus area. However, instead of blazing stories of great success, we encountered obstacles, setbacks, and a church split. These trials severely tested our faith. I believed that life with Jesus meant no more troubles, and if we did incur trials, then we must have sinned somewhere. This belief served as a Big Lie, clouding my ability to respond appropriately. Discouragement fueled my shame, guilt, and rejection. The promise that God had plans and a future for us—a rose garden life—proved not to be true in our life.

After our new young church had been split by an elder, just after the birth of our first and only daughter, my husband became devastated. I was crushed but endeavored to provide loving support to Pep and raise our daughter. I had resigned from a good job to remain a stay-at-home mother, a family value of ours. Our income had been cut by two-thirds within six months, from combined 27K (substantial earnings then) straight to 11K annually. With our income stripped, living daily grew tougher and tighter. Even so, we always had enough on our table and saw miraculous provision. Without knowing if all our needs would be met, walking through this valley proved to be challenging and the instability daunting.

The pastor who sent us off to COSM mentored Pep and brought him on staff at his church as an interning pastor. In his wisdom, the pastor knew Pep had to stay in the saddle and not die on the vine. We both came to life again. Eventually, after three years, we were called to move on to another church organization, and Pep remained working full time in the insurance industry.

A Fire Begins

While my life has been seasoned with many more Life Influencers, both in the form of people and events, I trust I have given you enough to understand more of my story. At this point, our faith remained stretched, but hope always kept us believing in God.

Because Jesus says that we must put our hands to the plow and not look back, most of us do not take the time even to comprehend how our past can influence our future. Who we are, where we come from, and what makes us do shape and form our character. Many traits and behaviors gained through those Life Influencers are learned and can be unlearned.

In addition to being able to sort out those Life Influencers, it is sometimes necessary to take a step backward to be able to move forward. I had no clue that I would be required to do so. I went on with married life: happy-go-lucky, with high expectations for our future and a desire to do my best in all circumstances despite the bitter setbacks and disappointments.

An expression says that in relationships, iron sharpens iron, and our marriage will not disappoint you. Our dire economic situation stirred friction between my husband and myself. I made every attempt to remain a supportive, faithful wife throughout every curve ball thrown. The mounting strain of setbacks and road-blocks put tension on our marriage. On the surface, we were the lovebirds, but underneath, a destructive fire had begun to burn.

Scene 12

Sparks Ignite the Search

A mighty flame follows a tiny spark.

—Dante Alighieri

1994
Columbus, Ohio

As kindling lit with any lighter starts a fire, adding wood increases the flame. Should nothing dampen its initial spark, a thriving flame soon burns and glows. If not contained, an entire forest or city block can be consumed in a raging fire. In our hearts, lit kindling can set not only ourselves on fire but also our families and relationships. Many of us walk around ignorant of little embers just waiting for more fuel to burst into a blaze. We often never sense this undercurrent until its too late.

Turning Point Year

A bottle of champagne requires two stages of fermentation with a minimum of fifteen months to three years of preparation before it is ready to be uncorked and served. Champagne aged five to six years is considered among the best in the world and most expensive. As champagne ages in the bottle, the longer the fermentation continues, pressure builds within the bottle, and the outcome produces top quality champagne. Like these bottles of champagne, stressful situations accumulated in our lives, building pressure inside both of us, which fermented inside. As the champagne house places a wire over the cap to keep it from exploding before its time, I lived with a wire cap clamping down my buried emotions.

Despite our state of crisis after crisis, some due to our own ignorance, God continually surprised us with His kindness and divine provision. During the next season in our lives, we never went hungry. We never took government assistance. We never went without utilities or mortgage paid. With no stable income, we received free carpeting and installation, a new water heater, and cars. We were extremely thankful each time, even with our faith tested as if in the refiner's fire. We lived on the edge, although we balked every step. Ironically, despite these blessings amidst hardships, because of the mounting financial and marital tensions, the weight of deep anxiety, anger, and bitter disappointments threatened to destroy us. Underneath the surface, the glowing embers of a destructive forest fire burned.

While we were not acting with any amount of faith, at least not according to what I thought was faith, God's faithfulness to His Word remained faithful to us. A mantra prayer of mine, taken from I Timothy 2:13 and Mark 9:24, became,

"Dear God, I am faithless. I have no faith for _____ (mortgage, bills, marriage, fill in the blank). But You, Lord, are faithful and cannot deny yourself. Would You show yourself faithful? Help my unbelief."

The year was 1994, and Pep had just taken a new job which ignited hope for our future. Because his other insurance company was relocating out of state, Pep naturally accepted another position with another company. Catching us by surprise, due to no fault of his own, this source of income was snatched away within ninety days. He became unemployed for the first time since he started insurance work seven years prior.

Despite having the rug pulled out from under us, our faith remained high with expectations. We believed God would open doors for Pep to quickly land another career position. What we could not foresee was in the next five years, he would only be working two and a half of those years, but in short stretches at a time, divided into three periods. The first bout of unemployment would last about 14 months. For some reason, God never revealed the entire future to us, as He rarely does. As the year continued with no further job offers, this loss of employment, just like the loss of the church, would affect Pep and me more than I could have imagined.

My Search Begins

We attended a church conference whose guest speaker was Randy Clark, a pastor with Global Celebration Ministries. Randy previously had undergone a severe ministry burnout. He felt as if he had hit a brick wall spiritually and hungered for a new touch from God. At a conference, he received a fresh vision and outpouring of the Holy Spirit, which supernaturally lifted his fatigue and weariness. Renewed and alive with God's burning love and compassion, he came to share this revelation with those attending the conference.

As practiced in our church, Randy began to pray for people who desired to be touched by God. When he stood in front of my friend who stood to my left, I could feel an unexplainable but palpable power radiating peace and love from him. In my spirit, I recognized this as the Presence of the Lord. Before I could blink, I floated safely back onto the ground like a feather. No one pushed, pulled, or touched me, not even Randy.

Throughout my Christian walk, I had never experienced anything like it. I had seen others fall under the influence of the Holy Spirit, but not me. The phenomenon of falling backward often happens when the Holy Spirit ministers. Some say it's because our bodies cannot contain the glory or power of the Holy Spirit and become weak. Others describe it as His healing presence. For me, I think He quiets our bodies and minds so that He can speak to us, shower His love on us, and heal us.

That day, the Holy Spirit certainly got my attention. I had never been so overwhelmed by the Presence of God as I had been that day. It felt like gentle, rolling waves of wind being poured over me. I found myself giggling, overtaken by joy. I usually viewed such phenomenon with skepticism. This time I sensed something different and knew my experience was valid. As the noise in the room grew vague and distant, time no longer existed. It was Jesus and me, and nothing else mattered.

As I encountered the sweet presence of God, my theology and preconceptions dramatically shifted concerning how God chooses to move and act. I figured the Holy Spirit, the One sent to guide us into all truth, wanted to communicate with me, but something blocked my ability to hear Him. I reasoned He had to knock me off my feet to quiet my soul, to infuse His Spirit with mine so that I could listen to Him. As I laid there, like basking in the sun, God bathed me in the warmth of His love and the stillness of His peace. It's as if His heart touched my heart. In those beautiful, sweet moments, His Spirit communed with my spirit with unspoken words.

Quite unexpectedly, what had been a casual curiosity up to this moment became an earnest desire, for the very first time in my forty years, to know my real dad. A missing piece inside cried out for its resolution. This longing only grew in intensity during the months ahead. I could not quench it nor shake it.

The Fire Grows

Throughout that year, as unemployment continued, we continued to seek the Lord for His direction. Did God desire us to return to full-time ministry? Did He want us to leave Ohio? Should Pep change careers? What exactly did God have planned for our lives? Feeling beaten, we both made every attempt to appear full of faith and hope.

Later that year, Pep flew out to friends in Portland, Oregon so that he could check out jobs in that state. He arrived in time to learn that they decided to accept a missionary position in Hawaii. Without expecting this, he enjoyed a little R and R before flying home. Our goal to move out would have been to work with our friends in ministry in Portland, not to relocate only for work.

By fall, we decided to check out St. Louis and visit our friends from Christian Outreach School of Ministries, in Goldman, Missouri. When we arrived with our two children, Dave and Beth greeted us and quickly announced that Pep could go job hunting, or we could come with them every day and night to a conference with Rodney Howard Browne, a South African pastor who frequently imparted the joy of the Lord. Randy Clark earlier in the spring had spoken of Rodney's influence in his life. Of course, we knew then why we were compelled to visit the Martins that week. Instead of looking for work, we attended the entire conference. We returned to Ohio touched, rejuvenated by the Holy Spirit, and thoroughly immersed in God's joyful presence.

As days, weeks, and months marched on with no answers and no jobs, the euphoria of the trip to St. Louis waned, and we both began to crumble secretly—not even sharing how we felt with each other. This diminishing feeling did not negate the effects of our experiences at the conference, but we expected a quick turnaround for our problems, which did not come. Our faith and marriage held by only a thread.

Withdrawal and Shutdown

Surely, Pep would receive a job soon. After all, didn't we experience God's Presence and His power exponentially at that conference in St. Louis? My faith remained confident that if Pep could only get interviews, he would obtain a position. Who could refuse this hard worker? Back at the ranch, though, no jobs were coming forth. After leaving interviews, the human resources personnel repeatedly told him that he was in the top two, but he was never selected. This continual disappointment fueled fires of discouragement within both of us.

After hearing this several times, I began questioning God for wisdom. I wondered if my husband was doing something wrong to sabotage his employment. Was it his dress? His mannerisms? My problem-solving skills wanted to help my husband by analyzing his job search. One day after Christmas after one more time of his being in the top two candidates for a position and not being the one chosen, the realization came to me: he only had a pastoral degree, not a secular college degree. So, of course, I suggested he go back to college and get another degree.

My husband also began withdrawing from me, his soul mate and only earthly lifeline. In his depressed state, he became angry when I bought a new shirt and suit from a large department store. He pushed me away when I offered to review his resume. In his woundedness, he told me to stop being his mother. At which I yelled, "I am not your mother!"

Sinking further into despair, he retreated inside one of the man caves in his brain. By Christmas, the distance placed between us created an insurmountable chasm. Both our faith levels and coping abilities slipped to unprecedented lows. For once, I could do nothing to support him, except to stand by him and pray.

Loss After Loss

In addition to increased trials at home, three out of six spiritual fathers in our lives passed away within a year. Each one significantly impacted us directly and mentored us as a young pastoral couple. When I saw the pattern, I began to pray for the other remaining three.

These losses compounded the weight of sorrow and loss that gnawed within me.

Entering 1995, I feared not only losing my husband but our house, too. I cried continually on my knees before the Lord whenever I could. Over time, I even had grown weary of carrying the weight of praying for our family. Any tenacity I had possessed gradually leaked out, both spiritually and emotionally. I hit a brick wall, physically and mentally. I could not talk to my husband at all. If I tried, I spoke to a deaf ear. He caved in and lost his fighting power; he froze and did nothing except look for work and nurse his wounds.

Known as the kissing couple in Missouri, we were now the boxing couple. I presented myself well outside the home while my insides collapsed. The embers of discontentment and discouragement fueled fires within me. I got edgy with my children and always asked them to forgive me for being short with them. As a supporting wife, I felt helpless as I could do nothing for him.

I was being set up for my Grand Uncorking.

Scene 13

Three Famous Words

Death and life are in the power of the tongue,
Those who love it will eat its fruit.

—Proverbs 18:21 (MEV)

January 1995

Sandy's Story

Approaching New Year's Eve 1994, a gloomy dread draped over me like a weighted, black grave cloak. Fear of having the rug pulled out from underneath us one more time haunted my mind. Though light in comparison to many others, trials had been pounding us for years with little reprieve. I'd dive into petitioning and intercession before the Lord, only to come up for air, and then another obstacle or trial would come whipping around the corner. Pressed on every side, I suffered loss after loss, and battle fatigue overtook my physical and emotional stamina.

As best as I tried not to stir up strife with my husband, the polarizing tension between us kept thickening. Putting on a happy face, I pretended everything ran smoothly in the home front, especially at church. Living a lie, I became an imposter who covered up her brokenness.

Just a couple of weeks into the new year we received a call from Joel, a dear friend from Otterbein College and best man at our wedding. He had married Sandy, another Otterbein student friend. It was a call we did not want to hear.

"Hey, Pep and Marian, Sandy became weaker and weaker. Nothing more could help her. We've done all we knew to do. She is now in hospice. Just calling to let you know. I will get back to you about memorial services."

Nothing made any sense. In one year, Sandy's passing away made the fourth person integral to our growth as Christians to leave this earth. More difficult to fathom, she wasn't old.

Why would God allow a young mother with four children to die so young?

At the beginning of the prior year, 1994, Sandy merely went to the doctor to see if she had bronchitis and came out with a prognosis of lung cancer. Ironically and most puzzling, she never smoked. Once diagnosed, their lives resembled a roller coaster ride with agonizing times of prayer intermixed with a barrage of treatments. Both were bulwarks in their faith. Madly in love, they were the first in our group to be married in 1978. They lived and breathed the love and grace of Jesus.

During our college years, Sandy stood apart among our circle of friends on campus. Her face lit up consistently with a cute smile and twinkles in her eyes, with her long black curly hair bouncing off her shoulders. Others loved to be around her; her passion for Jesus carried a contagious fragrance. She understood Biblical truths when others did not and conveyed her faith through her daily living. We could not go anywhere without her talking to someone about the love of Jesus in non-intrusive, natural ways. Her maturity in the use of the spiritual gifts listed in the book of Romans and I Corinthians surpassed her young age. She walked in great wisdom, doused with gentleness, sweetness, and humility. Of course, we all knew she was not perfect, nor a saint, but she came close.

Sandy always took time for others. Not proud or arrogant, she remained quiet and meek, yet confident and steadfast in her walk with God and the authority of Jesus Christ. She found great joy in setting others free by bringing them into a personal relationship with God through the love of Jesus Christ. Sandy lived in such intimacy with God that the Holy Spirit naturally guided and flowed through her daily life, and people were attracted to her—like iron to a magnet.

To this day, I recall with fondness the time our college fellowship group ate at our favorite ice cream place on High Street in Columbus, Ohio, called Farrell's. Sandy left her seat to visit the ladies' room, but we began to wonder why it took her so long time to return. We should have known. When she came back, she shared how another girl had entered the restroom. Sandy recognized she was agitated and spiritually vexed. Sandy then spoke with this young lady, prayed with her, and set her free from the evil spirit's harassment through the power of God, bringing her to freedom in Christ. Sandy walked her talk.

Visiting an Angel

Much later in the fall, after Sandy had received months of treatments, I called Sandy and asked if I could visit and promised I would not stay long. She welcomed my coming and agreed to let me know should she grow tired.

During the hour and a half drive east in the rolling hillsides of Ohio, my thoughts went back to my past. In our early pastoring years, we had walked with Helen, a member of our congregation, through her cancer ordeal. We gathered a team dedicated to praying with her regularly for her healing. We saw victory; later, it had come back on her quite suddenly and unexpectedly. We watched what she and her family went through. She underwent a bone marrow transplant, and only Pep, her designated pastor, could visit. He de-contaminated himself to enter her germ-free quarantine room. Anything he brought her had to be wrapped and passed through ultraviolet light, including a brand-new Bible.

While under treatment, our friend witnessed patient after patient die around her. Her biggest question had been,

"Why me, Lord? Why am I still alive?" To this day, decades later, Helen remains healed.

This early experience ministering to our severely ill friend gave me insight as to what to say and what not to do. In and out of memory lane, I prayed that I would be a blessing to Sandy. I did not know what to expect. After nine months of aggressive treatment, would she be lying down? Would she be ultra-skinny with sunken eyes, no hair, and frail?

After traveling up and down the rolling hills, the exit to Sandy and Joel's house soon approached. Suddenly, I snapped out of daydreaming and found myself pulling up to their sprawling ranch home.

Knock. Knock. Knock.

"Hello! It's me, Marian!"

"Come on in." Sandy waved to me through the windows.

I found my way to the enclosed porch which featured white wicker furniture with flowery cushions. She sat facing her back to the wall of windows with an end table. Clean, crisp, inviting. Magazines, books, plants, and other décor created a cozy niche, full of sunlight and warmth, beckoning guests to enter.

I did not want our conversation to be about me, but her. Nor did I want to overstay and tire her. Sandy greeted me with her trade-marked grin and a twinkle in her eye. It seemed like I had just walked into the Holy of Holies, where God's presence is so powerful yet calming all at the same time.

I could see her body's weakness and the weariness from the fight. Although her face still sparkled, I could see the pain in her eyes.

"How are you and Pep doing, Marian? Would you like some iced tea? Help yourself in the kitchen." Just like Sandy, being the hostess and thinking of others before herself.

"Sandy, thank you so much for being able to have me come over at such short notice. I'm sorry I couldn't have come earlier this year. I don't want to stay too long to overwhelm you," I said as I gave her a gentle hug before sitting in the chair across from her.

"I'm fine, thanks for the offer. How are you doing?" I asked.

What began as a short visit stretched three hours. Sandy did not want me to leave. We talked as girlfriends and chatted for a while. Then, she pointed to a book lying on an end table near her. Titled *When God Doesn't Make Sense* by Dr. James Dobson, this book helped many people through trials in life. For Sandy, though, it was different.

"Have you heard of this book?" she asked.

"Yes, Sandy."

She lifted her head, leaned over, and looked in my eyes.

"A well-meaning Christian from our church brought this over thinking it would help me. You know what, Marian?"

"What?"

"I haven't read it. I don't need to. To me, God is making perfect sense," she said with a serious look.

I just sat there. My ears opened wide to hear what my friend would say next. Not to disturb this sacred moment, I did not ask her what she meant. I knew she knew something from God that none of us could even grasp.

"Yes?"

"Yes, He is making perfect sense." Sandy's cute smile lit up her face again. She continued,

"We believe for healing; yet, we are preparing, too," said Sandy. "You know what?"

"No, tell me," I said, wondering what she would share next. I never knew what to expect to hear from Sandy.

"Joel's mother had some special family heirloom jewelry containing precious gems to be passed down in the family. I decided I'd like to do the same for our children. So, Joel and I went to a jeweler where I carefully selected four pieces, one for each child. I then wrapped each gift with a note from me, so that each child would receive a gift from me on their sixteenth birthdays."

It took everything in me to hold back the tears. I knew each child from birth. No one this young in life expects their time on earth to end. She clung to life with each breath. I sat quietly listening. I needed to be strong for her. She continued and said,

"You know, Marian, everyone is used to coming to me for help, counsel, and prayer. Well," she paused. "They keep coming, expecting me to be able to give them a word or something. Don't they realize it? Don't they see me? They won't stop coming. After you leave, someone else is coming today and expecting me to counsel and pray with them. What do I have, who am I to give any more?"

The look in her face and tone indicated that she was drained, depleted, and weary. I could see it took all her strength to breathe and talk. Instead of them coming to minister to her, people still depended on her for help with their problems. But, being Sandy, she did not turn anyone away. My heart ached for her.

Time flew that day as if we were transported to another place and the clock stood still. An hour visit became three hours. I looked at my watch and knew I had better say goodbye and let her rest. Before I did, I asked,

"Sandy, may we pray together?"

"Sure, I'd love that."

At that moment, I held my hands out, and she grabbed my hands. Her feeble hands wrapped all her fingers around mine and clutched them. I do not remember how or what we prayed, but I do remember her grasp—she clung onto life with all the strength she could muster. I will never forget her look, her voice, and her grip. We finally said our goodbyes.

I sensed it would be the last time I would see her on this earth. Seeing her suffer was difficult, and yet the image of her sitting with unwavering faith remains implanted forever in my spirit. I visited an angel that day. An angel who kept clinging onto life. An angel who knew that God was making perfect sense. To this day, I still treasure the most amazing and hallowed three hours I have ever had with a friend.

A Pivotal Moment

In January 1995, three months after my visit with Sandy in the fall of 1994, I wasn't surprised when Joel called.

"Hey guys, I have to let you know that Sandy passed away. Her memorial service will take place in three days."

In central Ohio, winters are very unpredictable; that week, we never knew when snow, rain, or sleet would grace our landscape. As chance would have it, in a snowy blizzard, after having found a sitter for our children, we traveled over 110 miles to attend. Despite the dangerous road conditions, hundreds packed the church pews. Sandy knew no enemies, and many dearly loved her.

Sandy and Joel had both planned her service; it was the most remarkable service we ever attended or have attended since. We learned that among her preparations, she told Joel what she wanted at her own memorial service. Full of worship, special music, and story after story, we celebrated Sandy's life; and, the message of Jesus Christ was heard by all who came.

Following, we walked downstairs to the fellowship hall of the church. Balloons galore filled the room, and a celebration birthday-looking cake took center stage. Music and laughter resounded all evening. Yes, Sandy would have wanted it this way, a party celebration. Safe in heaven, she had no more pain or sorrow. Though short-lived, she lived life full of the Holy Spirit, which touched anyone within her reach. The rest of us would grieve and mourn her presence on earth, sorting out all the why questions.

On our way home, we drove home both stunned and shocked as we mourned the loss of this lifelong friend. We felt for Joel and his four children, all below 16 years of age, whom we had watched grow up from birth. The youngest had to have been only 4 or 5. Memories of Sandy, how many people she had influenced in their faith, and the life she and Joel lived, turned over and over in my mind.

Unanswered questions churned. You know, those bigger "why" questions. To Sandy, God made sense. To me, nothing made sense.

Joel, at his young age, would be left raising four children. Our sorrows could not begin to compare with his trauma and loss.

On the way home, we stopped at a restaurant with a couple we had met at the memorial service and shared our grief for a moment. The snowstorm added to the long trip back home. Sandy's departure only compounded the feelings of significant loss that both Pep and I, each in our separate ways, had been experiencing as we walked through this dark time in our lives.

Once home, before we called it a night, we sat quietly in our living room. Our dismantled lives seemed beyond repair. In our silence, I turned to Pep and said,

"Honey, why don't we simply give our lives, marriage, and entire situation over to Jesus, like we did when we first got married?"

Unexpectedly, three famous words came out of the mouth of a very broken and hurting man. He looked straight at me, abruptly, without an ounce of compassion, and said,

"You need counseling."

At that instant, I shut down to him. Those words cut me to the core and marked a pivotal moment. One more time, he pushed me away, discounted me, and wounded my spirit. We now joke about it. Understandably, it's not an example of what to say to your spouse or anyone going through a rough time.

Our words have the power to build up or tear down, to bless or to curse. In those three words, the one I loved pulverized my already tender, fragile spirit. My husband took my heart and love for him and ripped them to shreds with those three words. Profoundly aggrieved, all I knew to do was to withdraw into a self-protective cocoon—emotionally frozen, exasperated, and numb.

Scene 14

The Odyssey Begins

Indeed, the water that I shall give him will become in him a well of water springing up to eternal life.

—John 4:14 (MEV)

My Refuge

Awake, but no feelings or life inside, I became a walking zombie. Alive, but immobilized. Feeling pain, and yet numb. Living daily by rote, my days passed on autopilot. Those stabbing words "You need counseling" tore an enormous festering sore in my soul that I could not mend.

I didn't know how to pray anymore. I tuned out worship, listening but not engaged. Once regarded as the one exuberantly singing, dancing and shouting to the Lord during praise and worship services, I now sat halfway up the auditorium, stared into space, and wished I had the same joy the others radiated. Lifeless, I had nothing left to give. The death of Sandy and the fear of my marriage disintegrating loomed over me with ever-increasing heaviness.

I tried all I could do to assist my husband, but he stubbornly refused my help. He had lost vision, hope, and purpose. Having no fighting power left, he unwittingly chose to flee and hide.

My husband's misery spilled into our home. Feeling useless, I functioned with my children and others but retreated from my husband. At home, I rarely said anything of substance to him. A knife could cut through the thick tension. We co-existed in cold silence for a year and a half.

We lived under one roof; we shared a house, but not a home. I frequently took the kids places. Once homeschooling was done, field trips or visits with other homeschooling families occupied the days. A couple of times, I took the kids on vacation to South Carolina.

My brief conversations covered only family basics necessary for daily living:

"I'm going to the grocery store."

"We have chicken for dinner."

"I'm taking the kids to the zoo."

Honestly, I couldn't stand the thought of seeing an unemployed man waking up. Each morning, Monday through Saturday, I left at 6 AM before anyone woke up. God was my only refuge. I ventured to a new park each day to be alone with Him. I would listen to worship music and cry. Soon one hour with Jesus grew into two, then, into three hours over the next several years. He was my only answer and the only one on whom I could depend. I could not run anywhere, either. I had to stay in a miserable marriage, remain faithful to my marriage vows, and raise my children. In my comatose-like state, God became my hiding place.

What I did not know was that the Wonderful Counselor would be cultivating a special relationship between Him and me during these times in the parks. Not knowing what to do, the very first day I drove to a park ten miles from where we lived. Dazed, I played a worship CD while I traveled and cried. By the time I turned onto the long country road to the park, my tears had flooded my face. Abruptly, a man's deep voice thundered, interrupting my mental muddle,

"Ma'am, you're going too slow!"

I looked to my left and parallelled with my vehicle, a sheriff's car kept pace with mine. He had rolled down his window, so I rolled down mine.

"Ma'am, you're going too slow. I'm giving you a warning—go faster!"

Startled, I looked at him and nodded. Then, looking at my speedometer, I realized I was only traveling 10 miles an hour in a 35 mile an hour zone. No kidding—I almost got a ticket for driving too slow!

I obediently stepped on the gas. Once I arrived at the park and pulled my car into a parking spot, I sat with streaming tears. I asked the Lord,

"How can I love this man? How can I love Pep? He's pushed me away. How can I keep on loving him?"

"You love him because I love him," the voice of the Lord succinctly and firmly told me more thunderously than the sheriff's voice. No one else, not even the sheriff, was in the park or near my car. My spirit knew God had spoken, and He gave me a direct mandate, clear and straightforward.

Thus, began a journey of intimacy with God, which took me into new heights with Him, lasting well beyond those five years.

The Starting Gate

One day, I bravely disclosed our current situation to our senior pastor and conveniently omitted the fact I had quit speaking to Pep. The pastor knew most of our background with its highs, lows, and detours. Listening carefully, he said,

"Marian, I do not know why God has you and Pep on this path. It's like you and Pep started at Point A, and He wants you here at Point B, but He is not taking you in a straight line to get there. Your lives have been like a zigzagging path, going here, then going there."

As he said this, he drew his fingers in a crisscross, back and forth motion on an invisible chalkboard, from Point A to Point B.

"I don't have answers, but why don't you just jump in the River?"

Whew! Was I glad he did not recommend counseling! I did not even dare tell him what Pep had said to me. I strove to maintain Pep's dignity and defended him whenever anyone said anything about him not trying hard enough to find work. Deep inside, I knew Pep was doing all he could.

After listening to me, the pastor pointed me to the only One who could do all the mending and restoring. I still had no clue the origin of all my inability to cope stemmed from the loss of my real dad. So, naturally, I did not tell him this history. No one knew anything about how my dad died. Until the year before with Randy Clark, no persistent longing to know my real dad ever crossed my mind. Thus, his story never surfaced in any conversation with others. Our entire family felt justified because the FBI caught the killer, the courts tried him, found him guilty, and sentenced him to capital punishment for his heinous crimes.

"Jump in the River ... hmm..."

"Jump in the River" was a phrase our congregation used during this season of the outpouring of God's presence, love, grace, and joy. To jump in the River meant coming to the front of the church in the context of worshipping God through singing with your whole heart, soul, mind, and strength. With no distractions, you could focus single-heartedly on God alone. Since God inhabits the praises of His people, faith becomes ignited in corporate worship, shoulder to shoulder in adoration before Him. For me, jumping in the River symbolized being immersed in His presence, opening my whole heart to God and permitting Him to draw me closer, to take me into intimate places with Him.

Hence, jumping in the River seemed natural to me when the pastor mentioned it. In God's Living Water, I would meet God and find my answers. I knew to throw myself before the Lord, and each worship song became a personal prayer between Jesus and me. I kept saying to myself,

"If I could just touch the hem of Jesus's garment, I know I would be healed."

I identified with the woman with the nonstop bleeding who pressed in through a crowd to touch the hem of Jesus' garment (Mark 5:25-34). She heard of the healing power of Jesus Christ. Not wanting to draw attention to herself, she thought that if she discreetly inched herself through the crowd surrounding Jesus, that by merely touching His hem, His power would heal her from the twelve-year-long sickness. She risked making everyone, including Jesus, unclean according to Jewish Old Testament law. But she did not care. She was desperate. As she touched the hem, Jesus stopped. He felt power leave Him even though the crowd had pressed in all around Him seeking healing.

Did Jesus shame the woman? No, He could have for she was unclean according to Jewish law. She thought she could grasp his robe without being discovered. Instead, when He turned and saw who had touched Him, the woman told Him the whole truth. He lovingly told her,

"Daughter, your faith has healed you. Go in peace and be freed from suffering."

I felt that same shame and desperation. Wholly identifying with the woman, I thought,

"If only I could touch You, Jesus, I would be made whole."

Following the conversation with my pastor, I knew he was right.

My season of hiding and denial closed; another leg on my quest began. In God's River of Living Water, seeking Him wholeheartedly, I would touch Him, find my answers, and become free. At the starting gate of an adventure into the unknown, it was time to take the next plunge.

Scene 15

Jump in the River

Find me in the River.
Find me on my knees with my soul laid bare.

—Martin James Smith, *Find Me in the River,* Delirious?

The Plunge

The next Sunday, I took the pastor's advice, and without hesitation, I plunged into the River, pressed into God's presence, and knelt before Him during worship. Turning back was not an option, and I did not want to be superficial and religious. I meant business. I jumped in the River with a determination to leave changed each time. Touching Jesus' hem remained my sole objective. I got out of my seat, went up front, knelt, and cried endlessly during the worship time. In the hot pursuit of healing, I did this for weeks while the congregation experienced a season of great joy. I was falling apart before the Lord. It wasn't just weeping, but depths of sorrow, loss, mourning, and grieving. Tears drenched my cheeks; my eyes turned puffy and red.

I stood out from the other worshippers and for once did not care what others thought. By this decision, without realizing it, I reached a first pivotal point in my journey. I had finally come to the place where God was able to begin touching me. No person came to pray with me for weeks, nor did anyone ask me what was wrong. I assumed they didn't know what to do with me and I was happy with that.

I kept asking God,

"Why can't I handle these losses? What is wrong with me? I have always prayed for and encouraged others. Now, I have no strength for myself. While others appear joyful and full of life, I'm a crying basket case. I can't stop. Why, Lord, why?"

With an unwavering tenacity, strengthened with desperation, I specifically told God,

"I never want to leave Your presence empty-handed. I do not want band-aids to cover up surface wounds. I don't want temporary fixes. I don't want platitudes. I don't want to feel better. I don't want to feel goose bumps and leave the same. I want to be touched by You and leave permanently changed each and every time."

Sorrow and grief overwhelmed me with no end in sight. With no clue as to why I could not shake the tears away, I continued to trust God would eventually intervene in my situation. He was the Only One on whom I could depend. I could not count on or go to my husband. Only God could be my source of healing, purpose, and life. No more going around the mountain. No more going back to my former self. No matter the cost to my reputation, I kept pressing in toward the Great Healer. One day, I knew He would come. One day, I knew victory would come. I didn't know how or when, and like the woman who dared to touch His hem, I never gave up.

Engaging the Currents

Over those first weeks with constant crying, God graciously began to engage with my wounded spirit. Words started coming to my mind. First, the words were simple without substance or details: sorrow, grief, loss. I was mourning our marriage, the loss of Pep's job, income, and the loss of Sandy and the spiritual leaders who had left this earth the year before. Within weeks, while crying, pictures of myself in the womb floated across my vision, which I thought were rather odd and strange.

One week, I sensed my mother waving as the airplane took off from Philadelphia that day and found myself saying goodbye to my daddy. I had no proof at the time that she did, just an inner feeling. Blinded to these small clues, I did not make any connection that my inability to cope with life had anything to do with the loss of my dad. Other exchanges with the Lord during worship times began to occur.

Each week in church, whether during praise and worship or prayer ministry time, I never knew what to expect when I bore my heart before the Lord. Fully persuaded that God was the only One who could untangle and fix my predicament, I persistently sought His face.

By now, the heaviness inside could no longer be contained. Somehow, I knew I was safe with Jesus. He became my refuge. He was my only Hope. In a small church, I did not feel safe and continuously battled the shame of falling apart. Regrettably, gossip, judgment, and unsolicited (but well-intended) advice run rampant throughout human nature, even among those who love and follow Jesus. Kneeling in front of the church, where others could see me, left me feeling humiliated and vulnerable. Rarely in our church did you ever see anyone cry, revealing their struggles, out in the open. But I say, what is a church for if you can't be honest before God?

Pushing all those perceptions and fears aside, I learned to block out those voices of intimidation and to enter this special hiding place with the Lord and me. At first, this took much effort to drown out the movement and singing of others. In time, entering God's presence became more comfortable, and I looked forward to this time in the River each week, although with fear and trembling. In the context of open worship before God at church, I sensed covered by an invisible dome of the Holy Spirit. I could hide and feel safe there—me, myself, and Jesus—separate from everybody else.

In these times of worship, I focused on the woman pressing through the crowd to touch Jesus. I knew in my heart of hearts one day I would reach His hem, and all would suddenly be OK.

Downstream in a Lifeboat

Floating down a river without any equipment could find oneself in a heap of trouble. There are twists, bends, shallow and deep waters, rapids, and waterfalls. If you want to kayak, you first must learn the extensive kayak vocabulary and determine the type of kayak you want. The kind of kayak depends upon if you wish to float gently downstream with minimum bumps, or if you prefer the fast and exuberant rides through rapids. While I preferred the easier route downstream, the Holy Spirit decided to take me on the trip of my life, full of rough waters and surprises. He must have known I could maneuver through the rocky places and make it through victoriously.

Are you aware of the cliché which says, "God doesn't cause you to face anything you can't handle?" Well, I believe that should be said more clearly: "God doesn't allow you to walk through trials He won't carry you through." I certainly did not think I was prepared to face what lay ahead on my journey to freedom. Like a frightened child, I cowered in a corner—scared and broken. My trust in God registered nonexistent at zero, all the while His faith and confidence in me tipped the scale.

Spiritually speaking, at the time of my emotional release, which I call my uncorking, I didn't recognize I had any spiritual preparation for this season. In retrospect, I probably did, and that preparation kept me afloat and kept the bow of my boat steady.

During my younger years, I had learned to turn every hymn, each song of praise into prayer from me to God. Apart from worship, my favorite times had been with coffee, my Bible, a journal, and Jesus. To escape an unemployed man, during these healing years, I often left early in the morning with a worship cassette, a pen, a Bible, and my journal in hand. Despite these spiritual habits, I had no idea I had developed intimacy with the Lord, and neither did I believe God truly loved me. The prior development of such disciplines, whether I recognized it or not, brought me closer to God and Him closer to me during this hard season.

Once I collapsed and gained some footing, I decided to give God all the room He needed to bring me through the traumatic time I faced. Hungry for more of Jesus in my search to know my dad, I attended conferences offered through the church. Midway through my five "dark years," I began to audit theological classes at another church. Unbeknownst to me, these practices and settings would become my lifelines.

In the conference context, the Holy Spirit, the Almighty Counselor, met me on many occasions, bringing profound divine encounters and producing greater freedom. In the theological classes, I strengthened my inner man in the Word of God and made new friends. During both my private devotion times and public worship settings, my heart softened.

On the immediate front, small Bible fellowship groups offered a connection with others. Many churches gather into weekly small fellowship groups. In these small groups, relationships develop with others as the teaching of the Word, worship, and prayer ministry occurs. Our church was no exception. Desperate for healing, I chose to attend as many groups as I could. This decision in and of itself seemed ironic since I couldn't trust anyone. However, my spirit knew I needed to be surrounded by other believers whether they knew what to do with a troubled woman or not. Within small group settings, the Lord began revealing my innermost thoughts and feelings, but gently and tenderly.

All these contexts gave room for God to touch and revive me and built a lifeboat for me as I traveled in the flow of the River.

Maneuvering through Rocky Currents

A river flows as it wills, carving paths through rock and feet of soil, tearing down anything that gets in its way. The amount of rain and force forges new tributaries, creeks, and streams. The second largest river in the world, over 4,000 miles long, the Amazon River, begins in the Andes Mountains from smaller streams merging into rivers which then converge into the Amazon. By 2011, the Peruvian government declared one tiny spring—under a cliff three miles high—to be the source of this highly unpredictable river.

The Amazon River boasts over 200 tributaries covering four nation states. Carrying the most volume of fresh water of all rivers in the world, the Amazon measures as narrow as one mile or as broad as 20 miles. The river may flow serenely in places or its currents can be violent and highly tumultuous. I know firsthand about its luring mystique and danger. On a mission trip to Brazil, I could have lost my life in the raging Amazon if it weren't for an angel sent from the Lord.

Though rivers in the United States are much calmer in comparison to the wild Amazon, their currents move massive volumes of water which crash over large boulders, stones, and logs. Risk takers thrive on the exhilarating white waters for such excitement and adrenaline rushes. Kayaks, canoes, and whitewater rafts must be handled carefully and skillfully for their passengers to avoid crashing, getting stuck, or turned upside down when maneuvering through the rapids. The sport attracts thrill-seekers, and every twist, turn, rocky point, and surprise waterfall add to the adventure. Rapidly steering their small crafts, the adventurers travel until the next bend in the river, and the trip continues to gain momentum until they've reached their destination.

Jumping in the River, entering the healing process—no matter the cost of reputation—equally proved both profitable yet risky and daring. Much like the whitewater rafters, once I chose to jump in the River, I could only go where the Holy Spirit, my Counselor, took the River. Diving in with my whole being, surrendering myself to God, meant traveling with the currents, from bend to bend, even through choppy rapids. In His loving kindness, God brought me through each wave, each rapid, and each bend in the river.

Physiologically, pain can indicate the healing of wounds. So, why would it be any different for spiritual and emotional healing? Excruciating, painful emotions and truths surfaced when I began to immerse myself in the presence of the Lord. I searched for the root cause of my present condition; and faithful to His Word, He brought truth bit by bit into the depths of my soul. The revelation of these destructive emotions residing within my heart shocked my psyche. Touches by God inched restoration forward as I simultaneously had to confront the monsters raging inside. Like rough rapids, conquering these took me on quite an adventure, which I did not expect.

Boulders in the River

As the raging Amazon has its unpredictable currents, other obstacles tossed across my path meant to steer me off course and take me down another tributary. Often, once one embarks on God's adventure, the enemy of our souls sets traps and obstacle courses to prevent and slow us from arriving at our goal. As my journey into the unknown places of my heart began, boulders had been thrown across to thwart the plans of God for my healing. For me, these boulders came in the form of various inner healing techniques, meant for good, but which served as roadblocks to me. Since each person is not a cookie-cutter duplication of another, not every healing methodology brings wholeness to every person.

Let me explain. Early on, after pressing into my healing odyssey, several conventional methods within the Christian healing models at that time did not further my healing. Standing like giant boulders, they hindered the way through my trauma and piled on additional shame, guilt, and sense of loss.

During this season, the church I attended held inner-healing classes. Feeling very vulnerable and intimidated, I attended these courses but in silent protest. Over the weeks, I observed many people attending to work through their pain to receive healing. At the end of each teaching, trained members could pray over us individually. Sometimes, the leaders prayed over us as a group. I suppose minor victories had to have been gained.

However, because others never shared any healing breakthroughs, I concluded others were not being touched nor reaching ultimate freedom in their lives. They appeared to always leave crippled and depressed, with no end in sight. I sensed many, like myself, were labeled broken, requiring unending healing sessions, and their genuine healing unobtainable. If others did not exhibit any release from their inside pain, I questioned if I ever would. Being in a public setting merely fed my sense of embarrassment, shame, guilt, humiliation, and hopelessness.

What frustrated me most was whenever someone praying for me would say,

"Help her to see God's face;" or,

"Help her to hear Your Voice;" or,

"Help her to feel Your Touch."

Why? Because I couldn't see His Face. I couldn't hear His Voice. I couldn't feel His Touch. I wanted to shout,

"STOP praying that!"

But I didn't. These women meant well.

To add to this, worship songs during this season were very intimate. They expressed the cry of the human heart to "See God's face," to "Hear His voice," and to "Feel His touch." When the worship band played these songs, outwardly I sang passionately for in my heart I wanted to see, hear, and touch God; inwardly I yelled,

"But I can't see Your face, God—I never saw my real daddy's face;

I can't hear Your voice—I never heard my daddy's voice;

I can't feel Your arms around me—never had my dad hold me."

A person's image of the Heavenly Father generally mirrors that of their earthly father. This makes sense. Our dads, whether present or absent in our lives, whether perfect or not, characterize the mental picture a child possesses of God. In other words, fathers carry an important role in shaping their child's perspective of God. Is the father kind, gentle and easy to approach? Or, is the father gruff, rough, and distant?

Since I never had the loving touch and words of my biological dad, I unintentionally rationalized that I could not see, hear, or feel the Heavenly Father. In my early walk as a believer in Jesus, I approached every Christian friend and asked, "How do you hear God's voice? How do you know it's Him?"

I desperately wanted to hear God's voice in my life, but had no base, model, or framework from which to work. So, forty years later, whenever prayer team members asked me those questions with the lyrics of worship songs reinforcing them, the pain of never knowing my real dad intensified.

Another technique to bring someone through the emotional healing process also never produced any positive results in my path to restoration. When praying for someone divulging a painful event, a Christian prayer counselor might have chosen to ask,

"Where is Jesus now? Do you see Him? What is He saying?"

Whenever a lay counselor would ask me those questions about a particularly traumatic event or memory, I refused to conjure up an answer. I would say, "I don't know."

Inwardly, I would silently shout with all my might,

"HE IS NOT HERE. HE WAS NOT THERE. HE IS SILENT."

Meaning: Jesus allowed my daddy to be on that plane, never to come back, and I am mad!

My Only Lifeline

Despite my unbelief that I could discern God's voice, my spirit and heart genuinely did know when it was God speaking to me or not during this long season of restoration because God's sheep hear His Voice (John 10: 17). On the other hand, whether I had the assurance I heard Him was another issue. I had yet to discover that I did indeed hear His voice. I had been so shattered and lacked any confidence. I convinced myself that I modeled someone who did not have faith, who did not fully trust in God, and who could not hear Him. Why?

- Because I went from being an assertive church leader with answers to suddenly being a wounded person in search of answers.

- Because I spent years being discounted by men—my stepdad, husband, and bosses.

- Because I never heard my real dad's voice.

- Because.

My distorted viewpoint led to my belief that only whole, healthy, happy Christians were deemed worthy of anything. I had witnessed other pastors who had failed in pastoring or church planting (like us). None of them ever seemed to get back on the horse or to remain steady to the call on their lives. Some even fell into sin, like adultery.

From my observation, religious leaders rarely exposed themselves. Pastors had their subculture with its subconscious code, expectations, and requirements for successful leadership. They rarely let their guard down to disclose problems or difficulties. I am sure they had many reasons such as fear of not measuring up, fear of gossip, or fear they might lose their positions for portraying weaknesses. Nonetheless, whenever they gathered, each one acted like their churches and personal lives were doing well.

In this environment, to his credit, my husband could not put on a façade as if everything was peachy keen. Neither could he be authentic and transparent with his pastoral peers. Instead of my husband dropping his guard and self-protective mechanisms to seek wise counsel from others, he chose to make it through on his own strength. He attempted to father himself and hid.

According to my skewed vision, Pep and I wore the words *"has-beens"* on our t-shirts; and, I believed most other pastoral leaders regarded us that way, too. Once our small church closed its doors, Pep felt uneasy attending any more ministerial meetings because he believed he did not belong anymore. Whether or not the other pastors considered us "has-beens," "washed-out," and "failures" did not make a difference. He believed the lies. I believed the lies.

Consequently, our lives stalled. The perceptions I adopted fed the lies I thought were the truth. We failed in church planting. This season now found us failing again in life.

Who could we turn to and trust with our problems? No one.

Were we loved and accepted by others? I'd have to say "probably, yes." People followed us in outreach to the community. We developed and managed a food pantry through the church. We launched Servant Evangelism into the city which brought God's kindness to others by showing them God's love in practical ways. We taught others how to move in the gifts of the Holy Spirit and how to reach out to others with the love and kindness of Jesus. We hosted a small group in our home over the years. During the unemployment season, we never went without food on our table or our bills unpaid. Anonymous love gifts from this church body continually surprised us.

Outside of the local church, before my emotional standstill, I had also gained respect as an advocate for children and parents regarding educational policies. I served our community as an elected local school board member. Once I resigned due to severe persecution for being a fiscal conservative and for my faith, new doors opened, which thrust me into the public arena. I spoke before parent groups throughout Ohio, served as a guest speaker on nationally syndicated radio talk shows, and lobbied at the state and national levels. This transformation from a mom in tennis shoes to notoriety as a child-parent education advocate forced me to push all my emotional drama and private family life aside so I could function, write speeches and op-ed pieces, conduct policy analysis and legislation, and develop workshops. Much of this volunteer public service occurred during the years of my healing journey. I presented a polished professional appearance to the public, while I was secretly caving inside.

Since we were well-known, respected and loved, neither of us could confide in anyone about the turmoil in our lives. Every time I had a new set of people praying for me, repeating my dad's account, along with describing our problems on the home front, I felt extremely humiliated. Shame and guilt overshadowed me. Too many could not hear our story; by constantly repeating it, I would dishonor my husband and make myself look thoroughly foolish. I could only confide in Jesus, my lifeline, and run to Him.

And run to Jesus, I did. I stubbornly chased after Him. Thoroughly convinced, freedom from whatever was vexing me would come directly from Him. Later, I would realize the little glimpses He was showing me had just been an appetizer to the main banquet meal to come.

Scene 16

Determined Resolution

Whether in the body or out of the body I cannot tell,
God knows...

—2 Corinthians 12:2 (MEV)

Desperate for God

I resolved to cling to Jesus with my whole heart and would not stop until I touched Him. Tenaciously, I believed I would recognize the final release and restoration. I did not know how, what, or when, yet I staunchly sensed I would know. Forceful people lay hold of the Kingdom of God (Matthew 11:12), and I decided to be among the unstoppable. I willfully chose to stand against spiritual darkness and persistently pushed through it, while seeking God to bring His sovereign kingdom rule and reign into my situation. I never gave up, never surrendered until I knew without a doubt that God heard me, touched me, and my breakthrough came.

Determined to be free from my anguish, I pursued God with all my strength. Like the woman who pressed into the crowd, I had no thought about what others would be thinking. Desperation calls for desperate action. I stood resolutely firm, believed my healing would come, and I would know when it would happen.

My marriage and my heart required extensive repair. Amid petitioning God to intervene in these two areas, the ramifications of the loss of my real dad and his absence throughout my life surfaced. Oddly, I expected God to change my husband first to bring order into our situation, but my interactions with the Holy Spirit focused on me, not Pep. I was baffled but kept diving in the River. I couldn't figure out why God didn't deal with my husband first. Once on this wilderness journey, I had no other choice. The River, the presence of God, held my answers.

Although I sought complete healing with no band-aids to cover anything up, I was more concerned with our current predicament over Pep's unemployment to be solved first. Isn't this just like us humans? We have our human viewpoint, while God has His heavenly perspective. He thinks eternally, we see in the temporal, short term. God knows what we do not know. He discerns and foresees what we cannot. He sees the whole elephant; we see only our limited view of the elephant. I was seeking financial and marital breakthroughs; God had other plans. He looked beyond these surface issues and took me at my word: no more cover-up and no more quick fixes.

Despite the Holy Spirit speaking to me concerning the loss of my real dad, I still did not comprehend its connection with my marriage, my relationship with God, and my ability to cope in life. I could not discern the correlation of my present condition with my quest to know my real dad. Blindness cloaked this truth from my eyes. A considerable barrier stood between my head and heart, which prevented me from recognizing that God had been revealing the root all along: the brutal, tragic loss of my real dad before I was born.

That was, until the day God supernaturally brought illumination. Once He obliterated my barriers and penetrated my heart, I could see. I could understand, which encouraged me to lean harder into Him. Hesitantly, I willingly embraced His path, unaware that His roadmap would, in due season, enable me to rise above the tragedy and losses experienced in my life. True to form, His itinerary went beyond fixing our marriage and temporary trials. He knew where He was leading me.

The White Horse

In my all-consuming quest for answers, one Sunday, Palm Sunday to be exact, God surprised me. In the middle of worship, I stood with my arms opened wide before Him when a gush of the wind of the Holy Spirit swept over me. His powerful presence came suddenly and without warning. I fell back under God's power and could not stop falling. Fortunately, two people who stood behind me kept their eyes opened during worship. They caught me and made sure I landed safely. They stayed with me, silently praying as they must have sensed the Holy Spirit was ministering to me. I laid glued to the floor. There was no escaping this experience.

The Holy Spirit's presence continued to descend upon me in powerful waves of wind like the pounding waves of the ocean as you are lying on a beach, only I could not get up, nor did I want to. I knew it was Him. He had come like I knew He would, just not how I thought He would. His power riveted up and down my body. It felt like electricity. Surging energy jolted through me, in me, and upon me. Unlike anything I had experienced, the weight of His presence became so intense that I did not know whether to cry, scream, or be silent.

In a split second, something transported me. Not quite out of my body, I did not think—but taken to another realm. My body was present in the natural, but I was not. Again, I saw my mother at the airport, waving goodbye to my dad's airplane. She was pregnant with me, and my sister Nancy was not with her.

Next, running through my head, I heard the chorus from *"Leaving on a Jet Plane"* by John Denver.

"I'm leaving on a jet plane…don't know when I'll be back again."

Quickly, I saw my dad's airplane in the air and witnessed the whole plane blowing up. In this other dimension, the plane exploded right before my eyes. In the natural, I screamed at the top of my lungs, so I thought. I sensed my daddy's death and his body scattered on the ground. Feeling trapped and unable to escape, I re-lived the horror of the plane explosion and wept ferociously, without caring what others thought. The traumatic event unfurled before my mind's eye and brought devastation everywhere.

I heard the words *despair, hopelessness*, and *suicide*.

In the twinkling of an eye, I felt like my life had shattered into pieces, unable to be put back together, just like my daddy. Laying there, I couldn't understand why God couldn't put my dad back together. Therefore, how could I expect God to put my life back together?

Immediately, the scene changed. I saw my body lying on the floor with a dagger—a sword—right through my body like you see in the movies. It measured close to three feet, with a guard, hilt, and pommel. The sharp blade penetrated my heart. Fortunately, the Holy Spirit prevented me from feeling any pain. My spiritual eyes then saw two little imps (demonic beings) called *death* and *murder* sitting on me.[1] I cried out to Jesus,

"Jesus! Jesus! Jesus! Come to me on your White Horse! Save me!" As soon as I said this, the worship song, *We Will Ride*, by Andy Parks, zipped through my head, ear to ear.

He has fire in His eyes and a sword in His hand
And He's riding a white horse across this land
And He's calling out to you and me
"Will you ride with me?"
We say, "yes, yes Lord, we will ride with You."[2]

Suddenly from my right, Jesus came riding on a White Horse circling in front of me to my left. His right hand held a brilliant scepter, yielding His sovereignty and authority. His hair flowed down his shoulders, and He was wearing a robe whiter than snow. With his loving, fiery eyes, leaning from His horse, His left arm swooped down and lifted me behind Him on His stunning, magnificent White Horse.

In this realm, three of me existed: the physical me on the floor, a spiritual me raised above my actual body with the dagger and the two imps, and, thirdly, the spiritual me upon the horse.

After having rescued me, Jesus Christ looked down with piercing eyes at the imps hanging on me by the dagger in my chest. They looked at Him and shivered in fear; and, without Jesus saying one word, *death* and *murder* fled for their lives. Lastly, Jesus pulled the dagger out from my chest and poured His healing oil, the balm of Gilead, upon my wounds.

An all-encompassing serenity filled me. I felt safe and free at last. These words came crystal clear in a soothing, calm, and reassuring voice:

"The tormentors are gone. The tormentors are gone."

The feeling of an electric buzz, signifying the presence of the Holy Spirit, which ran through my head, ceased. I have no other explanation for that sensation. I got off the floor limp, tired, awed, and relieved. I flippantly forgave the man who killed my dad. While forgiveness is an expected response, it was not from my heart but purely paid lip service—a religious, expected thing to do.

The two people who prayed silently for me this entire time did not know anything about what transpired in the heavenlies. To them, my physical body laid still on the floor. They knew the Holy Spirit ministered to me, but not that He had taken me to another realm. Further, when they began to pray for the balm of Gilead to bring healing to me, they did not know Jesus was simultaneously pouring His healing oil upon me in the alternate spiritual dimension. Stunned and submerged in the Holy Spirit, I remained speechless and did not relay what occurred. Who would believe me? Besides, wouldn't others think I would be boasting of this out-of-the-body type experience? Who was I to have had this supernatural occurrence?

That morning as I left church dazed and in awe of what had happened, I heard a still small voice ask,

"Will you ride with Me?"

"Yes, Lord, I will ride with You," I silently said.

In it to Win It

After saying "Yes, Lord, I will ride with You," I found myself on a spiritual expedition which I could not cancel and get my ticket refunded. I had traveled with Jesus too far to turn back. Taken up into another heavenly realm, as well as the deliverance I received, seemed sufficiently climatic. Anyone might have thought ultimate healing had come after such a rich and vivid spiritual experience. Stunned by this divine, euphoric encounter, I shared it with one of our pastors who replied,

"So now, your healing is complete!"

After that dismissive, though well-intentioned comment, I did not share that out-of-the-body spiritual encounter with anyone for years. Best to keep these strange, heavenly side trips to myself.

However, I had a choice—to believe I had enough healing as that pastor thought and to close the door on God, or to take God's hand, trust Him, and allow Him to be my tour guide through my web of emotions until complete victory. I adamantly believed I would know when this would occur, but did not know how, when, or what that entailed. I yearned to know my real dad, to be able to cope in life, my marriage restored, and to have my husband employed. None of those requests had come close to being fulfilled. My emotional entanglement still weighed heavily and troubled my soul.

Something inside me, whether it was my spirit or intuition, recognized the White Horse venture had been just the beginning. Just a tip of the iceberg. Another door opened to more healing. Deciding to take God's hand, with fear and trembling of having any more third-dimensional experiences, these thoughts often rambled through my mind:

"What will happen next? Will I look or sound foolish to others?"

"What will the Holy Spirit choose to uncover next? Can I bear such disclosure?"

"Where is He leading me?"

My distorted images of God the Father, despite progressive healing, ingrained such fear. But, He knew I did not have a clear understanding of Him and His character, didn't He? Since God is omniscient, wouldn't He know my fears?

Humbled by these powerful encounters and revelations, my pride and ego were slowly stripping away. I had come to grips that my total dependence had to be on God. Not on my husband. Not on his job. Not on my ability to earn money. Not on my past performance and achievements. What others thought of my falling apart could not matter anymore. Their opinions could hold no power over me, nor could my identity be found in them. Fixing my eyes on Jesus, the Author and Finisher of my faith (Hebrews 12:1-3), I remained steady with an unforeseen and unpredictable path ahead.

Life Changing Revelation

Even though the White Horse encounter shattered my theological paradigms about how God works, this spiritual event served as a gateway toward many more similar interchanges with God. I left that morning changed, comprehending the character of God in a new way that has remained with me to this day.

Initially, when Jesus came on His White Horse, ablaze with His Glory, brilliant and radiant white, He took care of me immediately. He could have first told the demon imps to leave. Pull the dagger out. Then, put me on His horse, or, just let me be. But He did not. In His love for me, before He confronted the enemy of my soul, He placed me safely behind Him as He arrived on His White Horse. He put me first.

Second, Jesus' presence alone overcomes spiritual warfare. Although He had a sword in His right hand, He didn't have to wield it. Nor, did He need to say a single word to the demonic imps representing death and murder. When He came to the rescue, the demons left at the sight of His presence. Jesus did not need to shout or declare, "In the Name of Jesus come out." Jesus did not engage in conversation with the evil entities nor did He take up any fight between the Kingdom of Light and the Kingdom of Darkness. Jesus didn't have to wrestle to win over the darkness. Jesus held authority over the demons from the beginning of creation. When He walked on the earth, before His resurrection, He cast out demons from demonically oppressed individuals and demonstrated His power over darkness.

In Jesus' death and resurrection over 2,000 years ago, the Kingdom of Darkness was defeated once and for all. The demonic beings knew this truth and trembled. They hated the presence of the Lord arriving on the scene in my life. Jesus came on His White Horse, which represented His wisdom, power, and holiness. One look at Jesus, the demonic beings knew they could no longer oppress me, and they fled for their lives.

To make it clear, I am not advocating a method or even a style for ministry, nor am I making a doctrine out of my experience. But I am describing the victory and authority Jesus has over death and the demonic. Once and for all, Jesus Christ, when He descended into hell, He took the keys of hell and death and stripped Satan of any authority so that those who call upon the name of Jesus (Acts 2:23; Acts 16:31) shall be saved from the power of the kingdom of darkness and bondage to sin and death. Once He rose from the dead, His resurrection stated that He now had power over death and life. All who trust in Jesus, would now never die, but live eternally with Jesus Christ. With respect to houses and buildings, whoever holds the keys has the authority to use the keys. Jesus took the keys, triumphing over Satan and making a spectacle of him. Among Jesus' last instructions to his disciples, He declared, "All authority is given to Me in heaven and on earth." (Matthew 28:18, MEV).

We each have choices to make. We can either choose life with Jesus or choose to remain in bondage to sin, death, and darkness. Although Jesus always had the authority over the rule and reign of darkness and cast out demons while walking this earth, He gave His authority to all who believe in Him.

Through the grace of God, we are now under the authority of the Kingdom of Heaven, the Rule and Reign of God. I, of course, had no inkling that I was being oppressed in anyway by the demonic imps. In retrospect, regarding the White Horse experience, God desired me to know that the plane bombing and the terror of the thought that my dad was blown to bits could have no power over me. He knew that, but I did not. He allowed me to see what He saw, to know once and for all the stench of death and murder could not be passed onto my children, their children, or their children's children.

He allowed me to see the heavenly battle over my life and to see who had won. I could then move on, knowing without any doubt, He holds the key to life and victory.

This supernatural encounter further transformed my mind-set and attitude when praying for others. I no longer had any concern if they were troubled by demonic spirits or not. Many Christians mistakenly pursue casting out demons when the individual is merely undergoing severe distress. By confusing the two types—emotional healing and demonic oppression—many can become shamed into thinking they are full of demons who will never leave. That had happened to me in my early Christian walk. On the other spectrum, many blame the demonic, which removes the person's responsibility from their wrongful actions and negates the healing of their emotions.

I quit being concerned about knowing the names of the demonic spirits to cast them from influencing anyone, which is taught within certain circles. In my spiritual encounter, Jesus never talked to them nor spoke their identity. Today, all I do is call on the Name of Jesus and call for the very presence of the Lord of Lords and the King of Kings to touch the person for whom I am praying. Why? His presence alone scatters the enemy. It is Jesus who fights our battles for us. We only need to let Him.

Our focus must be only on Jesus Christ.

Lastly, God is sovereign, knows no time, and transcends time. He is the Alpha and the Omega, the Beginning and the End. To Him, one day is as a thousand years and a thousand years as one day. He is Lord over time. He could take someone back in time or even to the future. He did that just for me.

The Box

God knew what I needed and when I needed it.

A few weeks before the dramatic spiritual encounter with Jesus and the White Horse, a surprise box arrived at our home sent from my Uncle Hop, my real dad's brother, in South Carolina. He had no idea that our lives had collapsed or that I had been searching to know my real dad, his brother. When I opened the box, my mouth dropped open in amazement. Inside, Uncle Hop filled the box with various mementos belonging to my father. One by one, I lifted the treasures out of the box:

- His army patches from World War II;

- Old photos of him, some from WWII;

- Newspaper articles about the plane bombing and my dad;

- Two issues of Life Magazine dated November 28, 1955;

- Two funeral, memorial service books;

- A framed portrait picture of my dad which sat on a table in Uncle Hop's house; and

- Leather items with MPH initials carved into the leather.

I jumped with glee after I opened it. This box, arriving when it did, signified to me God truly knew my longings to know my real dad. Everything I touched made me feel closer to my biological dad, and I imagined him using them. God answered my prayers; faith, trust, and hope increased. This box confirmed my search to know my father, which had only just begun. As I continued to struggle through massive grief and loss, this treasure box further affirmed that God initiated this strange and unusual pathway of divine encounters to bring healing to my soul. He was not about to abandon me.

God Confirms the Encounter

After the awe-inspiring White Horse encounter, I questioned if the picture I had seen of my mother standing at the airport waving at my daddy's airplane as it took off had indeed happened. It was not the first time the Holy Spirit allowed me to see it. My sister was not standing next to my mother in both visions. Only my mother held that answer. Months later without telling my mother about the healing I was going through or the vision I had seen of her at the airport, I popped one of those late night questions about my dad when I visited her back home. In my childhood, I knew I could not ask her anything about him when Stepdad George was within listening ear. I always had to wait until Stepdad George went to bed.

"Mom, can I ask you a question before you head to bed?"

"Yes, Marian, what is it?"

"Well, I was just wondering, the day that you took daddy to the airport, did you drive dad, or did he take a taxi?"

"Yes. I sure did," my mom said. She smiled and gave me a look as if wondering where I was taking this conversation.

"Ok. Did you stand and wave goodbye at the plane until you couldn't see the plane anymore?"

"Yes. I waited and waved. I had a babysitter for Nancy so that I would not have to worry about her. Why?"

"uh...I was just wondering...that's all."

"OK. Goodnight Marian. I love you."

"Goodnight, Mom, I love you, too."

Divine Orchestration

God indeed orchestrated my road to healing. He made it clear; He was the driver and I, the passenger. God had given me an accurate vision mirroring a specific event in the past. With these initial confirmations of the box and my mother, I could trust Him through the complete healing process. I did not need to fear the healing journey anymore. I could trust God—He had not steered me wrong, nor would He. He would not do half-baked healing either.

My spiritual experiences do not fit what many would consider normal Christianity, even though our battles on this earth are not against flesh and blood, but *against principalities, powers, the rulers of the darkness of this world, and spiritual forces of evil in the heavenly places.* (Ephesians 6:12, MEV). Paul had been caught up into the third heaven and could not even speak of it (2 Corinthians 12:3). We cannot fathom how or why God chooses to reveal Himself when He does. Why He communicates with one person in one manner and differently with others remains a mystery.

Extraordinary spiritual encounters do invoke questions such as: Does God work this way today? Why would God have needed to take Marian up into the spiritual realm? Is this even Biblical?

Having a very analytical mind, I dissect everything I read or hear like a spiritual scientist. Does the experience counter Biblical truth, the character of God, and scriptures? Does it point me toward Christ or away from Him? What is the fruit of the results of the dream, vision, or spiritual dynamics? Was that person's life changed for the better as a result? Does it incite fear and terror, or render peace and increased faith?

Perhaps you may be wondering why you haven't had any heavenly interactions like mine. You may be saying, "This is great for Marian, but why hasn't God touched me like this?" For years after listening to other supernatural testimonies like my story, I have asked the same questions. Rest assured, He will answer every cry of your heart in ways you can hear and receive from Him.

What I disclosed honestly occurred. Why did God choose such a powerful means to break through to me? I have no idea. Maybe God knew I needed such revelation to tear down my walls, and to trust Him more. From that day on, my mindset, warped view of God, and how He works began to change. I knew without any flinching He was in the driver's seat, not me.

Extending mercy, through His appearing on the White Horse, Jesus placed my well-being and safety as the top priority. He affirmed He was guiding me in my darkest hour. The all-powerful One shielded me, and no darkness could keep me in its grip. Jesus knew my fears and met me in my brokenness. He covered me with His love and filled me with His peace.

I had such a long way to go toward full restoration, but after this grand invitation to join in with His plans to rescue me, I could safely proceed. I had no question from that point on that the answer to my quest would be connected to the death of my biological dad. What or how remained a mystery. While the adventure ahead seemed ominous and uncertain, I stepped forward, taking His hand in mine. I thought that the White Horse scenario would be the last of such intense and vivid interactions between God and myself. Wouldn't you? What could top it?

Little did I suspect—my journey had just set sail and left the port.

Scene 17

Babies, Mothers, and Trauma

You brought my inner parts into being;
You wove me in my mother's womb.

—Psalm 139:13 (MEV)

After saying yes to riding with Jesus and venturing onto His healing road, many unannounced stops along the way included moments back in my early beginnings—what I call my "womb trips." As you may recall, when I first jumped in the River, I experienced a few such excursions. No one guided me psychologically back to this port of entry, nor would I have allowed anyone to do so. God certainly would not approve of this method for bringing healing, would He? The only way for the Lord to reveal the source of my problems, as I kept asking Him, was to take me by surprise and break through my unbelief in womb experiences as part of one's healing path. Before I share how He did that and what He showed me, let's lay a foundation by examining some research on babies, mothers, and trauma.

What We Knew Then

In 1955, the research on the neurodevelopment of the baby in the womb during significant losses, tragedy, and trauma of the mother was not as developed as it is today. Findings from a study of pregnant women who lived through WWII and lived during the Netherlands famine correlated the effects of the lack of food with much lower birth rates.[1] For decades after this study, the mainstream medical field had not conducted any additional substantial research concerning how a baby in the womb responds to the trauma faced by the mother. I could find no stellar breakthrough medical studies dated 1945-1955 at the time of this writing. However, the medical field's counterpart professionals in physiology, neurology, psychology, and psychiatry had been investigating correlations between the mother and the prenatal. Later in the 1960s and 70s, newer technology opened the doors for studying the unborn, which challenged the Freudian belief that a baby did not gain personality until two or three years old. These newer studies indicated the opposite of that Freudian long-held beliefe: a prenatal does exhibit personality while in the womb.

Thankfully, in 1955, my mother's OBGYN knew enough that he had better be there the night she got the news. His attentive care and oversight for my mother through my birth became crucial for her and me.

What We Know Now

Since the 1950s, we know so much more today about the life of the preborn. In the 1950s, the 2D (2-dimensional) ultrasound became available, but it took until the 1970s for ultrasounds to become routine care during pregnancy in the United States. Since then, with the introduction of 3D and 4D technology in ultrasound, the scientific, medical and psychological world has produced many studies on babies in the womb from conception through birth, with emphasis on the physical and central nervous system development of the baby. The research, ever growing, makes a case for the importance of taking care of the pregnant woman and her child.

In the study called *The Role of 4D Ultrasound in the Assessment of Fetal Behavior*, two physicians studied fetus (baby) behavior within 144 healthy pregnant women throughout all three trimesters. Their conclusions on developmental stages mirrored similar studies conducted worldwide. Among their many findings, the baby in utero begins movement before a mother ever feels the baby moving. In the second and third trimesters, they observed the baby sucking, yawning, blinking, smiling, frowning, and crying.[2] This observance was impossible to record before 3D and 4D ultrasound technology. As early as twelve weeks, the preborn can distinguish tastes, and as the baby develops, he/she can respond to touch, practice facial expressions, react to light, and might even dream.[3]

We have known for decades that a baby in the womb responds negatively whenever a mother smokes a cigarette or takes illegal drugs. When this occurs, the baby can cry, cover its eyes, and other movements that display displeasure and struggle for relief. The trauma induced damage in these cases can be irreparable, and these babies require extra love and care, often throughout their lives.

What We Know Now about Trauma Affecting Babies in the Womb

By 2018, while many studied the physical, behavioral development of the in-utero baby, other specialists researched the effect of trauma on the pregnant mother and her child within. Please note that not every woman experiencing heightened stress in times of crisis displays symptoms of post-traumatic stress disorder (PTSD). The following compilation of research is not for any diagnostic purposes or medical treatment. It is recommended that any pregnant woman when facing an adverse situation, anxiety, and trauma may want to discuss her situation with her obstetrician.

September 11, 2001, marked a day most will always remember. During that atrocious, frightening day, approximately 1,700 pregnant mothers were at or near the World Trade Center. The entire nation became traumatized to varying degrees and those who were physically present experienced first level, intense trauma. A research team formed a study to see how this trauma affected pregnant women who were in the World Trade Center or near its vicinity when the buildings collapsed.

Out of 1,700 pregnant mothers who were at or near the World Trade Center on 9/11, the research team selected only 38 women (2.2%) who displayed post-traumatic stress disorder (PTSD) for the study.[4] The team followed up with the 38 women and concluded that their babies had been adversely affected. Under normal stress, cortisol levels in the mother tend to increase. In contrast, with PTSD, cortisol levels decrease in the mother. In either case, the mother's hormones, including cortisol, pass through to the baby in the womb, resulting in a chain reaction. After birth, the researchers tested the babies at one-month-old for cortisol levels, and their levels measured proportionately low like their mothers. These lowered cortisol levels gave the babies after birth a propensity toward exhibiting PTSD later in life, as well as other conditions such as ADHD, hypertension, insulin resistance, and depression.

Dr. Thomas Verny, a well-published author on the unborn and effects of the prenatal environment, founded the *Association of Prenatal and Perinatal Psychology and Health* and *The Journal of Prenatal and Perinatal Psychology*. Dr. Verny is considered a forerunner in modern birth psychology and one of the world's leading authorities on the effects of the prenatal environment on personality and development. He wrote, "Every time a child is traumatized or abused, the integrity of the circuitry of his brain is threatened; if the trauma is powerful enough, the architecture of the brain will be permanently damaged. Everything the pregnant mother feels and thinks is communicated through neurohormones to her unborn child, just as surely as are alcohol and nicotine."[5]

Another study, found in the Journal of Child Psychology and Psychiatry, reviewed the correlation between the stress level of the pregnant mother and the neurodevelopment of her baby. The results confirmed other studies, such as the one with the 38 women, that the child might exhibit emotional or cognitive problems. The child has a higher chance of developing ADD (attention deficit disorder), hyperactivity, anxiety, and even language delay.[6]

Regarding myself, when I read this, I saw myself as a prime example of a newborn whose mother experienced severe trauma while pregnant. I lived with passive ADD all my life; I discovered it when I was an adult. I have also struggled with low-level anxiety to some extent throughout my life; and, my body stores stress. As a toddler, I was considered a late bloomer in talking. The family always lovingly joked that although I began speaking later than average, I never stopped talking once I did. While I don't know if the trauma I faced in the womb contributed to these conditions or not, I felt relieved to understand this connection between my mom and myself.

Furthermore, when a pregnant mother experiences high levels of fear and anxiety, including trauma, her body develops a metabolic chain reaction which produces hormones known as cytokines. These cytokines affect the mother's immune system, which in turn affects the baby. Chronic anxiety in the mother may result in trauma-based conditions such as prematurity, complications of birth, death, and miscarriage.[7] In my case, I decided to come into the world ahead of schedule.

Many other studies confirm that the trauma and stress of a pregnant mother affect the baby's neurodevelopment and neurobehavioral development of the baby's central nervous system due to the exchange of hormones between the mother and the baby and its cascading impact. The results can be extremely devasting to the baby, with lasting effects through adulthood. Fortunately, given the vast knowledge on brain development and the impact of trauma on the mother and her baby, the professionals have recognized it is crucial to further research ways to protect both mother and her prenatal, including as early as the embryo stage.[8]

Can A Baby in the Womb Learn, Store Memory, and Feel Emotions?

The research on this aspect of the baby and the mother carries significance for me. As you have read, I had become unglued emotionally. From the range of 1 to 10, when I was uncorked and coming out of denial, my emotions would have registered at 20—out of the ballpark and out of control. Desperate for the Lord to take His axe to the root of all my distress, He began to answer my prayers.

I started to recall, whether real or imagined, visions and memories when I had been in the womb. As you may guess, the out-of-the-ordinary mental pictures turned me emotionally inside out and upside down. Without any framework or knowledge of available modern-day research on prenatal feelings and memory of emotions, I became fearful and hesitant of what strange occurrences I would meet as I traveled on my Road to Freedom. What peculiar womb scenarios would surface next? What emotions would I feel? Why do these images continue to flash in my mind? Why can't I get over it? Why couldn't I stop the tears and gut-wrenching feelings?

Since then, experts in the field of prenatal learning and memory produced findings that the brain of the unborn baby develops the ability to learn and record memories early in the womb. The prenatal absorbs taste, smell, and hearing, including the mother's native language. These senses and the mother's native language become stored in the pre-born memory. According to David B. Chamberlain, in *Birth Psychology*, "the baby learns and responds to the mother's emotional state, whether good or bad...these diverse findings are that memory and learning seem to be a natural part of being human, including the first nine months."[9]

A reason for this could be that neurotransmitters move inside the mother's body, leaving a chemical and physical imprint on the baby's brain and body. Dr. Christianne Northrup, in her 738-page book, *Mother-Daughter Wisdom*, explains this cascading effect. Not just negative messages are encoded, but when a mother is happy and healthy, she produces oxytocin, known as the "bonding molecule," which sends an imprinted, encoded message to the child that all is safe, secure, and well. This imprinting enables the prenatal to bond with the mother. Because of the neurotransmission of hormones between the mother and child, the babies have the ability to remember events—both positive and negative—of their birth and many other events occurring throughout their prenatal life. These events become "an indelible biological imprint that impacts us at some level for the rest of our lives."[10]

Concerning learning, the baby remembers songs the mother sang to him while in utero, prefers foods the mother ate while pregnant, and recognizes books read out loud to him/her before birth. The list includes the baby's ability to recognize the mother's voice and learn the mother's primary language.

In a study published by P. Thompson, *The Impact of Trauma on the Embryo and Fetus,*[11] the outside world (environmental world) and the mother's personal life, including her relationship toward her preborn, influence every aspect of her developing baby, starting with the embryo stage. The prenatal brain, as well as the postnatal brain, stores memory of trauma, feelings, and other experiences. These, in turn, are encoded in the memory of the preborn, within the subcortical and deep limbic regions of the young, growing brain. These encoded messages influence the baby's ongoing physiological and psychological development. These engrained, encoded memories then stay with the baby into the early days of infancy and beyond.

I must emphasize that while the brain encodes such experiences, not every pregnant woman will respond and react the same way. Some may never exhibit any developmental detriments, and neither will their babies. Everyone responds and reacts differently, each with their own story and capability of navigating through traumatic experiences.

Can memories which have been encoded within a prenatal's brain surface later in life after birth?

I wanted to know, and my analytical brain kept me looking for more answers. As I dug further, the University of Virginia's Medical School, Division of Perceptual Studies, states: "Some young children report memories from before or during their birth. In the case of reported memories before birth, some describe being aware of events that occurred when they were in the womb, while others talk about events from another realm or heaven. Occasionally, young children describe parts of their birth process that their parents say they were not told about. While current understandings of infant memory do not allow for such memories to be possible, some children describe them nonetheless."[12]

Dr. Verny, the author of *The Secret Life of the Unborn*, provides physiological, scientific evidence of a baby's ability to store memory, especially from 6 months in the womb through birth. When a woman goes into labor, her body produces oxytocin. Oxytocin enters the baby through the mother; this hormone blocks memory, which can account for why most people never remember their birthing process. However, another naturally occurring hormone called adrenocorticotropin (ACTH) assists in retaining memory. Whenever anyone—man or woman—becomes frightened or anxious, the body releases ACTH to regulate the flow of stress hormones. When a pregnant woman encounters anything that startles, frightens, or causes anxiety, her body also produces ACTH, which also flows into the prenatal system. This flood of ACTH enables the baby to "retain a clear, vivid mental picture of her upset and its effect on him."[13]

When my mother heard the news, her body's hormones would have gone into overdrive. Spilling over into my system, the ACTH produced would have enabled me to store memories of her trauma, agony, and fears, which laid dormant until triggered by my traumatic upheaval four decades later.

In his book, *Windows to the Womb—Revealing the Conscious Baby from Conception to Birth,* David B. Chamberlain documents three decades of research regarding life and memories in the womb and offers numerous case studies concerning the entire growth and memory processes of the baby from its very beginning through birth. One of his clients' father died months after she was born, so she did not know him. Her father, like mine, was reported to have been a very kind, loving person. During a session, the client recalled an argument her father and mother had when she was in the womb and reported that alcohol was involved. Within the next week, the woman inquired of her mother about whether she and her father argued over her dad's drinking. The mother was stunned; she had never told anyone. Her father came home drunk only one time in their marriage, and they indeed argued when David's client was eight months in the womb.[14] This case study represents one among hundreds recorded, validating my prenatal recollections.

David Chamberlain and Dr. Verny agree—much can be done to promote the importance of parents' pre-birth bonding with their babies. The wealth of scientific, neurological, and psychological studies reveals the precious and delicate mother-baby connection. Since trauma in the womb can impact an entire future generation and culture, Dr. Verny and David Chamberlain concurred prevention and minimization of the ramifications of a mother's trauma on a newborn should be a new focus of prenatal care. David Chamberlain wrote, "I am especially aware of the need to create babies that are mentally and physically healthy in order to have a world that is healthy and peaceful."[15] In context, Mr. Chamberlain speaks of providing all pregnant women with quality to care and assistance to protect herself and her unborn child.

Memories of Trauma Recorded

Decades later, upon reading the volumes of studies available, I discovered everything my mother experienced, felt, and thought after hearing the news of my dad's death had fed straight into my prenatal soul, mind, and body. Able to record memory, coupled with the hormonal transfer, while still in the womb, I had assimilated my mother's grief, sorrow, anxiety, and shock.

It was no wonder I became zombie-like and shut down when I came to the end of my ropes with little emotional strength to sustain all the recent losses. I was partially right; the depth of my pain bore a weight my body, mind, and spirit could no longer support. Unknowingly, I had also been lugging my mother's trauma and pain all these years. I heard and absorbed my mother's screams, cries, tears, pain, disappointments, and sorrow.

In the way a baby stores memory, these remained lodged and hidden until my soul could no longer contain the trauma of my losses. After forty years of repression, I released, like a volcanic explosion, every stored spectrum of distraught feelings without any hope they would cease erupting. At the time, in 1995, the death of my real dad did not appear on my radar as being a cause for my emotional collapse. I only knew to bring my crushed spirit to Jesus' feet.

Believing Jesus would heal me if I could only touch Him, He became my only Hope.

From a series of her letters tucked in a box, my mom did her utmost to guard Nancy and the baby in her womb. She expressed fears about being a single mother, with no income base and no father for her children. She daily struggled not only with the sudden tragic loss of her husband, our dad, and missing him but also our wellbeing. Her dreams and hopes shattered in one night. Her one true love, our dad, abruptly taken away, never to return. Combined with the battle with her mother-in-law, our grandmother, her anguish and emotional state ripped her apart. Despite these devastating circumstances, her belief that God would bring her through steadied her as peace and hope fought their way back into her heart.

However, profound questions constantly swirled in her mind. Physiologically, beyond her control, her deep crevices of grief, sorrow, disappointment, and fears found their way profoundly embedded within my brain, body, and soul.

Scene 18

Trauma Knocked and Walked In

Knock. Knock. Knock.

—Trauma

The night my mother heard the news about my dad's flight became her worst nightmare and consequently mine. According to medical research, at six-and-a-half-months in the womb, I would have felt everything my mother felt, heard her piercing screams, and absorbed her surges of anxiety, panic, and terror as they shook her entire being. The effects of her trauma would have spilled over into my prenatal existence. Biologically, we moved as one, and I would have reacted to her traumatized state. My safe world was no longer safe. Because scientific and medical research on trauma and babies had not yet crossed my path in 1995, I had no framework to correlate my sense of loss, abandonment, anger, and grief from that first night in November 1955.

Man's Approach

In Christian healing practice prevalent in the 1990s, some facilitators would psychologically take people back to the womb and invite Jesus into the picture. In the healing group sessions which I attended, the leader would sometimes guide everyone psychologically from the womb to their adulthood by saying something like this, very slowly:

"Close your eyes. Imagine you are in the womb. Your little hands and feet are forming. Where do you see Jesus? What is He telling you? Now, you are in the birth canal and coming out to see the world. What do you see? What do you feel? Now, you are age 3. What are you feeling? What are you doing? Now imagine, where is Jesus? How does this make you feel? What is He saying to you?"

I refused to participate, sat quietly, and observed. This visualization or guided imagery counseling technique did not fit my theological viewpoint, and I could not accept it. Instead, I viewed it as extra-Biblical, outside of scriptural boundaries and incorporating human psychology into a Christian healing model. I did not want to conjure up Jesus either. Frustrated, I avoided this unnatural approach. I did not want any person to manipulate me into a false memory by the power of suggestion. I didn't criticize others in the group settings for participating in this technique to bring inner-emotional healing, that was between them and God.

God's Approach

My reactions and my resistance did not stop God. What does the Almighty One decide to do? The One to whom a day is like a thousand and a thousand days like one day? The One who transcends time and who sees the beginning from the end and the end from the beginning? He caught me entirely off guard. He knew the source of every tear went straight back to my very beginnings, in my mother's womb, much to my chagrin.

During the months that followed, deep-seated emotions continually surfaced. Using imagery, God took me back to the time before I was born. These pre-birth and birth encounters clashed with my Christian experience, shook my theology, and freaked me out. Besides challenging my paradigm view on how

God works, these side trips (visions) had no chronological order. On one day, God would give me a womb vision, the next day, my birth, then back to the womb. Some of them I have already shared. These express womb trips, as I called them, became a norm. I just never knew when to expect the next visit. With each one, the sense of anguish, loss, pain, and fears grew with intensity. Feelings emerged, and my very fiber would quiver.

Since I never heard other people talk about their inner healing journeys, I assumed I must indeed be a basket case. I quickly began to feel quite weird for having these visions, pictures, and spiritual encounters. They were divine and came from the One Above. My spirit bore witness to their validity, because my natural mind never could have created such vivid scenes. Oh no, not at all. For one, I never liked fantasy movies, books, or cartoons. Secondly, I was not an artist and could not have conceived any imaginary vision or storyline. If I had my druthers, I would have been healed and set free from all that tormented me the very first time I cried before the Lord. I believed He had a magic wand and "poof" our marriage would be restored, and my emotional upheaval dispelled once and for all. Had I been guiding my healing process, I'd have none of this slow, painful journey. If we are all honest, don't we want instant everything?

Although God knew I never believed in a counselor taking me back to the womb, the Mighty Counselor Himself spared nothing. He knew me before I was born like He knows everyone before they come into being. God fashioned me, wired my circuitry, and knew what made me tick. He foresaw my thoughts and feelings long before I knew they took anchor in my soul. He also wisely assessed when I was ready to meet Him in the secret places of my heart.

God had His reasons for the timing of these images and visions, and His rhyme and reason made no sense to my analytical, human brain. I had no one to guide me back in time. The Holy Spirit was my only Counselor. Without respect to any timeline, the effect remained the same: God was changing my perspectives and belief systems with each time travel trip, transforming me from a skittish young lady, to the woman whom He created, confident and assertive.

Not everyone going through traumatic events will have these encounters and may never need to spiritually or psychologically go back to their prenatal existence. Many therapies exist in which the professional guides people back to their preborn states. Even the experts are aware of false memories and the psychological damage that can happen when taking people back to their life in the womb. I do not recommend anyone stirring up what may or may not be accurate memories. I balked at guided imagery practiced for many of those reasons, including within Christian emotional healing groups. My faith obstinately believed Jesus would show up if He wanted.

God, in His Wisdom, recognized I needed to take this route back to my pre-birth memory because He knew how I had been affected by my mother's trauma. He already knew since before creation what professionals have been discovering these past fifty years—that each child in the womb can store memories, learn, and feel. I had asked Him fervently to free me once and for all, didn't I? He wanted me released from all the baggage of emotions that weighed me down as much as I wanted freedom. He smashed all my preconceptions of the inner healing process, overruled my intellect and pride, and took me back to where all my struggles began.

The Recurring Door

The door repeatedly opened and closed. Each time, it opened quickly and sharply slammed.

"What is this, Lord? What does this opening and closing mean?"

I pondered this recurring image. Over time, my mother, still pregnant, appeared in the scene. I saw her, standing at the door which repeatedly swung open and shut. Gradually, this scene broached my limited understanding—this was the moment my mother had opened the door to the three men who came to give her the tragic news.

At a conference, a speaker gave the call for people to allow God to reach in and remove past pain holding them back, such as repressed feelings, hurts, and wounds. Well, that fit my description, so I went forward to the front to respond. Over that prior week, images of the womb kept floating across my mind's eye. So, I knew God wanted to speak to me. As I focused on Jesus, His power descended upon me, and down to the floor I fell, surrounded by His Presence. In my mind's eye, I kept seeing Jesus's hands on my mom's shoulders at the door. He was with her, too, at that traumatic moment. I saw myself, in the womb, cry out:

"O God, O God, No, No, no—this just can't be!"

"Why am I hurting? What's going on?"

Suddenly, I saw myself tightening up. A vision of my six-and-a-half-month-old prenatal self was writhing in pain and convulsions. As I saw this vision, anguish gripped my soul. I cried out to Jesus as waves of the Holy Spirit, like electricity, riveted up and down my physical body as I laid on the floor. At some point, I saw my spirit lift from my body, again, whether in or out of the body I did not know. My body was on an operating table. Jesus walked up to the table, anesthetized me, and opened my heart for me to see. He showed how shattered my emotional heart had become. I saw pieces of my broken heart with words like "fear of loss," "fear of abandonment," "anguish," "trauma," and "shock." Others were unnamed or hidden.

I wondered, "Will He remove them? What's He doing? O, God, help!"

Then, Jesus put everything back in and stitched me up.

In a New York minute, I was back in my body. The Presence of God rested on me like a weighted blanket, and I had become immersed with His Holy Spirit as in the first Chapter of Acts. Some might describe it as His Glory. I laid on the floor and giggled with joy unspeakable. Through this entire strange scene, peace settled upon me. I knew then that the time my mother received the news, when she answered the door, was when I had been impacted too. God had shown me the precise time she heard about my dad killed by that plane explosion, and it was the entry point that held me captive to the bondages. God merely wanted me to see the extensive, web effect that one sinful act had on me. The source of all my pain went straight back to the vicious and horrible loss of my dad.

Isn't the kindness of the Lord beyond our preconceived expectations? He showed me He was with my mother and myself when she opened the door that evening of November 1, 1955. No one guided me into my imagining Him being there. Jesus, Himself, revealed that He truly stood there with my mother and me. I responded,

"I see you, Lord, standing there with Your hands on my mother's shoulders. Oh, and there you are also reaching inside and holding me."

He must have known what I could handle and not handle. In His mercy and compassion, He only revealed what I could receive and absorb at that moment.

By the time the Holy Spirit brought the image of the door to me, He had already been nursing my soul back to life by gradually grounding me in His love. His love was the key, His primary objective. He cared more for my knowing His love and being more confident in Him than any of the inner traumatic struggles I was facing. He had already won the battle and foreknew the ending of my healing adventure, whether I believed one was even possible. He passionately wanted me to know in the depths of my heart, without a doubt, that He loved me.

While engulfed by the Holy Spirit on the floor, I recalled when He threw me onto His White Horse first before confronting the strongholds which had been harassing me. He knew I could accept more truth hidden within my inner self. Through taking me back in time to that night of November 1, 1955, the beginning of all my emotional upheaval had finally come to light. In His love, the Almighty Counselor was preparing me for further healing and freedom.

I Love You, Too

At a small gathering in a home, people began to pray for me again, and the power of God ran through me like a stream of electricity. God showed me a picture of my birth again. Fortunately, it was not graphic, but instead symbolic. I wept as the words "loneliness and grief" flowed like a digital banner across my mind. Seeing the Cross of Jesus before me, I found myself releasing more grief, sorrow, and pain to the Lord.

These emotions had been buried deep within my inner being and meshed with my personality. No matter how many times I had cried, I could not shake off these thoughts and feelings that tortured my mind. Like the replayed tapes, their haunting and taunting would not stop. My identity had become twisted. I fought the lies swirling in my mind—I was not **loneliness**. I was not **grief**. My name was not **abandoned**.

Then, it happened again.

"My little one whoever you are, this is Daddy. I love you. Can't wait to meet you and hold you."

"Daddy, I can't hear your voice, I'm having such a hard time hearing you," I said.

A picture of my real earthly dad traveled through my mind. He was talking to me in the womb, with his hand on my mother's tummy. I remember it vividly—he was smiling. Friends had been praying for me, and this moment from the past, whether real or not, came out of left field. I did not conjure it up, and neither did the ones praying with me. Perhaps symbolic, perhaps a real memory, it did not matter. What did matter was it reflected a truth: my real dad was happy to have another baby and loved me. At the same time, this visual interaction assured me I had heard my daddy's voice when I was in my mother's womb.

Friends continued to pray for me as God's presence and power pierced the years of darkness, loneliness, and emptiness I had felt throughout my life. In my spirit, a sense of peace entered my consciousness, whether it would be permanent, that I did not know. It sure gave a moment of relief. While they prayed for me, I quietly prayed,

"Please God, can you replace those years I've missed having with my real dad?"

A few moments later, I walked into the kitchen, still feeling lonely and alone. For no reason, the words from the 1945 Rodgers and Hammerstein musical *Carousel, You'll Never Walk Alone,* repeatedly played through my mind, as if God himself sung over me: "You'll never walk alone."

Peace flooded over me. The comfort of these words resonated within and re-assured me that God had not abandoned me, saying,

"You'll never walk alone. I am with you. I have you in the palm of My hands."

God's power and love, using that familiar song, began to penetrate my years of darkness, loneliness, and emptiness. Later that evening, back at home, I whispered,

"Jesus, I love you."

"I love you, too, Marian."

As I laid down, I felt Jesus kiss on my cheek for the first and only time as He said,

"Goodnight."

He Felt No Pain

Once again, on a Sunday morning, lost in abandoned worship before the Lord, I was either like the woman who poured her saved tears upon the feet of Jesus, or the woman with the issue of blood pressing toward Jesus in the crowd. Unreservedly, my arms wide-open, I looked up as if gazing into heaven, tears streaming down my face. The noise of the outside world closed off, and I was not aware of my surroundings. Immersed in His presence, every noise in the room sounded muffled. Jesus and me. Nothing else mattered. Others clapped, danced, shouted, or laughed with joy while others knelt or sat in silence. What God was saying to them did not matter to me. My eyes and heart centered on Jesus, desiring to give Him everything and to be touched by Him. I never wanted to leave the throne room empty handed. I pursued significant change. No more bandages, coverups, and no happy, temporary feelings. Once the living God had touched me, I would leave different than when I came. In desperation, I called out to Him,

"How I love you, Jesus! Come, please come save me, touch me, heal me."

Suddenly, I saw an image of a chair that had been blown up by the bombing of my dad's flight. I recognized it as my father's passenger chair. I doubled over in the horror of it all. I hid my face in my hands as I screamed with terror at the thought of my dad's pain and death. Breaking in, the Lord gently spoke,

"He did not feel any pain. I suffered on behalf of your dad. I took his pain."

Next, a whoosh of the presence of the Holy Spirit over-whelmed me, and my frail body could not stand against His Power. On the floor I went. Flat on my back. Again, the picture of the chair flashed before me, and despite the comforting from the Lord, I began identifying with my dad and imagined his pain. Sobs deeper than any deepest point in the ocean tumbled forth from within me. I could not stop the tears.

Just as suddenly as the image of the chair had come the first time, I saw the strong, loving arms of Jesus reach down from heaven and swoop my dad's spirit up and out of the seat, the very instant the plane exploded. My dad was limp in His arms like a father takes his sleeping child to bed. Jesus took my dad, at the exact time of the explosion, straight up to heaven!

Comfort came. Tears of terror changed instantly to tears of joy and assurance, which then rolled down my cheeks. Jesus saved my daddy. I just knew it. Without a doubt, he didn't feel any pain. Unexplainable peace replaced my feelings of terror and anguish.

His Protective Arms

As quickly as the Lord showed me how He scooped up my dad, the "holy movie" changed. In the next scene, I found myself smack back in my mother's womb as a baby all curled up in the secret place. I know this sounds bizarre, but I began to accept that anything outside our natural, rational minds would appear strange to our limited and logical minds. Our material-based and scientific worldview contains no place for the supernatural. But not to God, who formed and knitted every person in the womb. He calls us by name and knows every number of hairs on our heads. Assuredly, He saw not only what my mother was going through, but also what happened to me when my mother received that life-changing news the night of November 1, 1955.

In the image, a strong sense of anxiety welled up within me, hidden in my mother's womb. The intense feelings of panic and fear overwhelmed me so much that I wanted to scream but could not. My voice froze. I began to quiver like a scared rat and said,

"I don't want to be born. I don't want to be born."

"I want to be safe inside my mommy."

"What am I going to do next? What am I going to do without my daddy? It's not safe out there; I don't want to be born."

The realization I had not wished to be born shook my inner core. Before I knew it, the Lord's protective arms wrapped around me, right inside my mother. This idea of not wanting to be born reflected all my fears of coming into the world. Another layer of the onion peeled, and an inch toward victory unfolded. I could face the world, with God's arms around me, holding, protecting, and loving me.

I Was There

It was another Sunday, and as customary, I lost myself before the Lord in worship. Jesus was the central focus. The worship band, with guitars, piano, and drums, played on a middle school stage while the congregation stood and raised their hands while they sang to God. The worship wove in and out from slow and intimate songs, to happy, expressive melodies. Much time was taken to allow anyone time to quiet themselves from the outside world and to commune with the Holy Spirit. The Word of God says that God inhabits the praises of His people. I never quite knew what that meant, until seasons of worship in the unity of the Spirit would sweep into our midst. I gradually became aware of the sweet fragrance of His Presence overflowing into the room. Dedicated to uncovering the root cause of my woes, I remained steadfast, seeking to touch the hem of Jesus' garment. Tears streamed my face—with sobs so deep, aching for the Lord to break into my heart and free me from what was eating me up inside.

Then, it happened.

With my eyes closed, the Holy Spirit brought me back to my birth, some forty years earlier. In my mind's eye, I saw an image of my mother in the delivery room and the doctor holding me in my swaddled blankets. I began crying harder. I grieved the loss of never having my real dad hold me or smile and look at me with his soft, tender eyes. A doctor cradled me, not my dad.

A person came near me and prayed,

"O, Jesus, let her see Your face."

I said to myself, not out loud,

"But I can't see Your face! I can't! I never saw my dad's face, felt his touch, or looked into his loving eyes. So, how can I see you, Jesus?"

A calm, firm, loving voice which I grew to recognize, interrupted, and said,

"Your daddy is with Me."

Suddenly, something only the Holy Spirit could have done, images from my childhood (where my real dad could not have been) quickly flashed across my mind like a family movie in fast forward, warp speed. God was showing me various times and stages in my young life where He was with me. I saw Jesus with me at school, camp, and play. I saw Him swinging with me. I saw Him standing near me while weeding the gardens, when my stepdad yelled, and when I escaped to my neighbors. He stood by my bed all the nights I cried myself to sleep. He was with me at my high school graduation, college graduation, and wedding day. He showed me how He was with me all my life. I felt Jesus holding me. I heard His voice and sensed His comfort. As fast as it began, the clip of memories ended.

"See, Marian, I was there when your daddy couldn't be with you and where your stepdad never was."

"Ahhh," I sighed relief. I felt hugs. Jesus' arms held me. I heard His voice, sensed His comfort, and bathed in His peaceful presence. He was there, whether I could accept this truth or not. He was.

The back-to-the-womb, spiritual excursions puzzled me and troubled my spirit. Each time the curtain was drawn open, my soul caught a glimmer of what lay backstage, off stage, and behind-the-scenes. Never having walked this path before, I should not have been so shocked. After all, hadn't I asked God to dig out the root of my emotional bottleneck?

God, the Almighty Counselor and the writer of my script, did not disappoint me. Instead, He kept me in suspension. Act One laid the foundation. Act Two delved into deep dark places, full of inner turmoil. Act Three remained a mystery script and left me spellbound with each scene change. Would there be an Act Four? During the times of intense inner work, God wisely guided the tour of my heart, showing me only what He knew I could handle each time—all the while, nudging me closer to the Father's love.

Scene 19

A Milestone Breakthrough

And it breaks the heavy yoke, breaks the heavy yoke,
When you shout, you shout to the Lord.

—Kevin Prosch

Reaching a Pinnacle

Over a year had passed in my search to know my real dad. I still could not shake off the powerful feelings of loss, sorrow, loneliness, abandonment, and depression. Sometimes I would sense those feelings would lift; only to have them rolling over me like a wave again. Meanwhile, the Holy Spirit enjoyed taking me on those occasional trips back to the womb, most of which were too emotional, vivid, and bizarre to share. Assuredly, He was in the driver's seat, not me.

The womb trips disturbed me tremendously. Was I making them up? Were they real? Was my imagination too wild? I did not question them coming from the enemy to throw me off. Good fruit always came from each image and imparted more of His heart to me. My spirit bore witness that they were from Him. But, on the other hand, the womb visits did not fit my intellectual, logical reasoning, and I had nowhere to place these mysterious preborn visions. I couldn't talk to anyone about them; the womb visions simply were too out-of-this-world. I asked myself often, "Am I OK? Do I imagine things? I am losing my mind?"

I continued to attend any event available to further my spiritual journey. Because I did not want to look like a groupie or needy person, I rarely approached any guest speaker—until one conference. After listening to a speaker from Desert Streams Ministry,[1] I learned about his years as a counselor and had a hunch he would be a safe person. At a break, I felt comfortable giving him a brief account of my story with all the bizarre supernatural interactions.

"Am I going crazy?" I asked him.

He looked at me with tender fatherly eyes and said,

"No, you're not! What you are experiencing is normal. I'd love to pray for you after the next session. Just meet me in the side room, OK?"

"OK!"

I was speechless and stunned!!! I managed to get back to my seat. I had not been so affirmed—ever—by any guest speaker, pastor, or anyone—during that year. I could not focus on the next speaker and topic. My heart and mind raced. I was finally receiving as close to professional help as possible.

"I'm not going crazy! I'm not losing my mind! I'm going to be OK! I'm going to be free!" I kept thinking.

All those thoughts circulated throughout my mind, and I could not wait for the next session to end. Once the speaker finished, I slipped out to the side room off the stage. We had only a 15 minute break; I knew our time together would be short. I did not want to waste precious moments. I told no one about this private counseling—prayer time with the conference speaker.

"Have a seat. What is your name?" This gentle, fatherly voice said.

"Marian," I said.

"I assure you, Marian, you are not going crazy with images from the womb. Now, you said that your mother was pregnant when your dad died on that plane with the bomb?"

"Yes, I was about six months in her womb and was born several weeks premature. About two months after my dad's death."

"And, you say you have been crying incessantly over the past year?" He asked.

"Yes, with all these pent-up emotions. I just can't stop. I'm falling apart inside. I don't know why. I don't know why I can't cope with life, get over it, and move on," I said, crying.

"I know a place to start when I pray with you today. What you are going through is normal. A prenatal, a baby, the unborn, feels and senses everything the mother undergoes. All her emotions and reactions poured over into you. You have been hauling a burden you were not meant to bear. You have been shouldering not only your own buried emotions but those of your mother, too. When she screamed, you felt it. When she cried, you felt it. When she went through her anger and grieving process, you did, too," he said.

"Wow, that makes sense." I said as I sat there, looking into his kind eyes, thinking to myself, "Someone understands me! Someone finally who knows what to do!" I felt relieved.

"What we need to do is to break off and separate you from your mother's emotions. Until now, it's no wonder you became so tossed around and overwhelmed. You couldn't help it! You had taken on both sets of emotions. Once her emotions that entangled with yours are broken off, you will be free to begin to heal for yourself. Up to now, you've had to heal for the both of you, and you were not meant to carry this double burden. Ready?"

"Oh, yes, I am so ready," I responded as tears dripped down my cheeks. I bent over with my head in my hands and closed my eyes. I thought, "At last, someone knows what to do."

"Holy Spirit, we invite you in right now into her mother's womb with baby Marian," He began.

At the instant when he started to pray, I had an image of the time I cohabitated with my mother—in that safe, dark place. I saw myself curled up, afraid, and upset.

He continued, "Now, in the Name of Jesus, I break off all emotional ties between Marian and her mother that occurred in the womb and separate her mother's emotions from hers."

I saw Jesus hold me in the womb. At the moment the man prayed those words to sever the emotional ties with those of my mother, I sensed the separation occurred. I can't describe the feeling—it was like a jolt, as if something shifted inside. A huge load lifted off of "me" in the womb as well as the adult "me" who was sitting next to this compassionate, understanding man who walked with loving authority. The weight of bearing my mother's emotions for all those years lifted! Relief at last!

When I walked out of the room, something significant had changed within me. A dark cloud dispersed, and a milestone breakthrough occurred in less than 15 minutes. I left freer and lighter than ever before; hope welled. Though not completely fulfilled, my quest continued. Only now I could breathe and would only need to deal with my wounds. He—Jesus—did it!

Although times of weeping overcame me sporadically throughout the next years, the intensity of feelings would not be so debilitating. I began to thrive again. To use a cliché, light at the end of the tunnel became possible for me to envision. Strength, both physical and spiritual, increased each day. Joy crept back into my countenance. My song returned and I walked with a lightness in my steps. A pinnacle reached.

I loved my mother dearly, but I was not meant to carry her burdens and emotions. She had no idea about any of this, neither did I ever tell her. She did not need to know. Secretly, I knew that God answered one of my desires: to have a breakthrough.

Act III had arrived. Unencumbered, I could safely skip onto the Road to Freedom.

Act III
Into Freedom

Scene 20

The Fatherless

"But You oh God, do see trouble and grief;
You consider it to take it in hand.
The victim commits himself to You;
You are the helper of the fatherless."

—Psalm 10:14 (NIV)

Needing a Father

The Fatherless. That was who I was. Although my mother poured her love and acceptance into my life and sought her best to fill my father's role, even after she remarried, a large void resided in my heart. You see, God created male and female. He established marriage between man and wife, going back to the Garden. He fashioned the father and the mother. Both reflecting the image of God. Both representing Himself. Both exhibiting different aspects, attributes, and strengths.

The father role fashions a child's heart in ways the mother's role cannot, and vice versa. When the father is absent, whether due to absenteeism or death, the hearts of their children incur damage. All yearn for a good, stable, and loving father to run to, whether we can admit this innate need or not, whether we know it or not, including me.

Throughout my childhood, I knew the story of my real dad and how he died. Both Nancy (age 6) and I (age 5) remember seeing our mother at the dining room table with her head in her hands, leaning over and crying. When we asked what was wrong, she said while sobbing, "I miss your dad so much."

Five years earlier, the instant my mother heard the news Hobby—her husband, my dad—would never come back, she knew she would forever need to be both father and mother to Nancy and me. In her letters, she questioned how she could fill both roles for us. The task she was suddenly assigned seemed too overwhelming and impossible.

By the time I was about two years old and still in diapers, my mother began dating this man we called Uncle George. When Mom brought him home to meet us girls, she recalled Nancy and I ran into his arms calling, "Daddy—Daddy." It's impressive how toddlers, at such young ages, could have such longing for a father—a consistent, male presence, and even recognize missing a father in their lives. Knowing my little spirit felt the lack of a father confounds me. My tiny soul hungered for a father's embrace and elatedly welcomed him.

By age 6, I knew my real dad could not come back to life. Thus, when my mother remarried, Uncle George became the only Daddy I knew. That was a happy day. No longer fatherless (so I believed), my young heart rejoiced.

I called him "Daddy" and never viewed him as "Stepdad George" until my Great Uncorking in 1995. Regrettably, he could only fill so much. When my sister and I became teenagers, he did not know what to do with us or how to parent teenage girls.

While I had a dad in the home, I did not have a father. I could not freely jump on his lap and give him a great big hug. He wouldn't put his arms around me and hug me for no reason other than he was a dad and I was his daughter. He was not the type of dad figure to whom I could go with my problems and receive comforting guidance. And, I certainly could not have cried on his shoulders. No, not at all. When he came home, I avoided ruffling him. He was the sort of dad who had his assigned seat on the couch and no one could take his spot. I felt rather sorry for him, because he did not know how to love or how to attach himself to others.

Whenever I had a special event at school, only Mom came. Stepdad George, a perfectionist himself, repeatedly would say, "Why would I want to go hear an amateur play? Why would I want to go to hear amateur musicians? Why would I go to hear amateur singers?"

His rage combined with the sting of those words he often shouted, "Marty, they're *your* girls," echoed inside with an ache deeper than hell. These words fueled rejection and increased my insecurities. I confess; we loved it when he left on business trips. Peace would temporarily return, and for a few days, we had a reprieve. We dropped our guard and relaxed. We could breathe, laugh, and enjoy one another.

When I became an adult, I learned from my mother that Stepdad George insisted our father's social security checks pay for all our needs, including food. Up to that moment, I always wondered why my mother carried two wallets. They had their money, we had ours. Thus, I never had a living dad serve as a provider. They were even able to purchase every home because the original house in Hatfield was bought by the sweat of the brow of my mother and her savviness in managing finances.

As for college, I received no financial help from him, and yet his income blocked me from obtaining any scholarship which I had worked hard for. On my wedding day, he proudly walked me down the aisle with a happy grin on his face. Arm in arm with my stepdad, I imagined my real dad in heaven looking down on me and Pep that day. Honestly, the only money gift I ever received from him was $300 for a wedding gift, but with stipulations that we spend it on something substantial he could see in the home. My husband and I were thankful and bought our first washer-dryer set. Much to my stepdad's credit, he did hand me a couple of his valiums to calm me down on my first trip to France as a college student. I floated through the walkways of the airport!

Because of Stepdad George's jealousy over my real dad, my only recourse was to repress my secret longing to know my real dad. About every five years through my adult years, late at night when visiting home, after Stepdad George went to bed, I would ask my mother about our real dad. I saw pictures and home movies of them skiing, mountain climbing, dancing, picnicking, and socializing with their friends—how they were happy together! Mom would not say much, except that he was the kindest, most generous man, and the most forgiving man she ever had known.

In my young twenties, good friends of my real dad and mother lived near us in Westerville, Ohio, a nostalgic Victorian village with brick roads. While in college, Mother made sure I had met them. One day, after we married, my husband and I were sail boating with this couple on the reservoir they lived on. Spontaneously, Mrs. Ross began to talk about my real dad.

"Marian, I worked with your mother in the chemistry lab and met your daddy through her," She said, with her hand on the boom, maneuvering the sails. "I remember your father as being extremely warm, friendly, generous, fun-loving, kind, and very forgiving."

"Thank you," I said. Thank you! Is this all I could say? Taken off guard by this remark, I did not think to inquire if she could tell me more about my dad. Perhaps she longed for decades to be able to share this with me. Cherishing this comment, I tucked this new tidbit into my heart. She confirmed every recollection about him given to me over the years by others who knew him. I thought to myself,

"He must have been quite a man; I sure wish he was around today."

Years later, 1987, Pep and I were at a Conference of the Holy Spirit in Cincinnati, Ohio. In the early days of a nationwide church growth movement, the attendance was small and intimate. During the ministry time, the guest speaker sensed that God wanted to minister to those who had abortions and who had been adopted. Well, neither category fit me, although I had a sense of being orphaned that I could not explain. Remaining in my seat, I lifted my hands in worship to the Lord.

"God, what about those without fathers? Where do I fit in?"

With my eyes closed, I immediately saw hands reaching down from the sky. The hands unrolled a scroll, and the Voice said,

"Marian, see, you are Mine. I adopted you. Here are your adoption papers. You belong to Me."

These loving words imparted an indescribable peace into my heart. Although I felt like an orphan with no earthly father, God personally confirmed to me that I was His child and adopted forever. At that moment, satisfied that God had adopted me, life moved on. Did I comprehend the fullness of this truth? Not at all. Sinking this truth into my inner core would take at least another decade.

This most profound longing for my real dad and to know him never went away. After being touched by the Holy Spirit in 1994, the desire to know my real dad emerged, with more fervency. Questions began to surface from my subconscious which had lied dormant for a lifetime. Again, I spoke to no one about my secret quest.

I didn't dare question my Uncle Hop, the South Carolinian self-made man, my only real connection with my father, because he never got over the loss of his brother. He never offered any stories, either, even with all my trips down to visit. He buried his emotions, too, and got on with life. Tragedy and grief leave their marks on all who experience them. My Uncle Hop certainly bore his in silence.

Uncle Hop loved Nancy and me as if we were his own, and perhaps we served to be his connection with his brother. I equally loved Aunt Sis and him—my surrogate parents. I could not imagine having been the one alongside my Uncle Chap to view my father's remains for identification purposes. The two uncles had done this for my mother, which I learned in 1997. He also endured much suffering living in his brother's shadow when my grandmother moved into his house. As you may recall, she had placed my father on a pedestal. Who could compete with that? So, how could I ask him anything about his brother without causing him pain?

I am Not Alone

Over the past twenty years, I have wondered how many children live without ever knowing their father or having a loving father in their lives. How many lost their fathers through bombings and mass shootings over the past two decades? What about those orphaned by the same plane bombing as my dad? How many will never get to experience their real dads' love, just like me? How many children have been orphaned through heinous murders? How many law enforcement families are now fatherless or motherless? How about military families? How many mothers now travel the path my mother had been forced to walk?

In our society, multitudes of individuals go through life with an "orphan spirit." Orphan spirits carry holes and gaps in the development of the individual with a father missing in action. Young boys struggle to know what it means to become a man. Young daughters shuffle through what to expect from a father and often end up making wrong choices because of the missing or distorted role model of their earthly fathers. Our culture of divorce has spun out of control. Fathers walking out of families. Fathers not marrying the mothers. Mothers needing to separate from abusive or delinquent fathers. Results? Single parenthood is rising in our culture.

Although orphans and fatherlessness have been around since the beginning of time, and nothing is new under the sun, the number of children without fathers in the home in the United States continues to grow. According to the U.S Census in 1960, 8.0% of 64.5 million children out of a national population of 187 million lived in fatherless homes.[1] Comparing the percentage of 5.2 million fatherless children to the entire population of 187 million, 3% of the population lived with single mothers. My sister and I would have been two of those fatherless children counted in the 1960 statistics.

By 2017, households with two married parents declined from 85% in 1968 to 65% by 2017. The children living without fathers grew to 32%, with an estimated 24.7 million children have no father in the home. According to a new Pew Research Center analysis, another 3% of all children live as orphans without either of their parents.[2] In a nation with roughly 320 million people, nearly 8% of our entire population are fatherless, up 5% from the 3% in 1960.

When statistics are broken into racial categories, the percentage of children living without a father in the home exponentially increases within each population group. By 2017, 24% Caucasian/white families were fatherless, (pop. 8.6 M fatherless) and 41% for Hispanics (pop. 7.2 M fatherless; figures may include non-Hispanic of other origins), and 54% of American Indian (pop. 351,000 fatherless).[3]

Statistics further indicate a major shift in the Black American community. In 1970, 66% of the African American families had both parents in the home and 35% had no father living at home. Forty-eight years later, using latest data available, the figures were flipped. By 2018, only 35% of the African American families had both parents in the home. African American single-household, fatherless families with children (pop. 6.1 M fatherless) reflected an estimated 59% of 14.5 million African American households, with some sources reporting a higher percentage of 65% of the 14.5 million living without a father in the home.[4]

The criteria for arriving at a statistic depends upon the method used for collection of data and compilation and which base figures are calculated. I encountered this when I desired to verify conflicting numbers. On a news media program, it was reported that over half of American children were without fathers.

Since this number did not correspond to the overall national rate of 24% of children, I pursued to research the matter.

I discovered the figure being quoted as the rate of nationwide fatherlessness, the 59%, reflected the rates of fatherlessness within the African American community, not the entire nation. Other data showed a ten-year history, 2007-2017, of African American fatherless children at 65%. Upon further investigation, the entire population of African Americans within the U.S. was 44.2 million at the time the data had been collected. Within the 44.2 million, 14.5 million accounted for the number of African American households (e.g., family units). Therefore, to report that 65% of 44.2 million African Americans are fatherless inflates the numbers. We would indeed be in a societal crisis larger than anyone could imagine if this were accurate. Out of an approximate 44.2 million African Americans, 6.1 million fatherless children make up 13% of the entire Black American community. It is more accurate to report 59-65% of all African American households are fatherless, a reversal of the 1970 statistics.

Why is this important? Fatherlessness is a crisis and one that will not go away unless every segment in society works together to place value on men, fathers, and families. But, to report that 28.7 million (65% of 44.2 million) within the African American community are fatherless does injustice to the community and the many families that remain intact with fathers in the home.

One missing stat, which could not be found from all the data—from nationwide to ethnic population groups—is a composite of national statistics of all individuals who grew up without fathers. That is, I am no longer counted in any up-to-date stats on fatherlessness because once I passed my 18th birthday, I would no longer be considered a fatherless child and included among the national data collections for fatherless children. Should it ever be possible to establish the total number of Americans raised fatherless—no matter their age or ethnic group—the social implications for our culture would reveal many more patterns and trends and could possibly explain the continual breakdown in the American family.

While these stats may be slightly confusing to sort, the growing number of children without fathers continues to climb. It also must be said, that not every fatherless child opts for deviant behavior throughout their life. Such is my case. I have other fatherless friends who also do not fall into the at-risk statistics.

However, the effect of fatherlessness on my life had taken a toll on my emotional health, thoughts, and beliefs.

The Effect of Growing Up Without a Father

Why are these fatherless statistics important?

With an increase in fatherless families, our nation is facing severe crisis in our society. The National Center for Fathering reported that most social ills faced by America's children are related to fatherlessness: poverty, drug and alcohol abuse, physical and emotional health, lower educational achievement, crime, and sexual activity and teen pregnancy.[5]

In an interview with Alan Blankstein, author of *Failure is Not an Option*, on NPR, the growing number of fatherless children "poses the most serious problems in education today."[6] He confirms the findings of the National Center for Fathering: fatherless children are more likely to be poor, impeding their academic success; 7 out of 10 fatherless teenagers are more likely to drop out of school; and, fatherless teens are also two times likely to commit suicide. Coupled with the higher High School dropout rate, there is a correlation between fatherlessness and incarceration in their lifetime. Because of the damage done by distant or non-existent fathers, even in cases in which the mother must separate and divorce her husband for self-protection, Alan has witnessed the emotional destruction of children not knowing their real fathers.

When asked about how fatherlessness affects girls and boys, experts on this issue agree that girls and boys respond differently. For example, Alan Blankstein pointed to research revealing a correlation between obesity and fatherless daughters. Young women without a father figure in their lives are also four times likely to become teenage mothers. Fatherless boys, on the other hand, prefer to act out in a range of behaviors—such a violence, criminal activity, and destructive behaviors—which brought national attention to the issue of fatherlessness; girls, though, keep their hurts inside, and he says, "if a young girl is imploding, we don't see it."[7]

The father wound, father hunger, father loss, the father effect, and orphan spirit are among some of the terminologies which describe the hurts and emptiness left by fathers on their children. In the United States, according to Beth M. Erickson, PhD in her book, *Longing for Dad,* Psychiatrist and therapist, Frank Pittman observed, "For a couple of hundred years now each generation of fathers has passed on less to his sons. Not just less power, but less wisdom, and less love. We have finally reached a point where most fathers are largely irrelevant in the lives of their sons...we've gone from a toxic overdose of fathering to a fatal deficiency."[8]

Two women, Denna D. Babul, RN, and Karin Luse, PhD, teamed to author *The Fatherless Daughter Project—Understanding our Losses and Reclaiming our Lives.* To undertake their research, they interviewed 5,000 women (ages 15 to 80) and discovered patterns in the 50% who stated they were fatherless. These women had lost their fathers due to divorce and separation (28%), emotional absence (26%), death (19%), desertion (15%), addiction (13%), abuse (12%), incarceration (4%), with 6% who never met their father.[9] I landed in three of those categories. The missing grouping, probably due to being so rare, was death by murder. When you add verbal abuse regarding my stepdad, I find myself in yet another classification.

Regardless of how the fathers were lost, Denna and Karin's findings confirmed my reactions to being fatherless. I fit their description of a fatherless daughter, laden with "heavy emotional cost, a profound feeling of loss, and a deep-seated need for survival that is unlike other losses."[10] Their own words further describe the fatherless daughter, "The repercussions of this loss can show up at different times in life in the form of difficult relationships or confusing emotions; most women are usually unaware of how often these experiences relate directly back to their fatherlessness."[11]

In order to survive, most women will secretly hide the pain deep inside their heart, as I did, until their lives bring them to a crisis of healing with the strength to face their pain.

A Growing Movement

In response to the detrimental impact of fatherlessness on families and children, non-profits have been developed to educate on the social damages of an absent father, to provide resources for men to learn how to be good fathers, and to minister to the needs of fathers, families, and congregations.

Recognizing this father absence crisis in the US, in 1994, The Fatherhood Initiative, a 501(3C) non-profit, launched nationally with a vision of every child growing up with a 24/7 father—a father who is involved with his children, takes responsibility for his children, and remains committed as a father.[12] Besides providing awareness of the seriousness of an absentee father, the Initiative created fatherhood curriculum, assistance, and resources to churches and organizations to assist fathers with skills and knowledge to engage with their children.

Christian ministries, like Encouraging Dads and The Father Effect, developed by John Finch, have risen to the occasion to turn the tide on the absentee father syndrome sweeping our nation, to bring reconciliation between the fatherless and their absentee fathers, and to turn the hearts of the fathers toward their children. His father committed suicide when John was only ten years old. Later in life, when John hit an emotional brick wall, he realized he had become like his dad: a workaholic, distant from his family, and with addictions. Once he had the grace to forgive his father, freedom came to him in every arena of his life.

After John's journey to freedom, he filmed a documentary, *The Father Effect*, and later wrote a book with the same title. He traversed the nation and interviewed hundreds of men and women abandoned by their fathers through all circumstances.

Ever since, he became a mouthpiece for the importance of fathers and forgiveness.

Since John has several daughters, and through hundreds of interviews he conducted nationwide, he became aware of the basic God-given needs every daughter looks for from her father: attention, affirmation, affection, and to be loved.[13] Doesn't this sound familiar? These four summarize everything I lacked and so desperately wanted.

Ronald C. Warren, author of *Bad Dads of the Bible* and former President of the National Father Initiative, brings to light the outright assault on fatherhood by our adversary, Satan. Warren writes that fathers are "earthly mirrors of a heavenly reality."[14] All fathers, even those who are not born-again Christians, were created by God to reflect His image and goodness. By emasculating men, making men unloving, ineffective, distant, distracted, disconnected, or abusive, children have no godly example of manhood and fatherhood.

The lack of a loving father's example in a child's life shapes how he or she views God, which is generally distorted. This skewed perspective influences the character, development, and behavior of the child. Believing in a loving God becomes difficult, even though the child may sing, "Jesus loves me, this I know."

Many of us walk blindly with orphan hearts and wonder why life is not going the way we thought it should. We selfishly do life our way, apart from fully trusting in God for everything. We believe God moves and acts on behalf of others, but not ourselves. We find it difficult to reach an untouchable God, who is distant, uncaring and demanding. Our earthly dads or stepdads have disappointed us or left us. To compensate for this lack, we unwittingly take up the role of father and pursue fathering ourselves in a complicated and confusing world.

Parents who never marry or continually change boyfriends or girlfriends, complicate the child's concept of God amidst a life of uncertainty. The instability and inconsistency toss the child about, and makes trusting anyone difficult, including God.

Any family situation without a stable father compounds the fatherless and orphan-spirit dilemma facing our society. Many single mothers do their best to fill both roles, like my mother; yet the absence of the male father figure leaves gaping, emotional holes in the children. Even perfect dads are not meant to fill the empty spaces in our souls where only God can live.

Everyone is Searching

Each one of us longs for a father's love and affirmation, whether we recognize it or not.

I once dreamed I had gone to a local mall. In the mall, a group of teenage gang members loitered and stood in a circle. I then saw myself going up to them and engaging them in conversation. They were all ears. I told them that I knew what they were all searching for—the father's love. And, I shared with them who their true heavenly Father was, that He was someone who would never leave them or abandon them. Years later, I stopped at a convenient local store to fill my gas tank. Who do I see? A gang of male teenagers, dressed in black, some with long trench coats. I thought,

"Gee, its school hours. Why aren't they in school?" At first, I felt intimidated by the teenagers who gathered by the door where I needed to enter. While pumping the gas, some of them walked around the building. Others remained around the trash can in front of the store. In my spirit, I found myself drawn to talk with those standing out front. The Holy Spirit engaged and directed the words that came from my mouth.

"Hello, there! Isn't school on?" I asked one of the fellows in a black trench coat.

"Oh, it's a special day where us seniors get off because of ...." said the young man.

"Mmm...what do you like to do? What's your favorite subject?" I answered.

"Art, I really like art." he said.

The conversation took off, and I began to encourage him to pursue his dreams and to not allow anyone to take it from him.

Focused on him, I did not see the entire group had circled me, all listening to the words of life flowing out from me. All fear left; I knew it was their time. God the Father wanted them to know His love. I am not sure what all I said, but I had their respect. It was as if they never had an adult encourage them. The first teenager opened up about his family life, enough to let me know it was not easy. I told them about a father whose love for them was immeasurable and who would never leave them nor disown them.

After I sensed the conversation ended, I confidently walked past them and paid my gas bill. As I drove away, the Holy Spirit recalled the dream about reaching the fatherless.

Fathers Wanted

The need for godly father figures in people's lives could never be stronger than now in our present times. People are crying out for the father's love, but do not realize this. Their anger, resentment, hard exterior, and bitterness hide the deep ache within. For many, because of abusive fathers or mother's boyfriends, the thought of any male is too much to bear.

Perhaps you may not have had a father present in your home growing up. Maybe your father walked out on you, your mother, and siblings. Perhaps you had a father at home, but who was absent emotionally, who never showed any ounce of caring. Or, maybe you had a father in prison. Or, a father whose addictions turned him into a monster such that no peace ever reigned in your house. Or, like my father, murdered, killed in an accident, or lost in the line of duty.

Maybe you were blessed with a father who showed you love, who nurtured and provided for you. If this is you, count your blessings. However, even good fathers cannot be perfect and can only mirror the true Heavenly Father's character as best as they can. Maybe you, too, had a father who has passed away and you still miss his influence and presence in your life.

So, where am I taking this?

My personal desire and passion for knowing my biological father mirrored the same need in millions of others just like me. What I discovered, as I suffered in my disjointed state, is that God knew all about my longing. He knows that each of us yearns for a true father's love, for loving arms to catch us when we fall, for wisdom that can only come through a father who faced life's trials, for comfort when we need to cry and a hug from a father. God knew what I had been missing all my life. In His love, while turmoil surrounded my life, while painful healing was taking place, He also nurtured me back to life amidst my emotional firestorm.

God was about to lead me on an excursion I would never forget.

Scene 21

A Father's Surprise

*"I will be a Father to you, and you shall be
My sons and daughters," says the Lord Almighty.*

—2 Corinthians 6:18 (MEV)

Early winter 1996

Meanwhile, the battles raged outside and within, leaving feelings of utter nothingness.

Nevertheless, God, with His immeasurable, everlasting love, and patience, upheld me through His Word and in ways He knew I could receive from Him. So much was being stripped away from me and the emotional uproar at times became unbearable. Even my ability to live depended upon His strength. He had indeed become the very air I breathed. Apart from Him, I could not make it through each day. Overcome by weariness in the tug of war for my very soul, I cried out to God continuously for His intervention, deliverance, and empowerment.

In private prayer times, I poured my feelings before Him. I focused solely on Him, desiring to touch Him, to know Him, and to see Him. The hunger for my father's love grew stronger each day. I felt like I was grasping at straws, ever reaching, but never grabbing hold of him.

The Surprise of My Life

Thankfully, God responded beyond all my wildest imaginations and expectations. He knew I needed more. Was it because He enjoyed my seeking Him, that He chose to delight in me? Or, was it because I set my heart on Him, and in return, He delighted in giving me the desires of my heart—to know my real dad? Which came first? No man can fathom the mind of Christ or comprehend why God does what He does. His ways are surely not ours, and ours are not His.

What I can assure you—He is not an abusive dad waiting for you to screw things down here on earth. He does not shame us into becoming perfect nor does He heap condemnation upon our heads. Instead, He keeps no record of wrongs and offers forgiveness, grace and mercy to all who ask. Walking in forbearance, He joyfully accepts and welcomes all who come to Him. When we fall short, He reaches out to us, picks us up, dusts us off, and sets us back on our feet. And, never remembers what we said or did.

Months later, at another Holy Spirit conference, desperate for continued restoration, I responded to the altar call. My husband and friend stayed with me. Another trusted friend stopped to pray for me. He knew nothing about my journey of healing, nor the story of my real dad.

He did not have to pray too long. I floated down onto the floor, again overpowered by the Holy Spirit's presence, with the same rush of a mighty wind as before. A second time, whether in-the-body or out-of-the-body, I do not know. I could hear the muffled sound of the worship band, which grew fainter and fainter. In a flash, like through a time tunnel, I found myself back in time, four decades earlier, looking in on my dad's funeral in South Carolina.

My mother, in her black maternity funeral dress made by her friends, stood holding my sister's hand by the gravesite. The flowers poured in from hundreds of people, hid the casket and filled the tent which stood over the gravesite. An overall sense of gloom and mourning loomed over the family gathered around the tent.

"What a shame—What a shame—What a shame" resounded as a chorus from each one standing. Every head shook in disbelief and sorrow. The blanket of mourning, shock, grief, and bewilderment hung heavy. I saw them with their heads looking down, saying,

"Hobby was so young. What about his family? Look at Marty. What about the children?"

In the natural, I cried and began to scream in agony. In this alternate realm, I saw myself as a baby in my mother's womb and I relived the sense of shame and deep grief shared by everyone who loved my dad.

"Where's my Daddy? Where's my Daddy?" I asked the Lord.

While physically lying on the floor, others thought I needed deliverance from a demonic entity, because of my outburst, but my husband and a friend stopped them. While no one knew what was transpiring, as I could not tell them, my husband knew that more emotional healing was happening.

Suddenly, in the midst of my upheaval, the voice of God tenderly and kindly interjected,

"Don't you remember, Marian, how I showed you I scooped him up in my arms and he didn't feel anything?"

"Yes, Lord."

The words no sooner were spoken when I instantly found myself in another realm. Whether in or out of my body, once again, did not matter. My physical body remained on the church floor, while the rest of me was ushered to another place. As if I had been pulled by God through His stargate, I instinctively knew it was heaven. As I was lifted up, my real, biological daddy stood there like he had been waiting all this time for this moment. He welcomed me, leaned down, looked at me with loving eyes, and took my hand to bring me to where he stood.

"Marian, I have **always** loved you."

My dad's words pierced through my soul. I had always wanted to see him, hear him, and touch him and at that moment—there I was—meeting him for the first time! He told me he loved me!

Thoroughly taken by surprise, God's grace and love brought me to him. Holding his hands, hearing his voice, I looked up at him. My dad's silhouette stood as tall as he was here on earth. I knew it was him—Marion Pierce Hobgood, my daddy. He didn't wait for me to respond and said,

"But let me take you to your Real Father."

He took my hand and placed it in the hands of the other silhouetted figure—Jesus Christ, the Son of God. Instinctively, I recognized Him. My spirit and His Holy Spirit bore witness to each other. Unfathomable peace and wonderment overtook me—all my vexations drained, every ounce of fret, including my entire past, all disappeared—forgotten. Jesus said,

"Marian, let me take you to your Real Heavenly Father."

In a split milli-second, I entered the very throne room of God. My figure melted into the brightest whitest light ever. I never saw such brilliance and describing it is difficult. No new LED bulbs could compare. No sunlight. No daylight bulbs. No white lights. No glaring spotlights. The peace that surpasses all understanding engulfed me as I was swallowed up in His light. God, on His throne, emanated this all-encompassing, all-consuming light. You couldn't see my frame at all, nor God's. We were both clothed in this pure light. To think, the very Father of all fathers invited me onto His lap which I joyfully accepted. His right arm wrapped around me. I was lost in the brilliance of His light as I became light with Him. My frame enfolded into the light, hidden and safe on my Daddy's lap. At last, I was home. I was one with the Father.

No painting could be produced on earth that would capture the sight because radiant light enclosed everything that came into the light. God was light. His throne was light. I was light. His lap and arms were light. Every color of the rainbow combined into one glorious splendor of white light. If one took a blank white canvas and labeled it "Heaven," even that would not accurately depict the brilliance, radiance, whiteness, and brightness. Nor could it capture the essence of heaven's pure, unadulterated love, peace, and bliss. Wrapped up in His light, a blissful peace permeated me. I never wanted to leave.

He had a big book opened on His lap as if preparing to read a story to me, His child. I could not see the book as the light surrounded it, too. But it was there. I looked at the pages, which were also absorbed in the light, and laughed,

"Father, that's Your book!"

To which He lovingly said,

"Let me tell you about Moses."

I knew He was relaying a message to me. Moses beheld the Glory of God on Mt. Sinai and stood face to face with God, enfolded in His light as I was then.[1]

Instantaneously, I was out of the throne room and back with my earthly dad and Jesus. By instinct or religious training, I knelt face down to render honor and holiness to Him who created the entire universe. However, Jesus would have none of that and lifted me onto my feet. Both my dad and the Son of God remained silhouetted black against grey with the rest of heaven blocked from my eyes, a stark contrast from the throne room with God.

Feeling completely comfortable, but not very satisfied, I did what most of us might do—I complained. I asked,

"Why is everything silhouetted? Why can't I see more?"

"In due season, Marian, in due season," Jesus said and pointed His finger in a far-off direction. My dad remained with us.

"What do you see, Marian?" asked Jesus.

"I see a large tree with broad extended branches, full of leaves."

"Yes, that is the Tree of Everlasting Life. You must go back and tell others there is a Tree of Everlasting Life waiting for them."

"I don't want to go back, Please, I want to stay here," I said.

"You must. You must tell others there is a Tree of Everlasting Life waiting for them."

In a God-instant, with no forewarning or ability to bid Jesus or my biological dad farewell, the floodgates of heaven opened, and the River of Living Water gushed out from under God's throne. The River roared deep and wide with currents that a whitewater rafter would find exhilarating. I discovered myself floating on top of the rushing River of Life, undisturbed, and without a care as its currents swiftly headed downward toward the earth. It flowed from the right then to the left, winding back and forth.

Suddenly, my spiritual body merged back into my physical body. I had left the building, then returned. No one else knew God lifted me to heaven. I recognized the muffled sounds of the worship band and sensed it was their last song. Simultaneously, a song by David Ruis, a worship leader-songwriter, zipped back and forth through my ears:

"Let the River Flow. Let the River Flow. Let the River Flow."

My eyes remained closed. I did not want to get off the floor nor join the present world. I preferred to stay in heaven in that blissful, fully content state, with unspeakable joy. Gradually, I knew I had to move as I could sense that we were probably the last ones in the large sanctuary room. I opened my eyes and saw my friend and husband looking down at me. They knew something transpired but did not know what. How long I was in and out of my body remains a mystery. Time did not matter to me.

How did I manage to walk out of that building that night? Barely.

The glory of God rested upon me and left me in awe. The Father of all fathers surprised me when He answered a cry of my heart to know my real dad and in such a magnificent way. Not only did I meet my real earthly dad, but Jesus took me to God the Father. Experiencing an indescribable blissful state, I did not want to leave the dwelling place of the King of Kings even though I had been commissioned to tell others about everlasting life obtained only through faith in Jesus Christ.

Dazed by what I had seen and heard, readjusting between heavenly and earthly realms took time. Speechless, I staggered like a drunk out of the building under the glory of God's Presence.

Entirely submerged in pure liquid love, peace, and joy, I could not cheapen this sacred and holy experience with any human words that would be too inadequate.

I would not want anyone to be jealous or think that they must have a divine encounter to be made whole. Fix your gaze onto Jesus, not on having any in-or-out of the body experiences. Do I feel uniquely privileged to have had this experience? Yes and No. I felt humbled, privileged, and thankful the Lord allowed me to meet my biological dad and then to introduce me to my Real Heavenly Father. My passionate search to know my real dad ended, with an eternity to explore my real Father. But I am no better and not worthier than anyone else. I had not been seeking to travel to heaven. Instead, I pursued the One who created heaven. My Real Father pleasantly surprised me that day.

Is Heaven for Real?

I have since heard other accounts of people who have seen heaven. Each one I heard or read about reports a different aspect and setting. Each one shares a different depiction of heaven. We all look through the glass dimly. Our unique worldviews and perceptions can influence what we perceive as heaven solely because God speaks to everyone in ways that they can understand. He speaks French to the French, Spanish to the Spanish, Chinese to the Chinese, and so forth. Heaven sits in an expansive space, in another dimension unseen by the human eye. God alone has the discretion to reveal what He wants, to whom He desires, and when.

What is significant? Does the heavenly experience give glory and honor to God and His Son Jesus Christ? Does the person leave touched or changed? Does the person boast about their experience and puff themselves up? Does the person exhibit virtues of humility in sharing their heaven experience? Does their description correspond to what we know Biblically about heaven, the glory of the Lord, and the character of God?

I know personally two people who had been taken up into heaven in their lifetime.

My grandfather, Rembert D. McNeer, my mother's father passed away at the ripe age of 94 or 96 (his birth certificate was unclear). He served his entire life as a Methodist minister. At his funeral, we learned he was the last of the known circuit riders in the Methodist church. Circuit riders often rode on horseback, then later, drove vehicles, pastoring multiple churches throughout mountainous and rural settings. He situated his family in the Blue Ridge Mountains and pastored many quaint congregations tucked among the mountain ridges. He lived an extremely frugal life, and when he married his second wife, he stubbornly refused to upgrade their washing machine from a ringer-washer to modern electric machine. He insisted his oldest son, my Uncle Rembert, travel two hours to fix things on the house instead of hiring local remodeling contractors. He became quite cantankerous in his later years until God encountered him. When he was in his late 80s, he woke up one morning and told my step-grandmother God had taken him to heaven. The Lord spoke to him about a few things, then sent him back to earth. My grandfather turned to his wife and said,

"I am so sorry for the way I have acted toward you and others. God told me not to be so difficult, and I will not be like that anymore."

My grandfather returned a changed man in his last years on this earth.

Another friend of mine died twice on the operating table while undergoing a routine, standard operation. He had been a well-known pastor in the area, and his church expanded by showing God's kindness throughout the city. The best surgeons had been gathered to perform the operation and to save him when complications arose. When he died both times, his spiritual body lifted, God gave him a glimpse of heaven, and he reported he met an angel. God gave him instructions about changes he needed to make in his life and sent him back. While in this out-of-body experience, he witnessed the commotion and scrambling in the operating room to bring him back to life, including all the staff, their conversations, and all the cussing. The doctors confirmed this was true and were puzzled by his recounting every word and actions to save him. In his book, *The Day I Died*, Steve Sjogren humbly shares that he had hurt many people on his staff. God told him to go back, apologize, and ask for forgiveness from each one. As soon as he could, he did just that to the best of his ability.[2] Not long afterwards, he handed his pastoral position over to others. Known as the originator of the Servant Evangelism Kindness movement, he still speaks, teaches, and reaches out to the least, the lost, and the hurting. While Steve's recovery took years and still walks with permanent injury, he left heaven changed.

All I know, heaven is waiting for all who call upon His Name and say, "Yes to Jesus." Heaven does exist and is the most healing, peaceful place ever, with no comparison to the most beautiful spot on earth. God is not sitting up in heaven ready to whack anyone who jumps out of line. No, not at all—He is loving, kind, and merciful. In God's dwelling place, you will find no more sorrow, no more tears, and no more sadness.

How Did My Heavenly Visit Change Me?

I dared not tell anyone, except for my husband, about this heavenly encounter for over a decade. When I did, I carefully chose who and when I would share such a holy interchange with the Living Father. The pastors and leaders of that conference do not even know what happened. Some might have chosen to believe it while others might have discounted it—assuming I was delusional or making it up. It is only at the time of this writing, some twenty years later, that I felt released to put this encounter in writing in hopes to encourage others in the goodness of God.

My experience was not a vision like a movie playing before my eyes, watching it unfold from a spectator viewpoint. I had not been hypnotized nor in a trance either. God teleported (for lack of a better word) me as a living participant, only my body did not break into mini pieces of matter as in the transporter in a 1960s, popular, science fiction TV series. My entire spiritual being in my petite figure landed instantly in the dwelling place of the Lord. As you may guess, my transportation to heaven marked a significant turning point in my journey.

Seeing and touching my real biological dad and hearing his voice say, "I have always loved you," penetrated all the wounds of fatherlessness and silenced all my longings and yearnings. At last, I met him. God honored my seeking. He allowed me to see my father, to hear him, and to touch him. My real dad was safe in heaven and gave me the father's welcome I had been seeking. He loved me so much and longed for me, too.

More significantly, I learned who my Real Father has been all the time. Nothing and no one can ever take this truth away from me. Before, I struggled with calling God "Father." For over forty years, I struggled with the concept of a good father. I questioned hearing God's voice and knowing Him because I did not audibly hear my earthly father's voice, nor could I ever until that point, touch my biological dad.

Afterward, there was no shadow of a doubt. The Father's love remains indescribably, indelibly, and eternally engrained and etched into my memory. No words exist to convey this perfect love effectively. His peace does surpass all our understanding here on earth. God's loving-kindness does melt away everything. Do I long to be with both my earthly dad and God, my Real Heavenly Father, in heaven? Unequivocally, YES.

There is no place I would rather be.

Since that encounter, my passion for everyone to know and understand the Father's love for them burns within like a blazing fire. Once the head-heart connection sinks into their spirits, they will never be the same. They will fly like the eagles, soar over storms of life, and discover their purpose and calling.

People are desperately searching for something; but, they do not know who or what they are searching for, just like the gang members. Just like me.

<hr />

My prayer times with Jesus from that day forth radically took on a different direction. I heard His loving words back to me, succinctly and more frequently. My interior wrestling lessened, though not settled. I still needed to release and resolve much emotional baggage, but knowing He truly loved me made the trek toward the finish line so much easier. Further grounded in the Father's acceptance and love, facing my inner monsters could be possible, whether I wanted to acknowledge their existence or not. Before my visit up-above, I blamed everyone and anything for my misery. I lived in denial about my responsibility. But that was about to change. Being in the throne room of the Father established my D-Day, with my V-E Day advancing on an unknown horizon.

Scene 22

Blessings in the Battle

Thus, says the LORD to you, 'Do not fear, nor be dismayed because of this great army, for the battle is not yours, but God's.

—2 Chronicles 20:17 (MEV)

In World War II after the Normandy invasion on D-Day (June 6, 1944), the allies fought many battles before reaching V-E Day (May 8, 1945), the end of the war. Likewise, the trip to heaven marked the beginning of my last leg on a long, tedious, and painstaking path toward the finish line, full of skirmishes and wrestling with darkness until reaching final victory. One might think that once I went to heaven and back that my freedom would be complete. It seemed my quest to search for my father had come to an end. However, God, in His wisdom, had plans to eradicate and pull out the origin of my troubles once and for all, just as I had asked. Blinded and oblivious, I never considered I would have to be responsible for my actions and reactions. Neither did I anticipate a massive frontal attack against my soul.

The Battle is Mine

Achieving the Final Win requires courage to fight through obstacles which block reaching the goal. To choose not to fight, but to flee or freeze, surrenders you to remain stuck in the same rut and replaying the same loops. Battles—from people, spiritual, and within—usually come unannounced. We cannot escape or ignore these battles, although I had tried.

In my early Christian years, a booklet promised that God had a beautiful plan for your life. From this message, I surmised that my walk with Jesus would be like a rose garden—battle, trial, and crisis-free. With Him on my side and I on His, what could go wrong? As we began to face trials as a young married couple, I logically thought we missed God's will for our lives, and we must have sinned. I asked myself many times:

- Did we go left when we should have gone right?

- Did we miss God's will for our lives?

- Was quitting our good state jobs to go to Missouri for pastoral training the wrong thing to do?

- Where did we miss the boat?

- Were we even called to enter professional ministry?

Shame, guilt, condemnation, and bitter disappointment mounted because of this skewed picture of both God and life. My hopes and dreams laid smashed. My paradigm and premise for life had to transform as I grappled with the reality that God never did promise us a rose garden, for my garden had become only weeds.

The battles, disguised in many forms, can knock you over with one blow, taking the wind out of you. Blow after blow, disappointment after disappointment, crushes one's spirit, and dashes hope to pieces. Proverbs 13:12 (MEV) empathizes with the human need for fulfillment of dreams:

Hope deferred makes the heart sick, but when the desire comes, it is a tree of life.

Through times alone with Him, Jesus strengthened my weakened condition. His truths began to transfer from my brain to my heart. I could not have possibly made it through the battles encircling me without His words giving me life and hope.

My healing journey from trauma and its emotional bondages fatigued my physical and emotional body. The stress of facing deep-seated wounds and feelings and then releasing them took its toll on my mind, soul, and spirit, including my health. I so desperately wanted to be free that I threw my entire being before the Lord, at home in private and in church and prayer settings. The process required much "dying to myself" in which I would let go of doing life my way and allow God to renew my mind.

In the late 1970s, at our College Christian Fellowship, we often gathered in a circle and worshiped with all our might. In warm weather, underneath the stars, in the baseball fields, we often sang with acoustic guitar, these lines from a popular 1970s folk mass song by Ray Repp, *"Into Your hands, we commend our lives, for we must die to ourselves in loving You."*

In my youth, I didn't quite comprehend the depth of those lyrics, but the spiritual principle of giving everything to God stayed with me throughout life. Our innocent intent was to become so like Jesus in our daily lives so our flesh (human nature apart from God) and the enemy would have no power to rule in or through us. We were one hundred percent dedicated to following Jesus. Our passion for God was sincere, albeit perhaps misguided when taken to an extreme and without a full grasp of His grace in working out our salvation with "fear and trembling."

Forty years later, adopting the only model I knew to reach Jesus' garment for restoration, I gave full permission to the Holy Spirit to examine my heart and reveal the causes of my inability to cope. While pouring out my heart with such passion, my body exerted an immense amount of mental and emotional activity. This developed physical fatigue, which in turn, limited my strength and endurance to fight the raging battles. Forced to cling to the Lord with all my might to live each day, total dependence upon the Lord developed. He became the very air I breathed.

After the separation from my mother's painful emotions, the breakthrough allowed me to face my painful emotions. Freedom from this heavy burden I had carried all my life opened the way for the Lord to uncover what resided in my heart. These discoveries were not all that pretty. Bitterness, anger, and hate had laid dormant for four decades, tucked deep in the inner crevices of my heart. They wrapped themselves around my very fiber and hibernated as if waiting for the time to be awakened. Meanwhile, the enemy, Satan and his cohorts, attempted to use all those exposed weak places and feelings of hurt to destroy me.

From the initial Great Uncorking period with the endless tears to the "whether in-the-body or out-of-the-body" experiences, no matter what bit of freedom came, I battled against my flesh, the evil darkness, and the sins committed against me. I was not yet conscious of my sinful reactions to the act of violence against my dad or the actions of my stepdad in my childhood. However, when unleashed, these truths triggered strong emotions such as fear of abandonment, fear of rejection, anger, and hate. These had unknowingly become interwoven into my psychological core and acknowledging their presence within me tore at my very spirit and soul.

The Word says that our battleground lies in our thoughts and we are to cast down every vain imagination that sets itself up against the Word of God (2 Cor. 10:4-5). In Christianese (what I call Christian language), these very thoughts and vain imaginations are called "strongholds." When left to flourish, the vain imaginations turn into beliefs which embed themselves into our minds and personalities, creating various kinds of footholds such as bitterness.

Overshadowed by our self-protective denial, we frequently are not aware of them. Our souls become enmeshed with the false beliefs rather than the identity God originally intended for us as His sons and daughters. Simple statements such as "I'm ugly," "I'm fat," and "I'm a failure" root themselves within us; we believe that we are those things, which we project onto others and into situations wherever we go.

My experience exemplifies the quandary we weave for ourselves. I not only contended with inner battles, but I also had an all-out war raging over my marriage, within my relationship with my husband and complicated by circumstances beyond our control. My whole being had become fighting grounds between good and evil, light and darkness, truth and lies, and my real identity and my false identity.

In the natural, my marriage and our economic future continued to be at the forefront of my prayers and tears. I prayed for grace and mercy for our children that they would not be affected negatively in any way by the crisis and trauma I was facing. God heard those prayers and organically provided for my children's nurturing in unexpected ways through spiritually mature and loving friends.

Because of the slow healing process, my frustration mounted as to why it was taking so long. I kept hoping for an end of the battles and believed complete freedom must surely be in sight, but no such chance. Living out of shame, I thought,

- Am I that bad?

- What did I do that was so wrong?

- Why can't I meet more frequently with a healing prayer team?

- Can't others see my pain?

- Why aren't others falling apart like I am?

My appointments with the church's specialized prayer teams were becoming too far apart. I had a different group of well-intentioned women each time. Months of having too many women knowing my business disconcerted me immensely. The lack of safety and confidentiality resulted in increased hopelessness, despair, and shame. My feelings of always being discounted, abandoned, and rejected compounded. The heavy weariness through the battle hung on me like Spanish moss hangs down on the trees in southern swampland.

Real or perceived it does not matter, because what is or seems to be a reality to someone in crisis or a broken state, is their reality. For me, I knew I wanted total freedom from all the lies I had been believing.

The battlefield was in my mind; I daily wrestled over feelings of inadequacy and fear over my blocking the healing process. This constant tug of war disturbed my soul and caused much distress. Unknowingly, I had become quite introspective (some might say narcissistic), taking scripture in the Bible to an extreme:

> *Search me, O God, and know my heart: try me, and know my concerns, and see if there is any rebellious way in me, and, lead me in the ancient paths (i.e., way everlasting, author comment).*
>
> —Psalm 139:23-24 (MEV)

In my journal, I rambled on about my state to the Lord. Laden with anxieties, I feared that I would have no more breakthroughs and that I would be skipped over by any prayer team. Here are some highlights of this continual conversation between Jesus and me.

> Me: *"Lord, set me free and let your Spirit of Truth come. Why I am such a mess, I don't know. All I know is that I cannot keep going like I am. You know what I need far greater than I do. Break down walls I've built barring You out. Help me to receive fully in my heart your view and truth about me. To know fully in my heart that You love me no matter what. You don't play favorites. "Oh, I am a blubbering idiot."*

Jesus: *No, Marian, you are not. I'm listening, and I will come. Even as I speak, I come. I will walk with you and repair the damage done by sin, shame, and guilt. I will wipe away the scars and the stings of your wounds. Your brokenness I have seen and heard. Allow Me to do to it. I will come. You will know my might, my power, my presence. Don't be concerned, distracted, or fretful. You're in safe hands. I've brought you this far. And, yes, it [the healing] has seemed so slow, distant and a long time coming. It will continue. Be at peace. I've ordained tomorrow. Give me the reins. Abandon yourself to me. My grace will carry you. The darkness will flee. Your hour of deliverance has come. Whatever I accomplish, know that I have ordained and purposed it. It will be enough for tomorrow. Rest in me. Be at peace. I am polishing you bit by bit, my cherished one from all the tarnish in your past—for My image is upon you.*

You feel like a battlefield, but I say to you—you are the battlefield. A war between light and darkness has been raging against you since birth. Allow me to enter your battlefield and win the war.

I stopped Him and asked, "But Lord, have I prayed enough or prepared myself enough? Do I have the right attitude?"

My insecurities, along with man-pleasing, pervaded these recurring conversations with the Lord. Although I knew Jesus had died for all my sins and that in Him, as a new creation, I was forgiven, my heart could not receive his freely given, perfect and pure love. Operating from an orphan spirit, I believed I had to do something for Him to get His attention. I worried if I had prayed hard or long enough. Like a loving father, He overlooked my confusion and distorted thinking about how He works. The Lord again responded:

"I have heard your cries from the depths of your being. I have heard them. Yielding is all you need to do. Allow me to work within you. Cry unto Me, and I will answer you. THE BATTLE IS MINE."

———⚬⚬⚬———

For the battle belongs to the Lord.
—1 Samuel 17:45 (MEV)

———⚬⚬⚬———

I savored these words in my heart. I meditated on them, not realizing what treacherous realms lay ahead.

Rejection

As my emotions were becoming unglued, things in the natural began to trigger bondages that had footholds my entire life, such as rejection. I seemed to attract rejection from others: in junior high school, in high school, from my stepdad, in my social life (I can count only five dates before I met my husband in my twenties), and from authority figures and peers as an adult. During this season, the enemy took every opportunity to harass this weak spot.

During one conference that first year, as I waited quite a while for someone to come and pray for me, but no one approached to pray with me. Struggling with rejection, I thought,

"It's just like me to be rejected. Rejected one more time. Why isn't anyone coming, can't they see me?"

I cried and then sat down in self-pity with my head in my hands just weeping and sobbing. Soon I felt a man's hand grab my hand, and his other hand gently stroked my hair as a father would his daughter. As he was gently praying, the Lord ministered through him and said,

"You are not forgotten. I have not forgotten you."

These simple, loving words broke straight through to my heart. I had not been forgotten by my real dad, nor by God. God hadn't ignored me. He moved through this man and held me in the palm of His hand.

"A broken heart and a contrite spirit, He will not despise," echoed through my head (Psalm 51:17).

He didn't look at my brokenness as a measure of my spiritual maturity. Instead, He was with me; He had been with me, and He will be with me. I had not been forgotten nor rejected by the One whose only opinion mattered.

Rejection Tested

Amidst making great headways toward becoming completely free, an unexpected turn took me off guard. As I grew stronger in who I was in Jesus and more self-confident through the transformation God was doing in me, I began to stand up for myself. My voice returned. Some of the inner-healing practices disturbed me, such as the use of guided imagery, and I questioned some of them. I wanted to know if I was on the right track with my beliefs or not. Being the man-pleaser, if I was not correct in my assessment regarding guided imagery and groupthink, I wanted to know. Because we were leaders in the church, I truly believed the leadership would consider my concerns and that we could discuss the issues with civility.

Remember how I stood against higher taxes and ran for office? My tendency to want to correct injustices carried over into the church. I won't dive into specifics, to safeguard that church and the pastor, but voicing my opinions proved not to be the wisest thing to do.

A conflict began brewing as a result of my search for answers, fueling my rejection syndrome. One day, a church leader said I was too damaged to be on any prayer team. This statement contradicted the very values of the church, based upon the premise, which said, "God uses broken vessels, and anyone can pray and minister." I fit that description quite well!

The very people whom I had trusted assaulted my character and spirituality. Without a doubt, the spirit of rejection operated through this leadership in full force to come against my person-hood at my weakest point: my high need for acceptance and belonging.

It's as if the enemy, Satan and his darkness, knew that when I obtained full victory, I would be a spiritual force to be reckoned with in the Kingdom Rule and Reign of God. The enemy did everything to thwart God's plans for my life. Destruction of my reputation seemed to be his MO, modus operandi. Why did Satan want to strike me in my weakest places? Why would the enemy even care about me? Was I that much of a threat to him? How could one lone person on the face of the earth matter? Wasn't I merely a mom in tennis shoes?

The Word clearly states Satan does come to annihilate and to keep anyone from following Jesus, as John 10:10 (MEV) says,

The thief does not come, except to steal and kill and destroy.

The good news is that Jesus finishes this statement,

I came that they may have life and that they may have it more abundantly.

Satan's mission is to devour anyone and everyone, to prevent them from knowing God and becoming all God has purposed for them. He uses those closest to us, circumstances, and our shortcomings against us. Although he lost the battle over two thousand years ago, he continues to use his only weapons left—intimidation and harassment—to devour and destroy God's people. In my case, my most definite weakness was my highest need for belonging and acceptance by others. In turn, this need fed my tendency to be a people-pleaser. The enemy then used leadership to target those weaknesses.

My story of rejection by the church leaders is not to bring shame or ill-will toward anyone but as a learning example for all involved in the inner healing and pastoral ministry. It serves as an utmost reminder to guard always the person's value, dignity, and worth.

In your healing journey, when you do find your voice and begin to stand up for yourself, others may find ways to attack you mentally, spiritually, and relationally. When this occurs, and others may attempt to marginalize you as I was, be at peace. Your battles are **not against** flesh and blood but **against** the spiritual principalities, powers, and rulers in this earth—the enemy of God. The church people are not your enemy. As God rescued and defended me, He will likewise do for you. Our response is to forgive and release all hurts and wounds to Jesus. He is your Defender, your Advocate, your Healer, your Vindicator, and your Redeemer, not man.

God, who did not cause the conflict, nonetheless used the entire clash for working His purposes into my life. He became my hiding place, and I ran toward Him for shelter, guidance, and identity. He indeed fought my battles while I cried to Him on my knees.

Just as that church (no church is perfect) became an unsafe place for me, God led me to a different church where I began attending its classes and conferences. The atmosphere exuded warmth and excitement. Although its congregation held thousands of members, it seemed more like a family. New friendships were forged, and an attitude of grace permeated the atmosphere. People treated me as a person, not a broken object. I was genuinely loved, nurtured, and accepted. Faster paced and increased healing occurred. Life, at last. Hope. Acceptance. Had that conflict never occurred and I never discovered this new church, I could have been stuck in a vicious, downward spiral instead of rising upwards toward Christ.

While the enemy plotted to destroy me, God built me up. He used the new friendships and environment to breathe new life into me. While I still struggled and remained an emotional wreck inside, I received impartations from the Holy Spirit in hearing His voice, evangelism, and revelatory knowledge. Most importantly, in the safety of this new environment, I could receive, in more considerable measure, the Father's acceptance, which permeated my soul and nurtured my love-starved heart.

Eventually, my husband and I switched church homes and flourished, blooming in our new church family. Restoration and redemption revived us as we set our feet on a different path.

What about those church leaders who had betrayed my trust? I had already forgiven them a long time ago. They knew not what they were doing and only acted out of their insecurities and brokenness, like myself. In my case, it took almost ten years for anyone from that former church to seek forgiveness for that conflict. When they unexpectedly came to me with all humility, it meant everything.

Suicidal Thoughts

In another phase of this healing journey, thoughts of suicide fueled by the released feelings of rage and anger, coupled with feelings of worthlessness, haunted my mind. They would invade my thoughts, especially when I was driving around the city on the freeway. Deep in thought and highly distraught, I would suddenly be overwhelmed by the thought of ramming my car into the back of the truck in front of me to end it all. Because I knew this idea did not originate from me, I recognized them as coming from outside of me and not from my thoughts. I knew I did not want to end it all, even though despair gripped me. Knowing my authority in Christ, I combatted the suicidal thoughts through the Name of Jesus and did not succumb to the enemy's wishes. Even if the suicidal thoughts came from within me, I still would have stood against them in the Name of Jesus. Why? The Holy Spirit, residing within me, gave me the power, authority, and restraint to not ever execute that urge. These attacks scared the daylights out of me.

This battle went on for a short season until the enemy gave up and stopped the intimidation and harassment.

The Knife Fixation

Another strange battle reared its ugly head; again, fueled by the anger, frustration, hate, and bitterness that kept me in bondage. Without any warning, the fear of throwing knives consumed me. Fortunately, this sudden compulsive urge only lasted a short period. I had become exceedingly angry at our present situation and even angrier with the killer for taking my dad. I had no idea why, but I had begun not to trust myself with knives, so I quickly put them away and hid them. To imagine that such wrath existed within me, the one who always tried to accommodate others for acceptance, horrendously disturbed me. Thankfully, anchored in both Jesus and the Word of God, I never threw a knife, nor would I ever. I do not recommend anyone allowing anger to overtake them to any heightened degree.

For the first time, I understood how unrestrained hate and anger could overtake a person. Persons without an authentic relationship with Jesus Christ or any moral restraint, for that matter, could easily murder someone in a fit of uncontrollable rage and deep-seated hate. Before you jump to conclusions, I am not justifying such evil acts, but the intensity of these dark emotions can consume and embody anyone apart from the Holy Spirit's intervention. Only hard hearts and seared consciences can commit such evil. Such was the unrepentant state of the man who killed my dad along with everyone on Flight #629.

Why I journeyed through this phase is incomprehensible. The fear could only have been instigated by the demonic forces desiring to destroy me. I recognized the battleground for my mind and stopped it by the power of God through the Name of Jesus, by casting down all vain imaginations and trusting in the Lord. The more I resisted, the more the urges to hide all the knives left. The enemy of my soul lost another round.

In all honesty, I shamefully went through a period in which I threw pots and pans in anger bursts, but no one ever got hurt, and nothing broke. I had been told in those inner-healing sessions

217

to tap into such feelings of resentment, anger, and hate and to hang onto them for a while, which I did. In my vulnerability and pain, I applied the teaching to an extreme and nursed them as if my life depended on it. After all, I earned the right to hold onto them, didn't I?

As I went to the Holy Spirit in prayer, I quickly stopped projecting my anger onto inanimate objects and recognized I should not project anger or hate onto my husband or anyone else. I had become someone I worked hard all my life not to be—an angry, bitter person.

The battle for my very soul and existence raged over me, and with each skirmish, Jesus and I won.

The Ultimate Evil Visitations

The deceiver of all deceivers never tired of tactics to thwart me from my pilgrimage toward freedom. Not content with those bouts of harassment—the suicidal thoughts and the knife episodes—which bore no lasting effect on me, he chose other means to intensify the hate and anger in my heart toward the man who killed my dad. As I grew in touch with my true feelings, these destructive emotions consumed me. How I hated the killer! I could not even say his name. He took my daddy. He ruined my mother's life, my sister's, and my life. He was the thief that came to kill and destroy without any remorse. His sin against my family left us void of a father's love forever. My anger and hatred appeared highly justified in my own eyes, and I was not ready to relinquish them. After all, he did get the death penalty, didn't he? How could I forgive someone so evil, who is dead, and most likely in hell?

One Sunday morning, out of nowhere, while I pressed into worship, an actual 3D holographic image of the killer's head appeared right in front of me, a little left of the center of my vision. The November 28, 1955, Life Magazine article, found in the box, contained photos of the killer, which allowed me to identify the entity.

"I got you now," it said to me, with piercing black eyes and a mouth stretched out in a wicked evil sneer.

Trying to ignore it, I focused on singing to the Lord with all my heart, mind, and soul. It would not go away. It repeated, with a voice full of evil,

"I got you now."

I finally stared directly at it and declared,

"Oh, *NO* you don't. I belong to Jesus."

As I continued to worship with my eyes firmly fixed on Jesus, it eventually left.

Over the next six months, the same entity appeared several times. Each time I would respond the same, and each time it would disappear just as it came. I refused to allow it to swallow and intimidate me. Eventually, the enemy of my soul gave up the harassment, and the 3D hologram visitations ceased. Sadly, despite these sci-fi-like, ominous visitations, I still had not been ready to do the thing I most needed to do—relinquish the consuming anger and hatred toward that killer.

> *Therefore, submit yourselves to God. Resist the devil,*
> *and he will flee from you.*
> *Draw near to God, and He will draw near to you."*
> —James 4:7 (MEV)

In His grace and mercy, God placed me under His wings and fought the spiritual battles on my behalf. His loving hand guided my healing journey. He made sure I knew He had never left and would never leave me. I belonged to Him, not that evil, demonic spirit. My anger and hate did not shock the All-Knowing One. Instead, He patiently waited for me to arrive at a point in which I could and would relinquish all my deep-seated emotions. Instead of shaming and condemning me for harboring such hatred, He relentlessly showered me with His kindness and blessings in the battle.

Scene 23

Kindness of the Lord

"Do you despise the riches of His goodness, tolerance, and patience, not realizing that goodness of God leads you to repentance?"

——Romans 2:4 (MEV)

Kindness Amidst the Battles

Our battlegrounds exist within various spheres—spiritual, physical, emotional, and life circumstances. Some battles we create ourselves; others come in like a flood from outside forces. Like an all-out war on every front, my life at this juncture resembled Christian's journey to the Celestial City in John Bunyan's *Pilgrim's Progress*. Christian's quest to reach the Celestial City met with various kinds of resistance, detours, and battles. I learned to persevere through each plan to thwart my Road to Freedom. An individual living in the freedom that God can only give becomes a target for the enemy who loves to keep us under his bondages.

In C.S. Lewis' *Screwtape Letters, Scene VIII*, Screwtape, a devil, mentors a younger devil named Wormwood. Their aim is devoted to thwarting the lives of Christians. Among many valuable lessons,

Screwtape teaches Wormwood the stark difference between how God and how the dark world views humans:, "We want cattle who can finally become food, He [God] wants servants who can finally become sons."

Once I opted for complete liberation, a tug of war, with me in the middle, between light and darkness plagued my soul. The closer I came to the Father, the more intense the enemy raged against me, so that I might become devoured by him. I felt like one of those rubber, stretch toy figures—pulled and stretched in both directions. The worst inside me surfaced, often making me not want to be around myself.

Venturing outside of denial can be treacherous if one is not ready to examine the ugly truth which may reside within. Our society, especially within the church walls, encourages the masking of reality, taking on the imposter role, and removes accountability from us. Deceiving ourselves, we become proficient stuffers and hiders to survive in this world. We live on the defense, not walking in who we are in Christ. The greatest danger in the slippery slide away from the grace of God is the ultimate denial of Jesus, which the enemy wants. We then become the cow that Screwtape and Wormwood eat.

Consider an iceberg; the human eye can only see what is above the ocean, an estimated ten percent, while the rest of the berg remains under the surface. As the tip melts or chips off, more of the underwater glacier floats to the top. Like the iceberg, most of our junk stays submerged and buried. I believe God shields us from what lies underneath because He knows if He allowed us to see everything wretched within us, we could not handle it. My healing process followed the iceberg analogy as the Holy Spirit only exposed certain areas in my life in stages. Once the realization of suppressed emotions surfaced, apart from the prevailing mercy of the Father, I could not have survived. Coming out of denial suddenly can shock and rock one's psychological being so hard that you want to bury the pain even more.

God's kindness keeps our well-being in the forefront, just as He placed me first behind Him on His White Horse. His goodness and mercy soften hard hearts and draw us to Himself. While the darkness attempted to accuse and shame me at every turn and tossed me about in the spiritual tug of war, the Lord showered me with His patience and forbearance despite my damaged emotions. Only He knew what lurked within my soul, yet He drew me out with His loving kindness. He did not see all my debris; He saw only His daughter.

His Presence Brings Healing

When everything crashed, and before my Father encounter, my conversations with God were rather one-sided. Straining to hear and too distressed to listen, I stayed focused on how miserable and lost I was. I did most of the talking. Of course, He knew this, but that did not stop Him.

Afterward, conversations with God turned a new corner. I quit the complaining (more or less) and the fog lifted. I could hear from Him more clearly, and my journaling became two-way conversations filled with intimacy. In His kindness, as I drew nearer to God, He drew nearer to me. Even though I had walked with Him for over two decades, that heavenly excursion transformed my thinking and perception of myself and God the Father. I knew without a doubt that He was my Real Father, the one I had been seeking. Yes, the desire to know my real dad as a person remained but meeting him in heaven settled the matter; I learned my earthly father always loved me. I saw him, touched him, and heard him. My spirit calmed, and hope abounded; one day, we would be reunited.

My Real Father wooed and anchored me tightly to Himself. I could now receive His love, accept His fathering, and relish His presence—for who He was—not for what He could give me. Fears of approaching Him or what He might say vanished. My struggle with double-mindedness ceased, and my orphan spirit no longer questioned hearing His voice. He was my Real Father and me, a princess in His Kingdom.

From my observation, God makes it easy to enter His presence. Through Jesus, His son, we have full access to the throne room and can approach the Father boldly. Moreover, He longs for an intimate relationship with us—a deep friendship—with two-way conversations. However, because He is a gentleman, the Holy Spirit will not force us to come to Him; instead, He patiently waits. The problem originates from our end. Our broken religious spirits make it difficult for us to draw near to Him. Like so many do, I had lived under faulty religious thinking:

- If only I were perfect, then God would hear me.
- If only I prayed harder, He would answer me.
- If only I knew the Bible like the pastor, then God would surely bless me.
- If only I were worthy enough, God would help me.
- If only _____. If only _____. If only _____.

Many don't even believe that we can ever enjoy His presence on this side of heaven. His very name, Emmanuel means "God with us." It is not, "God with us in the way up yonder," or, "God with us if we pray hard enough." It is "God with us" in the now, the present and future. The hymn *In the Garden*, which my earthly dad sang, encapsulates this truth:

He walks with me, and He talks with me, and He tells me I am His Own.

When Jesus took our sins on the cross, died, was buried, and rose again, He opened the door for everyone to have intimacy with God as once was available in the Garden of Eden. As Adam and Eve had walked and talked with God in the garden before the fall, so can all who call upon the Name of Jesus today. He stands at the door, inviting us to fellowship and dine with Him.

After I had been taken into heaven, my special quiet times with my Real Father took on a fresher outlook. With coffee, pen, notebook, Bible, and worship music, I delighted in spending hours with Him early in the morning when the children slept and my husband could watch them. I heard God's voice clearer than before. My heart, once laden with grief, began to flourish. My journal entries from the time of the heavenly encounter portrayed this newfound friendship with the Father. During my journey to complete healing and freedom, words from the Lord like the ones below sustained me. His reassuring words of love would prove to guide me through the intricate paths which laid ahead.

One day in the spring of 1997, as I journaled my prayers to Him with seemingly endless battles circling me, He responded gently with these life-giving words:

I have known you from birth, from before you were conceived. I have known you. I have guided and shielded you all your days. You have cried out to Me many times, have I not heard you? Have I not answered? I won't stop now. I will guide you. I will comfort you. I will lead you. I will pick you up as a father embraces his daughter. I will do these things and more. Turn to Me. Turn to Me fully. Lay aside your fears. Lay aside your past. Release all to me. I am making you new. I am bringing forth the child that I created, fashioned, and intended you to be. Come to Me. Run to Me. Let Me pour Myself into you, as a loving father wraps his arms around his child and imparts himself into her being. So, shall I be with you.

Throughout the following months, He continually spoke many such personal, encouraging, and directional words to my heart. One day, in response to my plea for relief, His loving and merciful words pierced my heart and soul, bringing me hope and encouragement. He said,

Bask in My presence. I will seal upon your heart all I accomplished in the past ministry time and all that will take place. I will envelop you. In time, I will grant you more and more wisdom, understanding, anointing, and insight.

Rest now, my dear. ENJOY MY PRESENCE. I am here. I am walking with you. I am with you. Lift your eyes and see My glory! Feel My presence. Hear My voice. Obey My Voice. Follow My voice. I have so much to teach you, my daughter. There are years to be redeemed. Bask—Bathe in My presence—Draw forever near to me, and I will draw near to you. I will give you a new song. A new song will be written on your forehead—a new understanding. A new revelation of Me and My love.

Often, God would merely remind me of His love and acceptance with words such as:

I have always loved you, my child.
You are mine and no other.
You belong to Me; I shall never leave you. Come, My child.
and walk with Me.

Other times, the Lord repeatedly reassured me with words of hope for the future:

Behold, I am doing a new thing—now it springs forth!
Winter has passed; but look—spring is coming.
Like a plant in the desert, which forces its way through the hard soil, life bursts forth.

My love encounters with the Lover of my soul carried me through all the wickedness and evil that battled internally and externally for my soul. God was not standing over me to shame me for being broken and for not being "strong in the faith." Instead, He stayed with me, steadfastly reviving me, building my faith, and most importantly, planting my identity firmly in Him. Throughout this season, He devotedly sang from D.J. Butler's song, *I Will Change Your Name,* to my spirit,

> *I will change your name. Your new name shall be confidence, joyfulness, overcoming one.*

He doesn't see as we see and looks past what we see. He doesn't see our junk. He did not see mine. What a mystery and marvel——how could the King of Kings, the Lord of Lords, who sits on the throne accept us in our frailty and humanness?

Interwoven with the surfacing pain and battles, God's kindness drew me closer to Him which strengthened my fragile spirit. Reinforced in His love, He could take me places I had not traveled before on my Road to Freedom. Since He never revealed the next stops on my healing odyssey, I held onto His hands tightly with each bend in the River. These stops would lead me closer to the finish line but would require much fortitude to face even fiercer battles through the canyons carved by the ripples of trauma.

Scene 24

Ripples of Trauma

"Something is traumatic if it causes terror and helplessness that overwhelms usual defenses."

—— Dr. Lee Norton, Center for Trauma Therapy

Trauma Knows No Bounds

Most of us in our lives at one time or another have thrown rocks into a pond or lake. Where the rock lands, small rings of water expand out from the center, creating ever-increasing ripples of water. Stones may also be skipped across the water. Searching along the shore for the flattest and smoothest stone becomes a game. With one quick flick of your hand, often with slightly bended knees, the rock skims the surface before it plops into the water. Skill at flicking determines how far the pebble hops across the water. No matter if it's a rock or a thin piece of slate, the same effect happens. Once it stops skipping and lands in the water, rings of concentric circles create a beautiful picture to behold. It's a peaceful pastime with you and nature. The blue sky meets with the green trees and grass surrounding the pond.

All else fades away from your mind. Rejuvenation occurs, and you return to the real world refreshed.

When it comes to trauma, though, its ripple effects do not bring life. Instead, the traumatic event sends shockwaves throughout your entire being and influences those around you, including strangers through vicarious trauma. For example, in the Oklahoma City bombing, April 19, 1995, 176 persons were killed by two men with vengeance on their minds. Not only did the immediate families of the victims become traumatized, but with the one degree of separation principle, over 3,000 persons received what is called tertiary trauma.[1] This figure omits the calculation of the additional traumatization of the entire nation with the national news coverage, much like the national media attention which spread the horrors concerning my dad's bombing and shocked all Americans at that time.

On the night of November 1, 1955, the first witnesses to come onto the fields after Flight #629 crashed were mere teenagers. In an interview with a news source, in Denver, Colorado, October 13, 2005, Conrad Hopp recalled what happened that night and what he and his then girlfriend (now his wife) stumbled upon. Fifty years later, the images of seeing a body still strapped in an airline seat still haunted him. He openly shared with the reporter, "It was tough, you never forget it. Every time I fly, I think about it."[2]

My Uncle Hop, L.G. Hobgood, had experienced severe PTSD (once called shell shock) when he returned home from WWII. He served in the Pacific arena and had witnessed his friends lose their lives at Iwo Jima. For years, my aunt had to wake him up from nightmares. Merely ten years later, he again witnessed extreme atrocity when he and my Uncle Chap had to identify my dad's body because my mother, pregnant with me, was prohibited from her OBGYN. In an interview with one of my cousins, I learned that he, like Conrad Hopp, was very traumatized after viewing his brother. My cousin said, "Marian, are you aware, that your daddy was not buried a whole person? Daddy reported that he could barely identify Uncle Perry (Hobby's nickname). After that, he experienced nightmares and never got over it."

Trauma is trauma is trauma. We cannot escape when it strikes.

With the increase in shootings and bombings in our nation, the study of trauma and how we treat the traumatized has become critical. According to Dr. Lee Norton, a trauma expert, an incident in which three or more persons are killed classifies as a mass killing in the USA. These happen every eleven days, she reported in an interview with Don Miller's Storybrand.com podcast, episode 102.[3] While trauma experts like herself work with the court system and the families of victims of mass killings (as exemplified in the October 1, 2017, Las Vegas shooting), discussion among the experts also center on prevention. The shootings in Dayton, Ohio and El Paso, Texas in 2019 have brought everyone's attention to what can we do better as a nation and society to stop and prevent any more senseless, hate-filled acts of violence. The issue is complex, with no simple solution.

The ripples of trauma go beyond the circles of people influenced by the traumatic event. The entire traumatized person, from head to toe, undergoes physiological changes beyond their control. Depending upon the level of trauma, the ability of the individual to process, and having a safe place to run to, the brain's chemistry changes. In severe instances, individuals without the ability to resolve their traumatic events might exhibit various disorders and conditions such as bipolar depression, borderline personality, ADD/ADHD, obsessive-compulsive disorder, phobias, and even fibromyalgia and migraines.[4]

Since the Vietnam War, professionals pioneered the study of trauma and post-traumatic stress disorder (PTSD). The number of experts in trauma, including childhood trauma, grew in numbers alongside the increasing volumes of research. More is known today about PTSD, and more help is available than previously. Government studies record 15% of Vietnam War veterans have been diagnosed with PTSD, but up to 30% of all Vietnam War veterans exhibit some degree of PTSD in their lifetime. An estimated 12% returning from the Gulf War and 11-20% from the Operations Iraqi Freedom and Enduring Freedom operations (Iraqi and Afghanistan) have been diagnosed with PTSD.[5] Even though the number of trauma specialists have increased, many more are needed to reach those suffering from PTSD who are not vets as well as to adequately serve veterans with PTSD.

Although we know more today than sixty years ago about PTSD, we have so much more to learn. The number of our returning military diagnosed with PTSD has helped push PTSD to national attention. After some unfortunate mass shootings by returned military personnel with mental disorders, the government and professionals have been compelled to further research and to develop more treatment methods. Furthermore, early diagnosis and treatment for PTSD have become paramount for the individual, his family, relationships, and the community. The development of new treatment methods continues to evolve, giving hope where there was no hope for those afflicted by trauma and its extreme form PTSD.

Because of these returning veterans, awareness of trauma throughout our society has grown with positive effects. These trauma specialists, including counselors, psychologists, and psychiatrists, fill an important role in providing a much-needed service. More specialists lend services to traumatized children, to adoption agencies in training parents in childhood trauma, to persons who have faced abuse, to families and victims of traumatic events of any nature, and to those traumatized by any cause. Recognizing the importance of treating traumatized individuals marks a major step towards healing families and communities.

Forging ahead, neuroscience and behavioral health professionals have been unlocking more discoveries about the body, the brain, the mind and memories when traumatic events interrupt life. Awareness of the severity of the impact of tragedy and trauma on infants, children, and women (through sexual and physical abuse) brings new perspectives into our society. For instance, judges, professionals in the court system, and those who work with troubled teens are becoming aware that childhood trauma (developmental trauma) or other traumatic events may be the foundational source of much anti-social and violent behavior.[6] Knowing this, fresh approaches to assisting these young adults might be on the horizon.

Whenever anyone experiences tragedy and trauma, any resulting behaviors effect not only that person, but those around that individual—family, friends, co-workers, and strangers. The ripple effect expands beyond the traumatized individuals into the very hearts, minds, and souls touched by PTSD's destructive nature, when left unresolved.

The trauma my mother underwent spilled into me. My unresolved trauma avalanched over time, influencing for the worse those who loved me, resulting in broken or strained relationships and painful situations.

Safety—Key to Healing from Trauma

Among many studies on trauma, a common denominator, which is recognized by professionals for a healing environment, is safety. The traumatized person needs to feel not only safe but must be in a safe place for healing to begin. Many remain in abusive situations. Their unsafe environments won't allow time for any healing from their tragic and traumatic events. Unable to heal, they either fight, flee or freeze, and hide their fears, pain, and sorrow until a safe person or safe place gives them space and time to heal.

The "Me Too" movement in 2018 gave women who had been sexually abused by others in their lives, including adult relationships, a sense of safety to come out after decades of silence. This national focus served to give a voice to many women who felt too ashamed to bring their abuse to the light earlier. Protection in numbers, as well as positive reception by the general public, created a safe and secure environment for many of these women to begin to heal from their traumatic physical or sexual assaults.

The lack of safety explains my reactions to the healing process. I had quit feeling safe when too many people knew my life situation, when a leader told me I was "too damaged" to pray for others, and when those I trusted with my deep, dark secrets broke that confidence. In contrast, the new place of worship gave me a sense of safety and became my oasis for healing and eventual full release into ministry.

In my mother's case, leaving the house full of memories with my dad and moving to Virginia to be with her dad became that safe place for her to pull back, regroup, and heal. Together, my mom and grandfather gave each other much-needed family support to process through their grief and losses. Nancy would no longer be separated from our mother as she had regularly been after our dad's death. And me? I was just a baby—nurtured by a grieving mother who struggled to survive her personal, tragic trauma.

Scene 25

Repercussions of Sin

Sin is too stupid to see beyond itself.

—Alfred Lord Tennyson

All of life's problems begin with one word: Sin.

Oops, did I mention that three-letter word? What do I mean by sin? Sin means both missing the mark by falling short of perfection and any immoral act, attitude, wrongdoing or nature that goes against divine law.[1] In other words, sin includes "everything that fails to meet God's perfect standards—in our language, our attitudes, our emotions, our actions, and our thoughts."[2] Sin is like yeast: it only takes a little to leaven the whole batch. Simply, sin keeps us from living in freedom that God intended and chains us to bondages that hold us back in reaching our potential, purpose, and destiny.

For some, when they think of sin, they picture the Ten Commandments found in Exodus 20. For others, it can be any vice which doesn't match their moral code of conduct such as smoking, not wearing a veil or hat in public, drinking, not reading the Bible every day, and even playing cards and dancing. Still, many view sin as only evil acts such as murder, rape, and stealing, while lying, envy, and adultery classify as sheer human nature. Our society has conveniently removed the word "sin" from our vocabulary, preaching, and conversations. In the era of relativism, in which no absolute truth exists, many who do not know God or His Word believe these sins are freedoms, rather than bondages, and do not see the need to be set free from anything that counter God's wisdom and His ways.

No matter how sin is defined, no one likes to discuss it. Instead, we love to sweep our sins—the bad things we have done, thought, or said—under the carpet until we get tired of tripping over them. We don't even like to admit when we're wrong. And, forget about confessing sin and seeking forgiveness when we have erred and hurt someone. Following in the steps of Adam and Eve in Genesis, human nature prefers to blame others, mask sin, make excuses, and ignore its wrongdoings. When have any of us been in a group and the facilitator gave the following ice breaker for everyone to answer: "Name your favorite sin?"

Why is sin the root of all problems in the world? Not trusting God. Disobedience broke everyone's relationship with God from the very beginning of the world. Adam and Eve chose not to trust God and did not heed His warning not to eat of the Tree of Knowledge of Good and Evil. Instead, they trusted the word of the serpent and trusted their own judgment when they took of the tree and ate. As a result, pain entered the world, and all creation has suffered since. Humanity traded living in eternal harmony with God the Father and Creator for living forever separated from Him. A legal transaction occurred——humankind's allegiance transferred from God, the Kingdom of Light to Satan, the Kingdom of Darkness. Death entered the world, just as God had told Adam.

How did this happen? Adam chose to believe Satan's words over God's warning to stay away from eating the fruit from the tree of the Knowledge of Good and Evil. To eat it would bring death to Adam and Eve. God knew they had to be banished from the garden, or else they would be always living eternally in their broken state. Leaving a place of eternal life with the Creator, mankind would now experience death.

Through Adam's offspring, all men and women came under the rulership of darkness. From the garden down through the ages, evil and sin has existed in the heart of man. Throughout history, humanity has committed myriad atrocities with worldwide consequences and most within family and relational contexts, which feed into the greater mass evils, leading to the downfall of societies. The immoral breakdown within the Roman Empire led to its collapse. Good news—God provided a way out, which we will discuss later.

Whether your worldview allows for the concept of sin or not, when traveling through the currents of healing from grievous wounds, or walking through emotional impasses, the road through the damaging effects of trauma to the other side and into freedom must examine three underlying influences of sin and wrongdoing in your life. To confront only those who have harmed you will bring a mere two-thirds of the freedom you are meant to receive. You will be set free, but with a limp.

The hardest segment on my path to freedom and healing had been the acknowledgment of my responsibility for my failings, the empty wells I had built, and other sinful reactions to the sin committed against my father and family. Ever since I invited the Holy Spirit to be my Counselor and Guide, He brought me to the point of my being willing to address three areas which wrought havoc within me:

1) Sins committed against me, including my stepfather, the killer, and others;

2) My sinful, dysfunctional, reactions to the wrongs committed against me; and,

3) My sins and wrongdoings——secret and public.

Anyone seeking total freedom from the struggles within, must sooner or later face these same inroads of bondage. All three types of sin can only be dealt with at the cross of Jesus through acts of repentance—turning away from them and changing the course of thinking—and receiving His forgiveness. All three types of sin bring destruction to varying degrees, including secret sins, which no else knows except for the individual and God. Imperfect, adverse responses may be subtle, but often leave a trail of fallen dominoes with lasting impressions, infecting everyone in your sphere.

A person who comes home from a bad day at work may kick the dog, which gets the children upset, and then the wife then yells at the husband for kicking the dog. During the entire evening, tension mounts. Over time, the children grow to fear dad coming home, and the husband and wife quit any meaningful communication. The husband sweeps his anger toward his boss under the rug and ignores it until his wife is packing and walking out with the children. The husband can't figure out why. The husband's real root issue is with his dad whom he could never please, like a boss he can never satisfy.

Sin, when left untouched like trauma, brings destructive repercussions in all the lives it touches.

On November 1, 1955, the ramifications of the man's atrocious act of placing that bomb on the plane possessed far more reaching significance than just killing the 44 passengers. His selfish, wicked act destroyed the families of the victims, detoured their lives forever, and left an indelible imprint upon them. Friends, acquaintances, and co-workers of those who died experienced secondary trauma. The hundreds of rescue workers, including the farmers who arrived first, suffered their unique trauma, which would have had long-lasting consequences on their families. From the explosion through the trial, the entire community in the Denver area shared in the tragedy. Lastly, since the plane bombing had been the first ever in the United States, the whole nation reeled at the disaster through tertiary trauma. Do you see how the ripple effect kept extending?

Since the other 43 families of the victims have their own stories of recovery and rebuilding to be told, I can only speak for myself. This one sin committed against my family burrowed its poisonous tentacles into my entire being. When faced with the ugly truth of how this one act stole my dad and wholly changed my life, I grew to hate sin fervently. No matter how small or large in the eyes of man, sin, when not dealt with, gradually destroys everything in its path as a thunderous tornado roars through a town.

Facing the Ugly Truth Head-On

In my case, because the accused killer was found guilty and given the death penalty, I grew up not even thinking my dad's death had any influence in my life. Did I miss knowing him? Yes, but I kept that secret. My stepdad would hear none of it. Did I get a lump in my throat and want to hide when I had to tell anyone his story? Yes. Did I remain quiet in high school when we discussed capital punishment in a history class? Yes. No one knew our family's history, and I did not want to cry in front of my peers. I, the Great Stuffer, was not even aware of any repressed feelings or emotions which are not sinful in and of themselves. It is what we do with them—our reactions—that determines whether they trigger sinful, knee-jerk behavior, or not.

Through pastoral, prayer, and trauma counseling training, I had learned that children cope with tragic events and evil acts committed against them differently than adults. Having no voice, not knowing what to do, or fear of telling anyone, children can shut off the trauma, stuff it, and pretend it never happened. Many grow up thinking they caused their parents' divorce, their physical abuse, or sexual abuse. They carry the burden of guilt they were never meant to bear.

Children can also use other defense mechanisms for self-protection, such as daydreaming in school, disassociation (ex: it didn't happen to me; it was someone else), or even the development of multiple personalities. Others choose self-injury, such as cutting, or wild living with drugs, sex, and alcohol. In the Information–High Tech Age, addictions to gaming, texting,

Instagramming, or other online social media cloak their pain. Anger outbursts, troublemaking, daredevil seeking, even gang involvement substitute for the pent-up emotions of a traumatic childhood. Subconsciously, they project their anger and hurt onto others or themselves—anything to silence their wounds and pain.

Living as children in an adult world, these work well (minus the self-injury and permissive, addictive or violent lifestyles) to protect and defend themselves. An instinct for survival drives the need to be safe and protected. But as children grow up and become adults, these defense mechanisms no longer work and finally catch up with them in a variety of ways by the time they reach full adult age. These self-preservation tactics in the meantime build layers of patterns of reactions to people and situations that can bring harm not only to the individual but to those around them.

When my ability to cope with life caved, and God brought me out of denial, it was no wonder my emotions had been so painfully overpowering. My coping mechanisms, developed over a lifetime, no longer worked. Not counting the compilation of my mother's grief, the depth of my mourning represented over 40 years of repressed emotions; all bottled up and corked. When my self-protective behaviors crumbled, the darkness of my depression, the strength of my anger, and the intensity of hatred, mixed with a lifetime of suppressed bitterness, came bubbling up into massive explosions.

I had come to the place in which it was time to stop hiding. According to the founders of the Fatherless Daughter Project, to survive trauma encompasses reaching "past simply learning how to exist and hide from what is overwhelming to look at; it means finding the time and space to touch, hear, and feel the emotions that need their own validating and healing."[3] I veritably had become aware of my feelings and emotions and stuck in that stagnant place, a shut-down mode, and God was telling me it was time to stop "repeating those dysfunctional old coping skills that no longer work."[4]

During the weeks of ceaseless weeping, I could not comprehend what was happening. Unaware of the five stages of grief at the time, I pushed through all my emotions to reach the hem of Jesus. But it was in the weeping when the Lover of my soul could begin ministering to me in my most vulnerable places. With each touch by Him, my guard slowly dropped. In time, as He anchored me in the safety of His Father's love, He incrementally revealed why I couldn't cope with death, loss, or life anymore.

Gradually, I had to face the horrible consequences of the killer's actions head-on. The ripples of his sin traveled far into my heart, piling sin upon sin. God did not let me off the hook either. He heard my plea for no more bandages; in His love, He took me at my word, no matter how daunting the journey. I can hear Him say,

"It's time, Marian, to quit tripping over the carpet. Let's take a look, together."

Scene 26

Well-Diggers Anonymous

For My people have committed two evils (sins).
They have forsaken Me, the fountain of living waters,
and hewed out for themselves cisterns, broken cisterns
that can hold no water.

—Jeremiah 2:13 (MEV)

Lifting the Carpet

When the carpet lifted, what did Jesus and I find? A field full of dry, broken, empty wells.

From childhood to adulthood, I unintentionally dug many deep dark empty wells. To mask pain and shame—which I did not know I possessed, I ignorantly continued to drill one well after another. Some were shallower than others; some were more in-depth and well-established broken wells. These wells could not hold any living water nor give me any life. I ignorantly kept drinking from my broken cisterns instead of seeking the water Jesus promised that would become a well of water springing up into eternal life (John 4:14). My empty wells became my source of comfort, fashioned my identity, clouded my real personality, and kept me from being whom God created.

These patterns of behavior stymied my development and interfered with knowing my purpose and call, which limited the achievement of my optimum potential. Although I was seeking the Source of Living Water, my self-dug cisterns blocked my ability to receive the full benefit of the grace and love of God. I had become a Christian who ran on fumes, on one cylinder, by her own strength, instead of running on all eight-plus as God intended. Ignorance and denial kept me from recognizing their existence and devastating force.

As the Father's love penetrated my heart, the Holy Spirit lovingly and gently began to disclose these false alternative sources for love and acceptance I had adopted over the years.

What do I mean by empty wells? Each empty well represents doing life separate from God and seeking protection, provision, and purpose apart from Him. Cisterns in Jeremiah's time were dug by man, by the sweat of man's hands; they were shallow, would crack and could not hold water for very long. Since water would dry up, man would build more cisterns. The people had forgotten that God was their source for everything and decided to rely on themselves.

On the other hand, God's spring of living waters never runs dry; God provides it, and no sweat labor is required to be fully satisfied by Him. In the desert, when the Israelites complained there was no water, Moses asked God for wisdom. In turn, God instructed Moses to strike a rock and water flowed from it, which demonstrated God's provision for the Israelites (Exodus 17:1-7). The fountain, mentioned in Jeremiah 2:13, is an analogy of this rock, illustrating that God alone is our Source for life.

Instead of fully trusting Him, I hid behind various labels, vows, and judgments to cope in life. I knew Him as my Savior but could not fully grasp He was my sole Source for all I needed. My coping mechanisms served me well as a child, protecting me from an uncertain and fatherless world, but once I became an adult, they no longer worked.

My Field of Empty Wells

No one sets out to see how many empty, broken wells they can dig in one day or even one's lifetime. They naturally develop in response to people and circumstances. Subconsciously, I had built many wells as reactions to the one evil action which had taken away my earthly father. From those, empty wells within those broken wells sprung up. They not only hindered my thinking and responses to life but affected other relationships, including the one with my future husband.

Abandonment and Rejection integrated with me while in my mother's womb at the point of my father's tragic death. These were the top henchmen who collectively worked to bring about the destruction that hindered my potential, especially in interpersonal relationships. All the other various empty wells I had dug stemmed from abandonment and rejection.

Fear of Being Abandoned and **Fear of Being Rejected** distorted my view of God, men, and others. Subtly, my behavior expressed these fears. With these behaviors, many sub-empty wells appeared in my field of wells. I possessed a driving need to belong, feared being left behind, and lacked self-confidence with its low self-esteem attributes.

Those fears fueled **Insecurity**, and my image of God took on a warped view of His character. I saw Him as a faraway God, one who was distant and kept me at arm's length. My biological dad resided in another far-off dimension, so did God. He was one to serve, but not one who desired to be intimate with me. He lived way up in the sky somewhere. Unreachable. Untouchable. Not personal. I could not imagine Him speaking directly to me or fathom His extension of grace and love. I was determined to serve Him regardless of whether heaven existed or not. At that time, At one time, I even believed that those who gave their lives to Christ only to get into heaven and escape the reality of hell, had become born again Christians for the wrong reasons. I viewed entering heaven a fringe benefit of becoming a believer, not so much the right motivation to follow Jesus. After all, Jesus

Christ, the King of Kings and Lord of Lords, deserved whole-hearted, devoted followers.

In order not to be rejected by God, I dug an empty well of **Performance Orientation.** My stepdad's perfectionism drove my **Perfectionism and Fear of Failure,** which developed **Man-pleasing** behaviors. I worked hard to remain in the good graces of my stepdad and God. I wanted desperately for my real dad, my stepdad, and God to be proud of me in hopes that I would be entirely accepted by all three of them. While being a high achiever, I walked through many decades burdened with an **Inferiority Complex**, believing others were always better, stronger, smarter, and prettier than me.

During the hippie movement days of the 1960s and 70s, when most teens rebelled, I adopted the **Good Girl** façade versus being the **Bad Girl**. The **Good Girl** mask produced positive outcomes, and I wore it into my adult life. Unlike many during the 1970s, I chose not to rebel, not to live a promiscuous lifestyle, and not to do drugs, cigarettes, or alcohol. I did not want to hand control over my life to anything. Consequently, I was providentially kept out of trouble by God's grace (His divine power). Failure was not an option, and while the need to have all straight As in school was not a driving force, doing my best to excel had dominated my choices and decisions. Consequently, I worked hard throughout high school, was labeled a book worm, and it paid off—I graduated tenth in my class of three hundred. To be clear, doing one's best was not the empty well, but my motivation—**Fear of Being Rejected** and underlying **Perfectionism**—made being a **Good Girl** a stronghold. I dug a substantial well which leaked.

The façade of the **Good Girl** followed me into the workplace. Adopting the identity as a high achiever, I worked diligently and gave 110% in every position, often without additional compensation. However, when I needed some guidance from a boss or co-worker, I could not handle the criticism when its delivery resembled my stepdad's berating tone with put downs. I had one boss who thought it was cute to call me stupid by using the K.I.S.S. statement, "Keep it simple stupid" in a derogative manner.

Whenever this happened, my perceived inability to ever please an authority figure, no matter how hard I worked, would be reinforced. I would swallow what was said, then leave, hide, and cry. I simply could not ever measure up to any boss, nor ever be good enough.

Out of these, I developed a **Distorted Image of God.** To me, God was up in heaven waiting to smack me for missing the mark just once. I would see this large arm swing down from the clouds with a God-size baseball bat to whack me whenever I got into any trouble. I avoided conflict and rocking the boat at all costs. This warped image of God would appear in my mind frequently throughout my childhood. Unfortunately, because my stepdad ruled as a "rage-alcoholic," this image of God as an angry father carried over into my adulthood. Shame, guilt, and fear of men/authority figures thrived under this lens.

To further understanding, I include this mild example. As of today, I do not like gardening, which by the way is not a sin. Why? Our stepdad turned two-and-a-half acres of land into an estate full of all kinds of gardens. He forced my sister and me to weed a minimum of two hours every day in sweltering, humid, bug-infested weather, in gardens full of slugs and deer flies buzzing around our heads. If we missed one weed, he would rant, rave, and make us weed again with his fingers pointing. The hard labor in and of itself was not the end of the world, but nothing we did, no matter how well we did it, could please him. My stepdad wasn't a dad, he was a taskmaster.

Subconsciously, God became the taskmaster God.

To my stepdad's credit, he believed he was training us in discipline and self-control with a good work ethic. But his parenting skills backfired. Therefore, I could not truly understand God as a loving father. I identified with Jesus, but I could not relate to God as a benevolent father. My stepdad rarely gave compliments, and I had to gain his respect, so I believed I had to earn affection from God the Father. I knew the Bible taught God loved me; but it remained head knowledge only, not in my heart.

This warped father image produced more empty cisterns such as:

- I am Un-Loveable.

- I am Unworthy.

- I am Discounted.

- I am not Accepted.

- I do not Belong.

- I am Overlooked.

- I am always Left Out and Left Behind.

These empty wells severely affected my marriage. After three years into the marriage, I could finally receive my husband's love and believed my husband truly loved me. Honestly, I saw myself as unlovable. To have a young man fall in love with me was something I desired and something I knew God wanted for me, but my false, deeply buried mindsets did not allow me to receive the truth: that my husband loved me for being me, with as pure love as he could. I also feared he would die young, just like my real dad. After he reached the age of 31 and had not died, I was so relieved. My fear proved to be nothing and I no longer held that haunting thought. I must add: I never worried my husband would fall into adultery because he and I were both extremely grounded in Jesus Christ. Our faith in Him stood firm. Our marriage was anchored and centered on Him. Still, I needed my husband to constantly prove his love to me.

Fear of the Future hovered over me throughout my years and created additional empty wells, one of which was **Living in the Past**. My dad's premature death made me aware life is short and unsure, and I could only look back, not forward. Secretly, I lived as if I had no promise for the future, although I did hope, dream, and plan. With an uncertain future and an unpredictable home life, without intending to, I chose to escape to the past to wall myself in and to create a safe, imaginary world.

An angry and verbally abusive stepfather created an atmosphere in the home such that we walked gingerly around him, not wanting to rouse the "sleeping giant." I tiptoed softly, afraid of facing another emotional assault to my already fragile and hurting soul. I did not want to do anything to disturb my stepdad. Outwardly, I pretended everything was OK; but, behind our doors, I kept out of his way and always tried to remain in his good graces.

Inwardly, unspoken questions swirled in the background. Oh my, why couldn't he love me? Was it too much to ask or to hope for? Was I that unlovable? Other girls had fathers who loved them. Why didn't I? To dull my pain, one of my coping mechanisms was holding onto what was sure: the fun events in the past.

As a young girl, whenever anything good happened in my life, I would write down every detail and frequently re-read them, smiling and dreaming. I would also regale my friends with my exciting adventures, whether it be a youth group retreat or vacation. Until the next one. My friends humored me and listened for the umpteenth time, at least they acted like they weren't bored.

I lived in the past, not the present.

In another example, my life changed the first summer in 1966 our mother sent us down to South Carolina to meet our cousins, Aunt Sis, and Uncle Hop. For six weeks, we did not hear our stepdad yelling, and there was no weeding. Instead, Uncle Hop and Aunt Sis, having raised eight children, kept a very loose leash on us girls. We were free to be ourselves in a large family who genuinely loved one another and always had room for more people around their long dinner table. We witnessed a healthy family life for the first time. It was not a perfect family (my cousins can testify to that), but they loved one another, stood by one another, and held up one another through adversity and joys.

Back home again, I recited every detail of our time in South Carolina over and over in my mind because I did not want the happy memory to end. I reviewed my scrapbook of photos regularly until we would return the next summer. I recreated history, reenacted it and clung to it. Living in a home without any peace, reliving happy memories became my bottle to which I ran for comfort.

I gradually outgrew this coping mechanism once I married my husband. Unfortunately, I merely swapped recounting good times with replaying all the painful, hard times in our marriage and inadvertently dug more broken cisterns.

Empty Wells within Empty Wells

Because an empty well runs dry and never satisfies, more empty wells quickly fill in the gap. Mostly occurring on the subconscious level, these new sources for life further the expansion of our field of broken wells. We behave in specific ways without even thinking about how our behaviors affect others. These behaviors could be patterns learned from our family. Others could stem from our own created empty wells. Most of the time, we remain ignorant that we are either offensive to others or self-sabotaging ourselves. Oblivious, we assume these traits belong to us and believe "it's just like me to _____ (fill in the blank)" or "I always _____." Other self-destructive mantras can be as innocent as "I am just like my _____ (family member)."

We proceed with our lives, not realizing we can be free from unhealthy responses, reactions, and behaviors and stop our self-sabotage. None of us are exactly alike, and our sources for comfort will be different. In our human nature, everyone tends to drill their own dry, empty wells and respond from them, and nurture them. It's no wonder we have challenging office atmospheres, road rage, disintegrating marriages, and other social ills today.

We all dig our personalized cisterns which cannot hold water.

Jesus Christ alone is the exception: He had no empty wells.

The Power of Our Words

Empty wells generally reveal themselves in our negative self-talk or by the words we speak, in addition to addictive behaviors. Our words have the power of life and death. We bring hope and encouragement to ourselves and others, or we communicate death and destruction. With our mouths, we either bless and build up or destroy and tear down. We innocently create vows, judgments, or self-inflicted curses. Our words, including our self-talk, reflect whether we live optimistically or pessimistically.

When we speak life, our bodies respond in positive ways. A wise old proverb says that a cheerful heart does good like a medicine (Proverbs 17:22). Sebastien Gendry, founder of Laughter Online University (www.laughteronlineuniversity.com), compiled over 350 research papers on the benefits of a happy heart and laughter.[1] Positive thinking, kind thoughts and laughter alleviate stress factors and counter stress's adverse physiological reactions in our cells and body. These studies confirm what God wrote through King Solomon almost 3,000 years ago: that a joyful heart leads to a happy, prosperous soul and body.

Have you ever met senior citizens in their 90s and asked what is their secret to a long life? I worked directly with senior citizens for over six years in the hospice industry and always asked that question to vibrant, happy, and content senior citizens. Whatever their responses, no matter their age, they shared a common thread: their faith in God and their easy-going approach to life.

Our choice becomes: Do we want to see the glass half-full, refillable or half-empty?

According to the Mayo Clinic, positive thinking (an optimistic viewpoint) lends to effective stress management, which results in many health benefits.[2] A person with an optimistic outlook on life speaks positively and views difficult situations as challenges for solutions rather than hopeless problems and trials. Physiologically, the ability to handle stress appropriately hinders the production of cortisol and its destructive domino effect on the body's health.

The counterpart, pessimism, reaps mayhem over time within the cells of our bodies. A person who is regularly angry, bitter, and carrying a chip on his shoulder sends signals to the brain to produce more cortisol to cope with the stress. Elevated cortisol levels correlate to higher fat production and a weakened immune system, which causes more inflammation and chances for any disease to form and thrive.

Living in an era in which society values transparency and authenticity, I thought telling people the truth about how I was feeling when they would ask, "How are things going?" meant being honest and truthful. If they asked how I was, wouldn't they want to know? I took them literally and responded with honesty by sharing my woes of the day. Of course, somedays I would be uplifted, happy, and light-hearted and say the typical, "I'm fine."

On other days, whether I faced depression or trials, I would be honest and tell them whether or not they wanted to know. It took me years to realize people do not want an honest answer when they ask, "How are you?"

Inadvertently, by being transparent when sharing my current trial or struggle, I allowed my words to send death signals to my cells, instead of communicating life to my body. My words, likewise, sent negative signals to the listener. Now, I make every effort to respond, "I'm blessed!" That seems to satisfy their greeting. And, both of us receive a positive uptake to our brains and cellular structures.

In an article by John Hopkins Medical University, a positive outlook on life renders hope which in turn may reduce the inflammatory causes of stress in the body, thus improving health. Likewise, studies have proven that negative emotions hinder the immune system and the body's ability to ward off sickness and disease.[3] An eight-year study from the Harvard T.H. Chan School of Public Health found that optimistic women had a significantly reduced risk of dying from several major causes of death compared with women who were pessimistic leaning and less upbeat. The list included cancer, heart disease, stroke, respiratory disease, and infection.[4] Learning early to manage stress and to view life optimistically may very well improve our well-being and prolong our lives.

The famous quote from Proverbs 23:7 (MEV) comes alive today, especially since findings from scientists and the medical field substantiate its resounding truth:

As he [a man] thinks in his heart, so he is.

When we choose to think or speak negatively, our bodies react negatively. If left unchecked, the resulting stress weakens the immune system and builds harmful inflammation, which may produce disease. We may feel a euphoric release by exploding our anger or hiding in our depression or acting out with negative behavior; but each time we do, we silently signal death to our body, mind, and spirit. At what age this catches up with us is uncertain. Both explosive anger or suppressed anger plays Russian roulette with our future.

The medical field has proven that what and how we think influences not only our psychological well-being but emotional and physical health as well. Empty wells bear rotten fruit. Life-giving patterns and thoughts produce healthy fruit. There's hope—without regard to how long anyone has been stuck in negative ruts and empty wells—everyone can be free. A joyful countenance can replace grumpy, complaining, angry attitudes.

The Law of Sowing and Reaping

> *Be not deceived. God is not mocked. For whatever*
> *a man sows, that he will also reap.*
> *For the one who sows to his own flesh will from the*
> *flesh reap corruption,*
> *but the one who sows to the Spirit will from the*
> *Spirit reap eternal life.*
> —Galatians 6:7-8 (MEV)

The principle of sowing and reaping applies to both the good and the bad, from feelings to reactions, including our words and actions. Since empty wells represent doing life our own way and finding support and comfort apart from God, they sow to the flesh, which then reaps corruption. The flesh represents human nature without any regard for God. Given free will, we all have choices to make—to sow healthy, happy good thoughts or to plant unhealthy, depressing, or negative thoughts. Often, we see the empty wells and bumps in the carpet in others first and judge them; yet, we fail to look at ourselves and realize none of us escapes creating artificial means to get what only God can give.

A Case Study

A man I know very well had chosen, early in his life, a path of rebellion. He took LSD, speed, and anything to have a high. A true-blue hippie with a laissez-faire outlook, he opted for drugs to seek higher spiritual dimensions. His choices led to his dropping out of high school and he enlisted in the US Army during the Vietnam Era.

Once honorably discharged from the Army, he re-enrolled in high school and proudly graduated a couple of years older than the average senior. In his quest for meaning and purpose in life, during and after the high school years, he explored most religions under the sun, including the occult and new age philosophies. To be inclusive in his search, he also studied and read the Holy Bible, along with the satanic bible.

In the height of the Jesus Movement in the 1970s, he surrendered his life to Jesus and all desire for drugs and alcohol left instantly. He became a new creation in Christ, ignited with a passion to follow Jesus who saved him from his life of destruction. He gained a fresh start—a second chance—and freedom from his past. He lost his only friend because he made a decision to give his life to Jesus. He experienced no LSD flashbacks. No withdrawals. No cravings. No desire for alcohol. No jitters. A fresh and clean slate. All ties, with the occult, other religions, and new age, broken. That night, he heard God call him "son" for the first time, something he never remembered his earthly father call him.

Years later, his laid-back approach toward life no longer worked for him. Only doing enough to get by in life, doing minimum requirements, became an underlying, subconscious attitude. While he had an excellent work ethic, was likable, funny, and served the Lord, his subconscious lack of drive crippled him and affected his entire family. He would work hard but rarely achieved higher positions or salaries in work. He often expressed that he felt like he was like a hamster—stuck in a hamster wheel and going nowhere. Then one day, God revealed to him an inner vow he had made at age 13.

By the time he was 13 years old, he had his eyes set on a brand new shiny motorized minibike. He got up early every day for months delivering newspapers for two paper routes to save money for it. When he accumulated enough, he went to his dad. His dad, without any discussion, flat out said,

"No, you cannot buy a motorized minibike, but you can buy a bicycle."

This abrupt minimization by the father, without any chance to present his case, crushed this young man's spirit. He had worked diligently at the two newspaper routes to earn that money. He received excellent tips and had been considered the best paperboy in the area.

Among many consequences to the rejection from his dad, this young man's mind registered a false belief. He subconsciously made several secret vows, such as, "It's not worth working my tail off and doing my best. I'll only do enough to get by in life."

Fifty years later, the Holy Spirit brought this memory to his attention. The grown-up man asked God to forgive him for making those judgments and vows, and the power of those words broke off him. His wife, who happens to be me, rejoiced because the atmosphere in the home changed and he changed. It wasn't long before his employer gave him a merit raise for doing excellent work. He has since been given another raise.

The childhood vows had brought nothing but a life cycle in which the rug would be pulled out from underneath him over and over. He would experience peaks of success, then valleys of minimum existence. Once broken by the power of God, prosperity and success started to find their way into everything he touched.

Also, the revelation of that past incident in his life unveiled the exact moment he turned to drugs and his wild lifestyle. It was that very day he felt discounted by his father. Before, he was not into drugs or alcohol. He was a paperboy, an average American teenager with hopes and dreams. After that one conversation with his dad, most likely the last straw of many prior rejections, he turned to addictive, destructive behaviors.

At the time of my Great Uncorking, we had been married sixteen years. Into our marriage, we both brought our emotional baggage with us. Mine culminated into volcanic explosions which uncovered the buried empty wells constructed of strongholds, vows, and judgments. Throughout the healing process, God, in His kindness, set me free. When He knew I could handle and face the destructive patterns hidden beneath my surface, He would shed more light into the dark places of my soul.

False Beliefs, Vows, and Judgments within Empty Wells

The law of sowing and reaping knows no boundaries and its principles played out through my empty cisterns. Like an avalanche on a mountain, each false belief, vow, or judgment tumbled over me.

My empty wells created an environment of doubt and unbelief, which made it difficult to trust in God. I believed God already had plans and purposes for me, with a hope and a future (Jeremiah 29:11). Did I honestly believe this truth deep in my inner core and that these words applied to me? No. Why?

On a subconscious level, it was just like me to be overlooked, discounted, stampeded over, and forgotten. I couldn't trust God who in my eyes might abandon or reject me because I wasn't perfect enough or who could beat me with a club. Trusting Him for all my needs proved quite a challenge. My faith said, "yes," my heart said, "No."

My distorted view of God and lack of trust in Him influenced my inability to trust my husband to do what was right or even to be the primary provider in the family. Since I couldn't trust God, I could not trust Him with my husband. When my husband had emotionally shut down and refused my input, my trust in man, in this case, my husband, disintegrated. My husband's actions and lack of inertia confirmed my twisted and distorted thinking. These mindsets and beliefs further blocked my ability to fully believe that I was loved and accepted by both God and my husband.

Often called vows or judgments, these false beliefs accumulated over a lifetime. They assimilated so much with who I thought I was, that I did not know they existed. Since they weren't on my radar, I lived unaware of how much they distorted my self-image and the way I approached life, people, and God. These patterns of thought and beliefs stealthily fashioned my being and identity.

The chart on the next page serves as an example of how the ripples of trauma and sin eventually played out in my life. In the first column, I listed my key empty wells. The second column contains some of their consequential vows, beliefs, and judgments. Perhaps you may identify with some; most likely, you will become aware of your own.

Sample Chart of My Empty Wells and Their Ripple Effects

Empty Well	Ripple Effects Empty Wells within Empty Wells— False Beliefs, Vows, or Judgments
Fear of Abandonment	I fear God will abandon me. I fear men will leave me and disappoint me. I fear my husband will die before me. I fear growing old alone.
Fear of Rejection	I don't belong. I am unimportant, overlooked, discounted, walked over, and left out. I doubt God or anyone close to me can ever truly love me. I can only trust myself since I will be rejected.
Perfectionism	I will never please God, man, or myself. I dare not fail or make mistakes. I fear God will reject me if I am not good enough. I avoid punishment at all costs.
Need for Justification and Self-Defense	I need to justify and defend my actions—good or bad. I want to fight or right every wrong that threatens me. I am the rescuer and peacemaker in our family.
Fear of the Future	I worry about all provision—safety, health, food, home, and finances. I fear that neither God nor man will take care of me. I have a hard time believing that God has a plan, a future, and hope for me.

The Way Out

False beliefs, vows, and judgments will vary with each person because we have different personalities, life situations, traumatic events, and losses. Likewise, various models and methods provide healing and liberation from these bondages. Here's what stays constant:

> The Road to Freedom—lasting freedom—
> remains the same.

Any attempts to break free in our human strength will be temporary, only delaying final victory God has waiting for us.

No matter how severe the trauma and pain, Jesus provides the way out of any subsequent, unhealthy thinking and coping mechanisms. In an instant, He can break the driving force behind the lies, vows, and judgments. Once free from reliance on self-made solutions, any person will discover they are viewing themselves and others differently.

Letting go and letting God be at the helm of one's life alters that person's life journey forever.

Walking through this process took longer than I anticipated. A spiritual mentor once said, "You cannot put a 100-ton truth on a bridge that can only hold ten tons." In His infinite wisdom, God knew I was that ten-ton bridge and took His time to uncover each well I had dug.

The Mighty Counselor's timing did not go as fast as my timeline, and neither did I realize how much healing I needed. I certainly had no awareness that God would be working on me and that I had to account for my dysfunctional, sinful actions in response to the sins and wrongs committed against me. I thought He would deal with my husband first!

Remember, we can only deal with the ten percent of the iceberg above sea level until it melts, and a new iceberg tip appears. We are to only respond to what the Holy Spirit shows us, nothing more and nothing less. I mastered introspection during those healing years, not realizing that hyper-critical, self-examination was my attempt to control the process instead of God. For me, looking excessively inward had become another barren well—the more I introspected, the better I felt. After all, didn't I have to prove I was doing all I could do to bring swifter healing?

Once the Holy Spirit showed me the false beliefs, vows, and judgments I made, freedom from the damaging mindsets required me to bring them to Jesus. Pressing through the emotional pain, I renounced each one as it surfaced, chose to turn away from it, and then received the mercy and forgiveness of the Lord for allowing it to control my mind and behavior.

Why would this be a painful process? Because coming out of years of denial shocks the mind and admitting I had harbored sin brought self-condemnation, guilt, and shame. Coming out of denial meant I could no longer protect the Good Girl. In time, I had to say "goodbye" to the persona of the Good Girl and embrace my imperfections and the truth that I did not need to be perfect to gain the Father's love or anyone's love and acceptance.

Only the power of God through the work of Jesus on the cross could break their patterns over my mind. Then, I asked Jesus to replace them with His thoughts toward me, with truths that bring life. I desired only to think as He thinks, to be transformed by the renewing of my mind.

The transformation may not come automatically in some areas, but as a person leans into Jesus and uses their faith "muscle," one by one, their mindset, heart, and thinking will be renewed. God did this for me, and He still does. Reversing a harvest of destruction, I began acquiring wholeness, healing, peace, and freedom. He makes this available to everyone—I am not an exception.

Transformational change through Jesus Christ brings permanent change.

My treacherous walk through the minefields of empty wells disclosed two major emotional strongholds that wrapped their tentacles around my heart. Unknowingly, they consumed my thoughts and strangled me. To imagine that such vile emotions could even reside within me tore at my gut. Despite the inner turmoil, desiring to conquer and relinquish them proved to be difficult, yet Jesus quietly waited for me to hand them over to Him.

Scene 27

The Hook of Anger and Hate

*"Be angry, but do not sin. Do not let the sun
go down on your anger.
Do not give place to the devil."*

—Ephesians 4:26-27 (MEV)

The Brewing Storm

Despite my minor victories, the anger and hate toward the man who took my father brewed. I remember having churnings so tight inside that I could have burst. I felt justified to hate vehemently the man who killed my dad. He destroyed our family and by all reports remained unremorseful clear to his end. He knew what he had done, and in his own eyes, he justified the bombing. As my healing progressed, I became fully aware of how this one evil act affected me directly; my husband and children undeservedly then suffered from my sinful reactions. My cognizance of the ripple effects increased my anger and hatred toward the man who took everything away.

In the process, buried resentment toward my stepdad surfaced, even though he never physically harmed my mother, my sister, or me. This anger and bitterness hooked me ever so clandestinely until God knew I was ready to come to terms with them. I kept sweeping the anger and resentment toward my stepdad under the carpet. I excused his behavior because I had rationalized that he loved me as best he could.

After all, he had introduced me to the nations through folk dancing. I became a French major, an advocate for missions, and always a friend to immigrants, all because of my stepdad's positive influence through international folk dancing. Nevertheless, his overall controlling and rage-alcoholic temperament skewed my image of man and God.

Ambivalently, I waffled between loving and hating him at the same time. I loved him because he was the only dad who raised me but hated his behavior. I resented how he treated my mother, who had showered him with love and took care of him until his final breath. He would verbally put her down at any opportunity. He would yell at a moment's whim. He would not let her visit us even when they moved down from the Cleveland area to Central Ohio to be close to us and the grandchildren. Then, as an additional slap to an already tenuous family situation, he developed Alzheimer's, making my mother's life even more unbearable during his last three years.

Before crossing the finish line of my long healing journey, my stepdad died. Through Alzheimer's, he had lost all control, and I grieved seeing this strong man deteriorate. I spent time around his bedside singing "Jesus Loves Me" as I gave him water with a sponge. In my love-hate relationship with him, love won overall. He had given his life to Jesus, and I had confidence he would be in heaven and, at last, full of peace. However, when we were at his graveside, everything in me wanted to dance on his grave, which I'm glad I did not.

My mother was now free, and so were we. My mother could relax and breathe, and I never saw her more alive, vibrant, and happy in my lifetime.

What's Wrong with Anger and Hate When They're Justified?

For every minute you remain angry, you give up
sixty seconds of peace of mind.
—Ralph Waldo Emerson

Regardless of anyone's faith or culture, most people have a profound understanding of the difference between good and evil, right and wrong. Only those with a seared conscience and hard hearts cannot and will not distinguish what is moral or immoral. Selfishly, these individuals become consumed with their selfish gain, and their hatred blinds any ounce of self-control. Without regard to consequences, they commit crimes, wound others, and leave a trail of devastation like a tornado ripping through a town.

When severely sinned against, it is normal and healthy to have righteous anger toward any immoral act, whether committed against yourself or someone you know. Persons victimized by atrocious actions by perpetrators possess the right to be angry. The violations committed warrant an angry response—whether it be the murder of a loved one, emotional, sexual, or physical abuse, or robbery, to name a few. While this list is not complete, an individual can legitimize anger towards freak accidents, long-term illnesses resulting in the loss of a loved one, or any significant sense of loss and victimization.

In the stages of grief, anger is a natural and healthy response. People grieve over the loss of a spouse—through death, divorce, or abandonment, loss of children, loss of pets, loss of careers, and dreams. No matter the source of loss, grief is grief, because loss is loss. Working through grief requires walking through all these stages, which includes the anger stage, but not staying in them, until arriving at acceptance. Once in acceptance, although the memories will be there, resolution occurs enough to allow the person to move on in their life.

What is unhealthy, which turns righteous anger into a destructive force, is how a person deals with their anger and how long

261

and in which manner they nurture the anger. Not knowing they can become free from the hurt and pain which underlies these damaging emotions, people cling to their anger, allowing it to birth bitterness and resentment. They project their hidden rage toward others, fueling and rationalizing their reactions because of the unjust and immoral acts against them. Others do not know that they have a right to be angry at what happened to them and keep that anger locked up. Conversely, often the person remains unaware of guarding such deep-seated anger as was my situation.

Unfortunately, in most cases of sexual and physical abuse, the perpetrator threatens the victims should they ever tell anyone. This intimidation forces the victims to repress the truth and the emotions, either consciously or subconsciously. Repression of emotions compounds their difficulties later in life until they find themselves in the right environment with a safety net to become free.

When my body finally told me enough was enough, I couldn't contain the pent-up feelings anymore. Our life events catapulted me out of denial, uncorked my emotions, and led me to face the ugliness inside. I had over-compensated by justifying my simmering anger and savoring my right to be angry over my dad's death, my stepdad's anger and verbal abuse, and the killer.

I had crossed the line. My suppressed, hidden anger toward the man who took my father away exploded in all the wrong places and onto the wrong people. During my healing odyssey, I nurtured this anger as it surfaced, which in turn progressed to hate. Rightfully so, I hated the murderer and detested the sin of murder. I loathed the very thought of the killer and could not speak his name. I felt righteous for my reactions, while the evil twins, anger and hate, locked arm and arm with each other in a plot to destroy me.

If left alone to fester, hate and anger become extremely powerful strangleholds over a person's mind and heart. This diabolic duo prevents us from receiving all God has for us, allows bitterness and resentment to rule over us, and deteriorates our health and well-being. We can fool ourselves into believing that we hold righteous anger toward someone who has injured us, but most of our anger, either repressed or expressed, remains unjustified. When left unchecked, anger can turn into seething hate.

Only an encounter with the Living Father can intercept and sever the ties with these two evils.

In the case of my dad's killer, he allowed his hate and anger against his mother, who placed him in an orphanage, to overpower him. His father had left his family at an early age. Fatherless, he sought revenge in multiple ways: he ran his mother's drive-in to the ground, committed crimes and larceny in his young adult years. In his twenties, he chose to vent his anger to such a degree that he connived the entire plot to seek revenge on his mother and collect the insurance. Consumed by the destructive path of rage and hate, he didn't care about the 43 other passengers.

The thief, the author of sin, comes to steal, kill,
and destroy anything in his way.

Ever since my memorable trip to heaven, I grew even more conscious of the anger and hatred I had squelched for 42 long years. I could not acknowledge these two deadly hooks beforehand. If the Holy Spirit permitted me a premature look at my harbored, destructive emotions, I might have crumbled under the weight of guilt and shame for giving them residence. Never forcing me, in His forbearance, God patiently waited for me to be willing to confront these damaging elements.

Once unveiled, I didn't know how to release them. Part of me never wanted to let go—my daddy was gone forever.

Right or wrong, books on inner healing and teachings at that time encouraged taking a good look at the anger before addressing it—to indeed own it. So, that is what I did. I clung to my right to be angry. Giving the benefit of the doubt to the professionals who wrote those books, perhaps my innocent, warped, and broken interpretation encouraged me to nurture those feelings. Clouded by my brokenness, I gripped these two destructive emotions as if they were a lifeline.

To me, I now had permission to justify my anger and hate. Driven by my propensity toward performance orientation, I held onto anger and its cohort with perfection. THEY WERE MINE. These two emotions simmered underneath the surface until they spilled out in behavior such as my fixation with knives. Since I could not project anger and hate onto a dead man, I threw them (not the knives) toward those around me, my husband taking the brunt of this venting. I also aimed them at myself and wanted so desperately to be with my real dad in heaven that the enemy of my soul took the opportunity to haunt me with thoughts of suicide. An extreme case of unresolved anger and hatred turned inward.

Physiological Effects of Anger and Hate

Anger, bitterness, and hate-filled emotions influence not only how we behave toward others, but also the physical well-being of our bodies, down to our cellular levels.

Even when anger is justified, as in the case of an abused individual having the right to be angry toward the perpetrator, holding onto that anger and not releasing it to Christ can produce disease and other adverse conditions in the body. Whether repressed or demonstrated, including short bursts of anger[1], unbridled rage:

- Can lead to heart disease
- Doubles the chance of having a heart attack
- Triples the risk of stroke from a blood clot to the brain or bleeding within the brain during the two hours after an angry outburst
- Weakens the immune system
- Increases anxiety

- Feeds depression

- May result in lung damage if you are a consistently angry or hostile person because stress hormones associated with anger create inflammation in the lungs and airways

- Can shorten a life span

To keep the peace, often individuals hide their anger instead of dealing with it appropriately. Not to be easily angered is a virtue and strength, but when a situation tips off anger, it is best to nip it in the bud. As stated by Mary Fristad, PhD, Professor of Psychiatry and Psychology at The Ohio State University, "Couples who hold in anger have a shorter lifespan than those who readily say when they are mad. Learning to express anger in an appropriate way is actually a healthy use of anger,"[2] Making every effort to never go to bed angry allows your body to sleep in restorative peace; compounding anger without dealing with it leads down a slippery slope to potential, future disease.

A compilation of studies conducted between 2000 and 2010, further concluded that anger—both suppressed or expressed—can determine specific diseases such as coronary heart disease, type 2 diabetes, and bulimic disorders. These studies further revealed that angry and hostile persons tend to have more car accidents and engage in road rage.[3]

Another study called *Anger Expression and Essential Hypertension—Behavioral Response to Confrontation,* links high blood pressure with "specific social skills that are ONLY apparent during the assertive expression of anger."[4] Anger, among the toxic and deadly emotions, causes a physical chain reaction that increases inflammation, which causes damage to your body. Despite decades of studies and innovative medical treatments, incidences of heart disease, hypertension, strokes, cancers, ulcers, skin diseases, and headaches continue to rise.

Many suffer from immune system deficiencies linked to negative emotions like anger. A weakened immune system leads to allergies, asthma, bronchitis, pneumonia, eczema, psoriasis, skin redness, and itching, Compromised immune systems can lead to Crohn's disease and autoimmune disorders, including lupus and rheumatoid arthritis, and fibromyalgia. Additional byproducts of a depleted immune system include depression, poor memory, phobias, panic attacks, fatigue, lethargy, exhaustion, insomnia, anxiety, foggy thinking, and migraines. While this list is not comprehensive, our bodies cannot withstand a constant barrage of anger, hate, and other toxic emotions, whether suppressed or demonstrated. According to Dr. Caroline Leaf, "Suppressed emotional pain doesn't just disappear. It can turn into lingering pain."[5] Accumulated in our bodies over time, lingering pain leads to mental and physical deterioration.

Have I painted a strong enough picture of the consequences of anger and its companions—bitterness and hate—in our lives? Is it even worth continuing to ignore emotional scars and suppressing emotional pain? After this summary of the impact of such negative emotions on health, what appeals to you? To cling to them, or release them?

I have had to relearn how to remain calm and not be quickly ticked off and angered; it is not worth the consequences. Not only does anger eat us up inside, we become toxic to those around us, who do not deserve to be our punching bags. My hidden, repressed anger hindered my walk with God and my husband, spilling into other areas in my life. I am now thankful that the Lord used the pressures in our lives to bring everything to light when He did.

If you struggle with depression, hurt, bitterness, and anger, you are worth more than being controlled by these negative emotions. You are worth more than any abused self-image imposed by others. You are worth more than being enslaved by your own unbelief, worries, and fears. Your life is precious, and your time deserves to be used to make a difference in the world. Holding onto grudges and disappointments keeps you from fulfilling the destiny and purposes God has for you.

If you are among the many who struggle with bitterness or anger, you can be free from anger and begin improving both your physical and spiritual life. Just as negative emotions spill toxicity into your body, positive emotions, such as peace, joy, and love, rebuild health. It is no wonder that we are called to think on whatever is lovely, noble, pure, and from above (Philippians 4:8).

Getting to that point of letting go, though, can be extremely difficult when the sins committed against us leave Grand Canyon-sized scars deep into our souls. "Just getting over things" and sweeping feelings under the carpet are not the answers but compound the repression of our anger. I could not merely "forget and let go," until God's grace crashed in on the scene.

When we have been so severely beaten, abused, used, and hurt, it can be difficult to come to God. We think we have to be perfect to come before Him with our sorrows. Shame and guilt keep us from approaching the very one with all the answers. I get it. It's painful to admit we allowed others to trample on us. It's traumatic to confront the demons within. It's humbling to ask for help. I can relate. I discovered that all my fears of letting go and coming to God held me back from the very freedom I so desperately needed. I learned that God was not waiting to punish me, but that He loved me with all my shortcomings, failures, and quirks. He had the way out all the time.

So, isn't it worth asking the Father in heaven who loves you to transform you and change you from wallowing in depression, hurt, and anger to living a contented, happy life?

Jesus Christ is reaching out to you with open arms to welcome you. He is the only One who can take the brunt of your anger, defuse it, and deliver you from the debilitating clutch it may have on your life.

Your wife can't. Your husband can't. Your children certainly can't. Neither can your friends, pastor, boss, co-workers, or strangers you encounter daily. None deserve to receive your misguided anger—not even yourself. None can withstand the force of such volatile emotions.

No one, but Jesus.

You are worth it.

You were not meant to carry any level of anger and its accompanying hate, depression, and anxiety. Had I known the repercussions of my hidden rage once it surfaced, I may not have decided to hold onto it. Instead, I nursed it for a long time. But I had forgotten a little bit of wisdom. John Wimber, the founder of the Association of Vineyard Churches, always said,

"Sin makes you stupid."

He was right.

We are not responsible for the sins committed by others against us, but only for our sinful reactions to them and the ones we committed. One day, our wrongdoings will be exposed. We might as well learn to give them up in the here and now, once and for all.

My sin of repressed anger then later explosive anger merely caused slow destruction within my physical body. I am now trusting God to redeem all that was stolen from me through years of pent-up anger—health, joy, a sound mind, peace in my heart, and the return of youthfulness.

Do not do what I did—I clung to that anger and hatred for as long as I could. As my day of decision approached, could I face them?

Scene 28

Preparation for the Finale

That He would give you, according to the riches of His glory, power to be strengthened by His Spirit in the inner man...

—Ephesians 3:16 (MEV)

Two monstrous footholds remained with penetrating attachment to my soul. By now, their identities and hooks had simmered to the forefront in the form of two ferocious feelings—hatred and anger—and reached a boiling point. I had to deal with them, once and for all. Before I could even accept that they existed within my heart, what God did not reveal to me, in the beginning, was that they were the source—the cause—the catalyst—to all my turmoil. I asked Him to dig out the root; He, in His gracious wisdom, waited for the perfect timing in my healing itinerary to draw back the curtain.

Just like any sports player or Olympic player undergoes rigorous training before the big competition day, God foreordained my training to prepare me for the Final Win. He needed to clear debris, demolish roadblocks, and strengthen my spiritual and emotional endurance. He rebuilt me from an old wooden ten-ton covered bridge to that of the 900,000-ton Golden Gate bridge that could handle the weight of truth.

After the milestone breakthrough, the Father surprise, and surrendering empty wells, barriers lifted, which opened the way for me to receive more from the Father. With expanding capacity to embrace the healing process, my fortitude strengthened, which allowed increased and rapid healing. The Father met me in times of worship; visions of dancing and frolicking with Jesus in meadows of flowers frequently waltzed through my mind. When I felt like dirt, He romanced me, pursued me, and drew me closer to Him. My well-engraved image of a distant taskmaster God changed to a father who joyfully embraces his daughter. I longed for His presence and to know Him better; He reciprocated. Instead of turning His back on me as I had expected, God, in His goodness, kindness, and mercy, restored me.

Tears of joy replaced sorrow and crying as Jesus spoke healing words, which anchored me deeper in the Father's love. Like a budding flower in the dry, desert sand, life began to sprout internally, and a wellspring of living waters slowly burst forth through the walls I had built. Hope mounted as feelings of despair lessened. I sensed my season of mourning—my dark years—closing. I thought it would never end. In its place, joy began to radiate.

Once separated from my mother's pain, I had to face my inner turmoil and the effects of my dad's death. Gingerly leading me, God knew when I could handle more revelation. The Almighty Counselor gradually exposed deeper inroads into the webs that this one sinful murderous act produced in my life.

False beliefs, vows, and judgments came to light; overtime, I gained the courage to quickly ask Jesus to forgive me for each one, without shame and guilt. Many had become my identity, my source apart from the ultimate source of life and living water—Jesus Christ. I had believed so many lies. Each falsehood damaged my self-image, which interfered with interpersonal interactions.

As an example, true to self-fulfilling vows, I often felt invisible. In many gatherings, it was as if I were standing on the outside looking in, unnoticed by those around me. At times, people would act like they were greeting me, only to ignore my presence and talk to someone else. Perhaps my short stature eliminated me from their vision, maybe not. Either way, the resulting feelings of rejection, loneliness, and unworthiness did not mirror what God intended for me as a new creation in Him. I dreaded certain social situations because of these overwhelming feelings but would press through them. These began to change as I slowly emerged into my own person, unencumbered by those alienating feelings.

When I brought my brokenness to Jesus, I made sure I did not leave the throne room empty-handed. In exchange for my ungodly responses—the lies believed, the vows made, and sinful reactions displayed—I received His forgiveness. In doing so, I asked Him to replace each one with His truth about who I am and what I have in Him. With each instance, I also forgave the person or individuals, who with their frailties had wounded me. In turn, I asked Jesus to forgive me for having held those individuals as a hostage. My unforgiveness toward them only kept me in bondage and blocked true freedom. I handed Him the jail keys to deal with them as He willed and gave up my right to be their judge.

With each dismantlement of an empty well, greater peace and a sense of worthiness blossomed. I discovered I was someone, not a nobody. My identity switched from the fearful, timid, little girl, to that of a princess, beloved by the King, fully confident, and looking forward to fulfilling dreams.

The one person I held nothing against was my biological dad—it was not his fault that he was on that flight and never came back.

My big V-E Day neared, although I did not know when. All that transpired the past years prepared me to face the most difficult challenge God was calling me to accept. Would I?

Scene 29

The Final Jump

Forgiveness opens the doorway to freedom.

—taken from my journal

Spring 1998

When Forgiveness is Difficult

I just could not let go. I was unaware that the anger and hatred I had carried for so long would eventually affect my physical health. Had I known my emotional upheaval could affect my health down the road, I might have dealt with these emotions sooner. Instead, the unreconciling pain of losing my dad plowed deeper burrows; subsequently, nurturing the vile feelings seemed justified, almost righteous. After all, didn't I have the right to be angry at my stepdad and the killer? Didn't I have the right to hate the killer and his sin of murder? Doesn't God hate killing and violence?

Throughout my road toward freedom, various individuals at seminars and conferences would make attempts to have me forgive the man who killed my dad. Fortunately, a friend stood by me and indicated to them that it was not time. Because they didn't have either the training or the full story, the platitude answer "just forgive the man now," fell automatically out of their mouths. In their passion for seeing freedom come, they had forgotten to walk in my shoes and to become empathetic with me as a person. They could only see a snapshot of me—extremely troubled, broken and crumpled over in tears.

Even the haunting 3D figure of the killer which taunted me did not bring me closer to being able or willing to release all my rancor. Instead, I became fearful of the moment I would choose to forgive the killer. Partly because I had had so many divine encounters and visions, I did not know what to expect whenever I would make that choice. Fear of having another cataclysmic battle with the dark forces intimidated me from stepping over the threshold of forgiveness.

At a counseling training class, I even asked the pastor if I had to forgive a dead person. The answer came back emphatically, "Yes." I couldn't get off the hook. No excuses. Nonetheless, fostering the wounds with their pain appealed more to me instead of relinquishing the bitterness—at least for a while.

All the heavenly Father's love and kindness lavished upon me during this season built up my trust in God. On the other hand, I also feared Him. Entering another year, the knowledge the Lord was calling me to forgive the killer churned in my spirit and gut. The relentless gnawing would not leave, and the wrestling over forgiving the man did not stop.

Over the months, the conviction over harboring these feelings intensified, and God repeatedly brought me closer to bringing this anger and hate to Him. The Father knew these heart conditions were eating me up inside like rust and hindered the peace and final resolution for which I had been seeking. Being the gentleman that He is, the Holy Spirit waited on my timing and did not force me to give up anything I did not want to. Instead, He permitted me to wallow in my deplorable self-pity until I could no longer bear the weight of these burdens.

Meanwhile, in my mind, I began to practice how I would confront the killer face to face, figuratively speaking, since he was dead. My speech commenced with venom, finger pointing, and a litany of the consequences his repugnant, vile action had on my mother, my sister and myself. Each time, my rehearsed rant escalated, and my list of grievances expanded. By this time, I had connected the dots of the ripples of his sin with almost every aspect of my life. I wanted him to see the devastation he brought to our innocent family.

"You knew, so and so, exactly what you did…you took my dad…and you didn't care one bit…you can burn in hell…blah…blah…blah…"

I realized this was a wrong approach, but I did not care. I hated the killer and what he had ruthlessly done. I detested him for yanking my dad from my family and derailing our lives. He never repented and did not care about any of the passengers. I never had the opportunity to face the murderer, stand up to him physically, and scream at him. Although I knew I'd be talking figuratively to a dead man, that didn't bother me either. He deserved my wrath and hating him was entirely justifiable. What put fear in me was facing him. The demonic 3D hologram face that had previously haunted me emanated pure evil, and I was not sure what to expect. Would I be confronting him in a vision, transported to another spiritual dimension, or what? Would God be there with me and what would He do?

During this final stretch of the journey, two deaths of significant people occurred: Uncle Hop, my last physical contact with my biological father, and Stepdad George. Both died within months of each other. An era in my life and link to my biological dad vanished. Hanging on by a thread, coming to peace and laying everything down dominated my thoughts. It was time—and God had been standing by, calmly anticipating the day I'd make my next move.

One evening en route to an inner-healing group meeting, I knew I had to take that step of forgiveness. I mulled it over in my mind—do I forgive that man or do I not? Is tonight the night?

What do I do? What will happen? In the midst of my quandary, the familiar voice interrupted, with a loving firmness that He meant business.

"Marian, why do you fear that which cannot take your soul?"

Hearing His voice stopped me in my tracks, and I realized God precisely perceived what was churning over in my heart. Like a child caught with her hand in the cookie jar, I froze. He only said it once, very sternly and with the same solemn tone He used when He told me to love my husband. Tears streamed down my cheeks.

Gulp. I swallowed. God, the Three-in-One, the Almighty God, the Prince of Peace, nailed me. His words echoed,

"Why do you fear that which cannot take your soul?"

He even used His own Word:

> *"Do not be afraid of those who kill the body*
> *but cannot kill the soul.*
> *Rather, be afraid of the one who can destroy*
> *both soul and body in hell."*
> —Matthew 10:28 (MEV)

"Certainly, a dead killer and his 3D entity cannot take my soul," I thought, "Only God has that right over my life."

"Only You can, Lord," I said.

"Why do you fear that which cannot take your soul?" resounded again in my head.

Whenever God speaks three times, He means business. One simple, direct question. I could not run or hide anymore from facing the greatest fear I had—letting go of 42 years of anger and hate. I drove with fear and trepidation to the church's prayer session that night. Pulling into the parking lot, I got out, took a deep breath, and walked inside, shaking inwardly.

While sitting and waiting for prayer time, the terrifying fear of finally facing the killer overwhelmingly rattled my mind and heart. I told no one. One of the ladies who often prayed with me sat nearby. Even she had no clue what I was about to do, though she knew much about my Road to Freedom.

Inside, I quivered—would this be my Final Win? Had my V-E Day, the touching of Jesus' hem, arrived?

A facilitator asked us to stand if we desired prayer. I stood and raised my hand. The lady standing close to me placed her hand on my shoulder. My heart raced, and my body trembled. I stood at a spiritual crossroad.

"Why do you fear that which cannot take your soul?" reverberated in my mind.

Looking back, I was like Frodo, in the *Lord of the Rings* trilogy by J.R.R. Tolkien, who bore the treacherous, heaviness of his mission and the foreboding force of the One Ring. Had Frodo not made it to Mount Doom and fought Gollum over it—causing both Gollum and the ring to fall into the fire—evil would have embodied Frodo forever. Like the One Ring, the pull of my hatred toward the man who killed my dad gained strength each day; and, the burden of carrying these intense feelings exacted all that was within me, weighing me down with an unbearable heaviness.

In that moment, I had a choice—to choose life or death. Hanging onto that hate would imprison me forever, bringing death. Choosing life meant doing the impossible. Frodo fought that same choice.

My mission? To completely forgive the murderer. And, the evil ring that held power over me? Hate, anger, and their companions—bitterness and resentment. I knew it was now or never or I'd be forever swallowed by those evil entities, digging deeper wells of resentment and bitterness. I didn't want to live a hateful, embittered life, yet to give up ownership of my right to be angry and to forgive the man seemed monumental, ominous, and too difficult.

I closed my eyes, held my hands out, and waited in the Holy Spirit's presence while the worship team played softly. Instantly, in my mind's eye, surrounded in that invisible dome of the Holy Spirit, I saw a courtroom conference table. The killer who I hated with a passion (I still could not say his name) sat across from me, with Jesus seated at the head of the table. Vile hatred spewed from my eyes to the man.

"Jesus, I can't forgive this man. I can't do it. Help! I need Your grace," I said.

No sooner than those words left my mouth, Jesus placed His hand on my shoulder.

In a split second, I looked at the killer across the table, opened my mouth, and expected my scathing speech to come spilling out as I had often rehearsed. He deserved to be given a piece of my mind, and I wanted him to know everything his selfish, wicked act had done. I had no time to think. Instead, these words flowed as I squarely looked the killer in the eyes.

"You thought, John Graham, that you killed my real dad, but you didn't—my real dad is the Heavenly Father. I forgive you."

In a millisecond, as soon as "I forgive you" left my lips, a blindfold lifted, and I was suddenly made aware: my sin of anger and hatred toward the man who killed my dad was the same as his sin of murder. I had been no different than he.

With God's grace overwhelming me, this truth smacked me between the eyes and in the depths of my heart. Immediately, I prayed,

"Father, please forgive me for harboring anger and hate toward the killer all these years. Take them. I don't want them anymore. I don't want to be controlled by them anymore. I give them to you."

All this transpired faster than we can humanly count seconds. With Jesus' hand on me, the power of His resurrection washed over me, and I experienced FREEDOM as never, ever before. The weights and chains broke. The shame and guilt fled. No more hate and anger. The root of bitterness had been uprooted forever. My V-E Day—My Victory Day had come!

What astonished me most was what had happened at that exact moment I looked at the killer. Instead of railing him, God gave me His grace—His undeserved love and power—to forgive, and I could speak the killer's name for the first time in my life.

The words that flowed shocked me:

"You thought you killed my real dad, but you didn't—my real dad is the Heavenly Father." It was at that moment, out of the depths of my being, I knew without a doubt who my Real Father was all along!

I desired to run around the sanctuary shouting praises to the King of Kings and Lord of Lords. He did it! No more crying. No more grieving. Joy splashed over me like an ocean of living waters from heaven. Dancing and leaping returned. My grave clothes fell off. Righteous robes went on. I touched the hem of Jesus' garment. I crossed the finish line, and my odyssey ended.

Jesus and I celebrated that night! Free from the pain of losing my dad! Free from my dad's tragedy ever defining me anymore! God took me beyond the rubble of tragedy through the heaviness of trauma and led me to the other side—through forgiveness—I leaped into lasting freedom!

My chains were broken, and I wanted the whole world to know what Jesus did for me. I didn't care if others in the room that night understood me or not. I started to jump up and down, but contained myself, wanting to be considerate of others. How could I run, dance, and leap with joy unspeakable around the sanctuary? Many were still walking on their paths to wholeness and processing through their pain.

It's as if Jesus gave me a private party, and an exhilarating feeling washed over me. Oppression left. Torment departed forever, never to return. No more torture! I forgave and I was forgiven! I wanted to shout at the top of my lungs,

"Thank You, Jesus! You did it! I AM FREE—I AM FREE—I AM FREE!!"

My longing to know my real, biological dad had taken me straight to the throne room to meet my Real Heavenly Father! At last—I found my Father!

Scene 30

Life Beyond Tragedy

Therefore, if the Son sets you free, you shall be free indeed.

—John 8:36 (MEV)

Ripples of Freedom

At last, after a great chase and battle, the weights and chains had fallen off! Genuine, ever-lasting, indescribable freedom smashed my world paradigm, transforming me forever. No longer defined by the tragedy, I walked through the trauma to the other side. Forgiveness! Sweet forgiveness! I tasted the goodness of the Lord. My search to know my dad ended as God honored my heart's cry. He brought me into His chamber to meet my Real Heavenly Father. The awesome power of His presence delivered me, demonstrating His passionate love for me. Like a prince charming, He swept me—a damsel in distress—onto His White Horse. His presence alone scattered the darkness which cannot stand His light. I rose free and no longer fatherless, no longer orphaned.

I began my journey from a place of desperation to know why I could not cope with life any longer and yet gained more than I ever could have imagined. I felt like I lived the past three years in a deep Amazon rainforest bat cave with many pathways going nowhere, only further into the darkness. The pitch blackness blocked my vision and demolished hope of making it out alive. As I came out of denial and confronted each of my empty wells, light streamed into the dark passages. Remaining oblivious that unforgiveness kept the main entrance of the cave hidden from my view, I followed that light out inch by inch. Then, when the obscurity overwhelmed me with groping blindness, Jesus called out,

"Take my hand; I'll get you out."

Trusting His guidance, with His hand in mine, we both walked out through the window of forgiveness which ushered me into a brilliant, liberating light. Once out of the dark cave, I stepped into living a life full of color.

These experiences significantly transformed how I live life. Just as trauma and sin induce destructive ripple effects in our lives, so also the goodness of God produces never-ending ripples, producing fruit for eternity.

True Transformation

Indeed, freedom in every which way broke into my life that day. I knew I had, at last, touched the hem of Jesus' garment, and my V-E Day of healing arrived—the victory of victories, ending the war within my soul and for my soul. The light dispelled the darkness in that instant. The axe was taken to the root cause of all my inability to cope in life—my unforgiveness toward the killer. The evil enemy lost—pure mercy, love, and peace won. God in His mercy guided me on this path, using circumstances and His Word in my life. He drew me so close to Him until He knew I was ready and utterly depleted of my strength to continue apart from Him. Then, He stepped in.

I knew I had forgiven once and for all the man who killed my dad and that the Heavenly Father had forgiven me for all those years of compounding hate and anger. The killer and the tragedy of losing my dad no longer held power over who I was and to whom I belonged. The haunting banished, never to return.

—— ⚬⚬⚬ ——

No torment is freedom.

—— ⚬⚬⚬ ——

The chains once stifling and suffocating my identity as a child of God, like a boa constrictor around a neck, snapped off instantly and could not stand against the forgiveness I extended and received. The anger, hatred, and bitterness no longer held me in their vice. The churning in my stomach ceased. Peace overwhelmed my soul, and my pounding heart calmed. Thoughts that brought shaming and guilt fled from my mind, no longer able to torture my inner being. The tapes replaying in my brain ceased; clarity replaced the muddle. The high-level anxiety which pummeled my mind soon quieted; the voice of the Father stilled my soul. Jubilation and thanksgiving instantly replaced the unfathomable sorrow and sadness. Faithful to His Word, I discovered joy does come in the morning (Psalm 30:5).

—— ⚬⚬⚬ ——

A joyful outlook is freedom.

—— ⚬⚬⚬ ——

I felt newly born, with a whole new license on life, and ready to live as God originally intended.

I became free to receive God's love for me and to freely love others with a renewed compassion. Hope for the future displaced despair.

Although I never obtained answers as to why my dad had to be on that fateful plane, I came to peace that I may never know this side of heaven. I had finally arrived at the fifth stage in the grief cycle: acceptance. Acceptance and forgiveness did not lessen the severity of the crime nor that man's responsibility in the death of my dad and the 43 others. Instead, the real me could emerge—free from the slavery of anger, hatred, and bitterness.

⚬⚬⚬

Fresh vision, hope, and peace is freedom.

⚬⚬⚬

My journey took me through the minefields of the broken cisterns I had dug. As I turned away from each well for my identity and looked to God as my source for what I lacked, patterns of damaging self-talk ceased. Each time I found myself slipping, I would ask God to forgive me and to free me from each negative mindset. Each time I did, I unknowingly walked out my ultimate healing, and my faith increased. Gradually, that pattern of behavior, reaction, or thinking held less power in my life and could no longer keep me hostage. I stopped replaying old tapes in my mind, and the crippling introspection ceased. Today, when I am tempted to fall into old patterns of an empty well, I can walk past it with a decided "no" and a smile on my face.

⚬⚬⚬

Ability to walk past temptation is freedom.

⚬⚬⚬

Trust and assurance in hearing God's voice grew exponentially, and my long walks with Him became much more meaningful and intimate. Journal entries turned a permanent corner—from a gloomy-self-absorbed-woe-is-me pattern to a love relationship and fellowship with the Father. Since I could now receive His love, I could also hear His loving words to me. My groveling, begging approach to prayer transformed from that of a child hoping dad will hear, to a child fully anchored in the goodness of a father. I laid my requests, desires, and wants before God as I had before, but out of a place of confidence, not out of wishful thinking or doublemindedness. I knew I could now hear His voice, and He hears me.

Confidence is freedom.

Full Restoration

As I changed, our marriage experienced restoration, my husband obtained an excellent position, and we settled into another church. There we found a whole new church family who accepted us for who we were, and we thrived for the first time in years. Ironically, when one pastor had rejected me, God placed us in a church with over fifteen pastors who welcomed us. Our children made new friends and blossomed in their walks with Christ and made new friends.

A restored marriage and close-knit family are freedom.

By divine circumstances, a pastor placed me on staff working alongside him in ministering to the poor—the least, the lost, and the forgotten in our community. He knew this had been my passion for years, so his acceptance, encouragement, and blessing brought further life to my once-shattered soul. I felt I had experienced my convergence and the ministry flourished. Upon the return from the visit to heaven, leading others to the Father became more integrated into my daily lifestyle. In this God-given position, I had so much joy teaching and leading others to do the same.

In reaching out to others, the way I approached them and prayed for them radically changed. Making sure I maintained their dignity and their trust; no person ever became an object of my ministry. Each person God brought across my path, I treated with value and worth. I sought to see them with the Father's eyes and compassion. I made this a habit, which became a natural outflow and integrated with who I am. As the Father did not reject me, nor does He reject anyone. Acceptance marks His character. I knew this truth with head knowledge and sought to live it, but now I had this written in my heart. What I was freely given, I was now free to give away.

God does not play favorites. When persons are brought into His Presence, freedom and healing naturally flow—not any formula or words. He is the lover of their souls and loves them much more than I or anyone ever could. What He did for me, He will do for anyone and even more.

I soon attended a school of ministry within the church and I discovered my calling. I took peer counselor training and mentored under the pastor overseeing pastoral counseling. As I freely received, I could now coach others beyond their tragedies, guide them through their trauma and connect them with the Heavenly Father, their source of ultimate, lasting freedom and life.

Leading others to freedom is freedom.

Living Freedom Out

Did life instantly become a piece of cake and we lived happily ever after?

No. That's a fairy-tale. Our future proceeded with the ups and downs of the normal flow of life. Trials and hardships frequently crossed our path, and seasons of feast or famine dotted our journey. Times of plenty. Times of leanness. Times when we made left turns when we should have turned right. Times when we traveled smooth, straight roads.

Armed now with tools to cope, turbulent times still served to test our faith and to strengthen our marriage as we clung to the Lord as our Source. We have also witnessed His miraculous provision and continual protection. As the years progressed, my husband and I have grown so much closer and more in love with each other. Each time I am tempted to be hurt or angry at anyone who wounded me, for whatever reason, I choose to forgive them, knowing that if I could forgive a murderer, I could forgive anyone.

Forgiveness is freedom.

By the grace of God, our children grew in their faith, married delightful spouses, and love the Lord with all their heart, mind, and soul. Hopefully, they learned forgiveness by the example I set—during the healing years, I continually asked them to forgive me when I failed them. They witnessed the faith of their father and mother who never turned their backs on God through difficult storms of life. Established in life, each confidently carries the torch of influencing others, their communities, and the world.

Me? I have had to learn how to live in my newfound freedoms which is a lifetime journey. Only now I know without a doubt, I am not alone. The Heavenly Father walks beside me. I'm His beloved daughter, a daughter of the King. Set free and renewed. And, I belong to Him.

This is *the* ultimate and lasting freedom.

Scene 31

The Father's Search for His Child

*No one, not a single human, is destined to be orphaned.
Many, though, walk this life as if they are. I know, because I did.*

—Taken from my journal

I believed I was searching for my father from the very beginning. In one way, yes. In another way, no. It was He, God the Father, who had begun the quest to find me—His broken, distraught little lamb. He went looking to bring me back, fully knowing I am His, when I forgot whose I am. He initiated the entire adventure which took me into deep, dark crevices of my soul, to bring me out into a wide spacious field of joy and elation. I used to call the years, between my emotional crash and my eventual liberation, my dark years. Today, I call them my freedom years. I had been dead inside—I emerged alive.

As He revealed Himself as the Lover of my soul, the very Father who sought me, Jesus promises to all of us:

I will not leave you as orphans. I will come to you.
—John 14:18 (NIV)

Since He favors no one above the other, He remains forever the One who loves you more than any other person could and the Father who searches for you. Whether you have walked with Him for a very long time, or perhaps not at all, He desires each of us to intimately grasp His Father's love. Once anchored in His love, understanding the depth of His love, we can live unhindered by chains that once grounded us, guided by His peace.

Through my lens, you have witnessed God's mercy and compassion fulfilling my long-sought desire to be loved by the Father. Little did I realize the Father had been searching to bring me home all the while I was seeking my answers. He never gave up either. When I viewed myself as faithless, He was faithful, and would not allow me to stay stuck. He heard the cries of my heart.

In the middle of an intense roller coaster ride, in my miserable state, He relentlessly pursued me with each mount, descent into the valleys, and turns. When others rejected me, He accepted me. When anger, hate, and bitterness entangled my soul, the Father romanced me to Himself. It was as if all He saw was His daughter, whom He loved. God gazed through my ugliness and clothed me in His radiance, fit for royalty. He brought me to my feet and danced with me like I was a princess, putting His arm around my waist and waltzing across a ballroom floor without a care in the world, with my hair, of course, blowing with each twirl.

When others regarded me as damaged goods, He immersed me—no, He lavished me—in His extravagant love. Instead of chastising me, He washed every bit of my shame and guilt away. Some call it "healing the father wound." Others, a "baptism of love." Some describe it as "liquid love." In any event, His love saved me in every which way.

Since God doesn't have any stepchildren and doesn't play favorites, He seeks after you.

No Longer Orphaned

I don't know where you have been, what has happened to you, or what you have done—whether you had a good decent father in your life or not. I don't know the tragedies, trauma, and losses you may have had to walk through or that you face today.

But I do know the One who does know. What God did for me, He will abundantly do for you. He stands ready with open arms to gather you to Himself and to bask you in His penetrating, perfect love. The Father is gentle and does not ever force someone to run to Him. He gave us all free will to choose for ourselves to turn to Him as our sole source for life and to know Him as Father.

Our orphan spirits, even those of grown men and women, don't realize we were never meant to walk this earth alone. Since the beginning of time, the Father has been persistently reaching out to bring everyone to Himself. Whether you are seeking Him or not, He searches for you.

He will lovingly pursue you like the good shepherd who left the 99 sheep to find the one sheep which roamed outside of his protective fence of love. He is like the father who patiently longed to welcome back the son who took his full inheritance and squandered everything. When the son returned, he did not even need to enter the gates of his father's home. From a distance, the father saw his son, filthy and destitute, and ran to him. In his shame, the son begged his father to treat him as a servant. But the father instead restored this wayward son to full status as son and heir.

Some of us may identify with the wayward son who stood on the outside, looking in and deeply wanting to be accepted and loved. Others of us may identify with the resentful son who stayed home and worked hard to earn the father's acceptance.

The remedy for both types remains the same—both sons and daughters require the same grace, mercy, and compassion of the Father.

No matter which one you identify with, the simple prayer below will open doors for God to take you on His journey of love and freedom. Your journey will not look like mine but will be gloriously tailored just for you. He stands ready to pour out His loving tenderness, to wipe away all your tears and sorrows, and to overflow you with His Father's blessings. He will understand you and will know what you need even before you ask. He will answer the cries of your heart and utterly amaze you.

It makes no difference whether you are female, male, a Christian or not, young or old; you can experience the same love of the Heavenly Father by sincerely praying a ten-second prayer:

> Dear God,
> I am tired of doing life on my own strength and fathering myself.
> I need your help. Please teach me how to let You father me.
> Come love me and father me.
> Amen.

Final Blessing

I am no one special, just someone who has walked through difficult times and gained more than I could ever ask or imagine. As I have freely received, I leave you with this blessing:

> May you be graced with the Father's blessing,
> That you grow in knowing God as Father and hearing His Voice.
> May you know how wide, how deep, how high the Father's tender love is for you,
> That the Father's glory, grace, and peace fill the longings in your heart.
> That you will live a life full of His presence, passion, and joy,
> Forever confident knowing Him to whom you belong.
> Amen.

I now thank you, Daddy, Abba-Father, that as You searched for me and brought me out of severe pain and sorrow, You will wrap Your arms around each person so they may find safety in You, see You, feel Your embrace, hear You, enjoy You, and walk with You forever—no longer fatherless. Amen.

ACT IV

Your Road to Freedom Story

Epilogue

My Mother's Faith and Never-Ending Love

My mother, Martha Pearl McNeer Hobgood Weber, imparted grace, mercy, and kindness to everyone she met. She never showed any bitterness in her life, but gratefully and joyfully loved life and others. In 1997, I first learned her entire story of what happened the night my dad's plane exploded and how she survived.

Years before 1997, in one of our midnight talks back home, my mom acknowledged that God had prepared her and my dad for what was to come. Following World War II, Leslie Weatherhead,[1] from Great Britain, had come to speak to churches in the United States to help Americans make some sense out of the war and bring healing to the nation. Prior to my dad's death, they studied Weatherhead's book, *The Will of God*, in their Methodist Young Adult Fellowship group. She kept their original book which contained his handwritten notes. She had told me, "I look back and see that God had been preparing us [she and Hobby] all during the year before he died. This helped me make it through."

Following the downing of the TWA flight off the shores of NYC and the Oklahoma City bombing, a local newspaper editor learned about the terror on United Air Lines Flight #629 and that my dad had been on that flight. He desired an interview with my mother and me. As shared, my stepdad never allowed her to discuss my biological dad. My mother agreed because the reporter promised not to directly quote her in case my stepdad read the paper. She brought artifacts my dad had worn that fateful day which I had never seen—cuff links and a watch, both with the FBI tags still attached. The Suburban Newspaper, in Central Ohio, February 1997, printed a two-page article entitled *A Daughter's Search for Her Father*.[2] The interview and article occurred in the middle of my journey toward resolution and freedom, which confirmed God was guiding me through the healing maze.

Knowing her entire account allowed me to reconstruct her story as found in Act I. I also learned more about her godly character and how she lived out her faith. After the reporter and photographer left, she spoke of deep things she had tucked away inside for over forty years.

Looking into my eyes, she said,

"You know, Marian, I always felt sorry for the wife of the man who killed your dad. She had just had a baby, who would be a little older than you. Yours and Nancy's counterpart is alive somewhere."

With a loving gentleness that adorned my mother, she said,

"Marian, while I had a bad feeling and did not want your dad to go on that company trip and shared my opinion with him, your dad and I only had one real argument in our entire life—we argued over which carriage to buy for Nancy when she was born."

In the next breath, she shared her well-kept, well-tucked secret. A wise friend of mine once told me that women carry secrets in their hearts, and my mother now revealed hers without any prompting.

"Marian, there was never a couple more in love with each other than your dad and me. Not a day in 42 years has passed that I have not thought about him."

That is love. Unending love. While Rose, the character in the movie *Titanic*, always held onto her love for Jack, my mother's love for her first love, my father, was real. It was true love—and she never let go.

After our stepdad died in the spring of 1998, my mother came alive for the first time. She told me one day that she woke up seeing a frown on her face—from the mourning of our stepdad and the burden of being his caregiver in his last years. She decided then and there that it took more muscles to frown than smile, so she chose smiling, joy, and laughter. When she told me this, she frowned and then broke into the widest and brightest smile that lit up her whole face and the entire room!

I had never seen her happier, more joyful and active. She was the one driving others to their doctor's visits and errands. She watched our eight-year-old son while I took my daughter and her friends to Monday night youth group meetings. We joined her at events at the retirement village where she and my stepdad had lived. Favorite times occurred on most Friday mornings when the children and I would bring in delicious pastries and share them with Mom and her friends in this elegant tea room.

That fall, she took off on a three-week trip back to her roots in the mountains of Virginia, insisting she did not need the kids and me to go with her. In fact, she was so active, I barely saw her as often as I would have liked. A free woman, she enjoyed life and her friends.

Suddenly, within a few weeks of her grand vacation, we got that call no one wants to receive—she was in the hospital on life support. Always putting us first, her final words I heard her say was, "I'll be OK." She passed away three days later, right before Thanksgiving, 1998. She was right; she is OK.

As most miss their mothers, I miss her to this day. However, I am eternally thankful that I am her daughter, that she was my mother, and that she shared her heart with me that day in 1997.

She is now reunited with her one true love. Without her knowledge of the significance of my "jumping in the River," I still hear her say her last words of wisdom to me—

"Go with the flow to the next bend in the river."

Appendix A

In Memory of the Victims

A List of the Passengers and Crew on United Air Lines Flight #629

November 1, 1955

Fay E. "Jack" Ambrose, 38, Seattle, Washington
Samuel F. Arthur, 38, Seattle, Washington
Bror H. Beckstrom, 48, Seattle, Washington
Irene Beckstrom, 44 Seattle, Washington
John P. Bommelyn, 53, Seattle, Washington
Frank M. Brennan, Jr., 36, Seattle, Washington
Louise D. Bunch, 61 Forest Grove, Oregon
Horace Brad Bynum, 32, Sherwood, Oregon
Carol Bynum, 22, Sherwood, Oregon
Thomas L. Crouch, 23, Wichita, Kansas
Barbara J. Cruse, 23, Aurora, Colorado
Carl F. Deist, 53, Hillsborough, California
John P. Des Jardins, 42, Overland Park, Kansas
James Dorey, 58 Whitman, Massachusetts
Sarah Dorey, 55, Whitman, Massachusetts
Elizabeth D. Edwards, 57, Providence, Rhode Island
Gurney Edwards, 58, Providence, Rhode Island
Helen Fitzpatrick, 42, Batavia, New York
James Fitzpatrick II, 13 months, Batavia, New York
Lee H. Hall, 38, Seattle, Washington

Vernal Virgil Herman, 69, Vancouver, Washington
Goldie Herman, 59, Vancouver, Washington
Elton B. Hichok, 40, Seattle, Washington
Jacqueline L. Hinds, 26, Eugene, Oregon
Marion P. Hobgood, 31, Hatfield, Pennsylvania
John W. Jungels, 57, Aurora, Illinois
Daisie E. King, 53, Denver, Colorado
Gerald G. Lipke, 38, Pittsburgh, Pennsylvania
Patricia Lipke, 36, Pittsburgh, Pennsylvania
Lela McLain, 81, Portland, Oregon
Suzanne F. Morgan, 40, Wilmette, Illinois
Frederick Stuart Morgan, 48, Wilmette, Illinois
Peggy Ann Peddicord, 22, Seattle, Washington
James W. Purvis, 45, Tacoma, Washington
Herbert G. Robertson, 43, Rutherford, New Jersey
Dr. Harold R. Sandstead, 50, Silver Springs, Maryland
Sally Ann Scofield, 24, Denver, Colorado
Jesse T. Sizemore, 24, Mumford, Alabama
James E. Straud, 51, Lansing, Michigan
Clarence W. Todd, 43, Tacoma, Washington
Minnie Van Valin, 62, Newberg, Oregon
Dr. Ralph Waldo Van Valin, 72, Portland, Oregon
Donald A. White, 26, Seattle, Washington
Alma L. Winsor, 48, St. John's, Newfoundland, Canada

Appendix B

Marion Pierce Hobgood Memorial Fund

A Public Thank You

We thank each person who graciously donated to the Marion Pierce Hobgood Memorial Fund in September-November 1956, which greatly blessed our mother, Martha P. Hobgood. We know how much your love, support, and generosity meant to her throughout the years.

We were adults when we learned about this Memorial Fund and look back with fondness and thankfulness for the 14 years of Christmas and the Savings Bonds. As the letter dated November 21, 1956, from the Memorial Fund Trustees to our mother, wrote,

> *"It is a true indication of the respect and admiration which Hobby's friends and colleagues held for him, and an indication of their desire to do something very concrete for you and the children. It is our intent that it be used to provide some special Christmas presents for the children as we know Hobby would have done."*

We remember the many times spent with your families and children when we were young, and how your love and friendship kept Mom going after the loss of our father, Marion Pierce Hobgood, on flight #629. We will forever be grateful.

From the depths of our hearts to yours,

Nancy Hobgood Kesterson (born July 26, 1954)
Marian Hobgood Poeppelmeyer (born December 28, 1955)

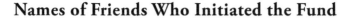

Names of Friends Who Initiated the Fund

William F. Given	T. Jack Heckelman	Morton L. Long
James L. Maddox	James E. Pitman	James B. Williams

Names of Contributors

Mary Virginia Babb	George Baker	James Beaver
Norman Bender	Stanley E. Benson	William Benz
Ed Biedrzycki	Daniel Biles	Unarda Boggs
S. Oscar Boughner	Charles C. Bradley	Preston J. Brewster
Frank E. Bristow	Frank Burson	Norman Caban
Ed Casey	Vincent Ciletti	M. Eugene cook
Robert Dahlberg, Mr. & Mrs.	Hugh J. Datte	Burton W. Dempster
John De Wald	Alan R. Dott	Fred E. Eichler
Dr. Gordon D. Ellis	Albert D. Emurian	Ed Fink
John M. Fisher	John Flynn	Harold A. Goodman
Philip Goldstein	W. M. Gourley	Ray Gratzner
Dorothy Harrison	John R. Henhoeffer	Henry E. Hockeimer
Art Hynes	Anne Jones	John Kelly
John Kingston	Ed Kletke	Eugene P. Lounsberry
Robert Lukens	Cathie Lyona	Eugene J. Herbert, Jr.
John Marsey	Dr. Thomas McCrea	Earl H. Moore
Vito Moreno	John Morrissey	Elsie Morton
B. G. Nead, Mr. and Mrs.	Anthony Pensabene	Anthony Petrilla
Guy C. Pierce	Jeannette Ranieri	Genevieve Reavis
John Regan	Wilhelm Reiss	Ivan Robinson
John Roth	John Ruddy	John Rutledge
Robert Ruth	Dan Sattenspiel	John Schofield
John Schull	Harold Schwartzberg	William Sentell
Robert Senulis	Howard Sheldon	Horace Sinclair
Gil Smith	Richard C. Smith	Thomas A. Sorber
Marshall Soura	Marion T. Speights	Sterling C. Spielman
Thomas Tatem	Claire Vattieri	Quentin Veit
Al Vick	John Vitaglione	Milton Weiner
Paul Whittemore	Lloyd Winter	Sterling H. Wright

First Methodist Church, Married Couples Group
Factory Personnel (Philco, Plant 18)

Appendix C

Interesting Facts About United Air Lines Flight #629

(This list is compiled from sources documented in the Notes, conversations with Marty Hobgood Weber and G. Gordon Liddy, former FBI agent, with special thanks to Andrew J. Field, *Mainliner Denver—The Bombing of Flight 629*)

1. The downing of Flight #629 ranks the first commercial airplane bombing and the largest mass murder ever in U.S. airlines history up to that date, November 1, 1955.

2. The sabotage of Flight #629 became the worst plane bombing and mass murder in Denver history. In 2005, the explosion's 50th anniversary, local Denver media remembered the tragedy through TV mini-documentaries and newspaper articles.

3. The delay of Flight #629 leaving Denver allowed the rescuers to find the bodies, the FBI to conduct its investigation, and the authorities to arrest John Gilbert Graham.

4. The explosion exerted such power that plane parts and bodies landed approximately one foot deep into the ground, leaving outlines and imprints. The following spring, crops grew around each outline of the deceased, leaving an eerie impression.

5. President Eisenhower took a direct interest in this case, not just because of its tragic, historical event that rocked the entire nation, but also because he had links with two of the victims.

6. The case was handed over to the State of Colorado because Colorado had the death penalty, and the Federal Government did not.

7. July 14, 1956, after John Graham's execution in Colorado, President Eisenhower signed into law authorizing the death penalty for anyone convicted of sabotaging a commercial airline which results in death and twenty years in prison for any sabotage not resulting in death.

8. John Graham was charged with one count of murder, not 44 counts. It would have been impossible to prove in court that John Graham knew each passenger and intended to kill each one. This decision sped up court proceedings.

9. The case of John Gilbert Graham became the first case to allow photographers and the filming of the court proceedings. A special booth was constructed for the press.

10. Baggage checks had not been required at the time. Although the airlines questioned Daisy King about an overweight piece of luggage, they did not inspect her luggage. John Graham paid the extra cost for the added weight.

11. Following the bombing of Flight #629, the insurance vending machines continued to be allowed in airports.

12. Philco Corporation had hired the best lawyers in Philadelphia to sue United Air Lines, but concluded it would be impossible, since there were no laws requiring baggage checks and the plane exploded due to sabotage and not a malfunction. A couple of families with victims filed lawsuits, but their cases were dropped with undisclosed settlement amounts. Marty Hobgood never received any settlement for her husband's loss.

13. The bombing of Flight #629 had become an FBI case study for training FBI agents for many years.

14. In February 2005, in compliance with the Aviation and Transportation Security Act signed by President Bush, November 19, 2001, Denver International Airport began automatic screening of every checked baggage for explosives.

This case contained many other interesting facts and represented many firsts within U.S. history about the sabotage, the court case, and the FBI investigation process.

To learn more details, download a free comprehensive *Flight #629 Interesting Facts Sheet* at: MarianPoeppelmeyer.com

Acknowledgments

I remember over twenty years ago, after I crossed into lasting freedom, the desire to put my dad's story into a book burned within me. I wanted to make my dad's life count so that his life would not be in vain. I desired nothing less than to reach thousands with the Father's love and message of the power of forgiveness. September 11, 2001 (9/11) had not yet occurred. After 9/11, I sensed my story—whose life started with tragedy—could bring much healing and hope to many affected directly and indirectly by 9/11 and to the nation.

Since then, the U.S. remains in a constant bombardment with traumatic killings, from mass killings to shootings of cops and individual murders. A nation that is continuously traumatized through the nightly news requires great healing on multiple levels. Having been through such an atrocious act of evil and over to the other side, I hope readers who read *Finding My Father* will find freedom for themselves.

Although it has taken over twenty years to publish my book, God's timing is always perfect. I could not have completed this book without the following people who believed in me, supported me, and offered guidance, prayers, and laughter every step of the way. When I first began writing *Finding My Father*, I did not realize many others would become involved in this project with a passion for seeing it through from beginning to publication. Each person who joined me to complete this book, grasped the vision for themselves, owning its message and desiring to see others touched and changed through it. So, while I am the author, this book represents the collective effort of the many God sent to further His plan and purposes to spread His word of hope and victory. May I remain faithful and loyal to them as they have to me. May the message of the importance of fatherhood, forgiveness, and redemption resonate with each reader and bring healing and restoration to many.

My Family Team

I thank my mother: You endured many hardships, yet never showed any bitterness. You taught me how to love, show grace, and give mercy to others. Your conversations and the trail of letters, photos, and keepsakes you left have helped me piece together what it was like for you on that fateful day and beyond. You were a courageous woman, and I will always miss you this side of heaven.

I thank my family: First, my husband, Colen (Pep). You walked with me through this tough journey of healing, supported me through this book, and stayed by me for over forty years. Thank you for loving me and believing in me. I love you forever. Second, my children—Amanda and Austin. You each told me separately, "I knew you were meant to write for years. It's about time, Mom." Your love, laughter, and presence kept me moving forward and still do. I will always be there for you and your families. Next, I am thankful for my sister, Nancy. You have been my best friend all my life, even when distance kept us apart. You reflect the sweetness, goodness, and mercy of our mother, please don't ever stop. Lastly, I am so grateful to the entire Hobgood family in South Carolina. Your love and acceptance of this Yankee and your fun-loving spirit tied me closer to my real dad—your uncle—more than you will ever know.

My Spiritual Oversight Team

I give thanks to Danny Meyer, Dave Martin, and Peter Yoshida. When I initially began to write my story, I desired spiritual oversight and guidance, and God had placed each of you in my life. You each readily affirmed the messages within *Finding My Father* must be written. I am thankful for your part in guiding, being my sounding board, and providing me constructive insight. I know I gained far more than anticipated. I will forever remember our friendship, your encouragement, continual prayers, spiritual oversight, and insightful conversations. To Danny, when I called you, you responded "It's about time." This confidence spurred me to keep on writing. Over the years, I have always appreciated your hand in the finishing healing work God had begun in me. Your willingness to review portions of the book for your guidance will always be appreciated. To Dave, whom Pep and I have known over 37 years, what can I say? Your spiritual insight, prayers, and many conversations brought much laughter and joy in the midst of writing such a serious yet victorious story. Your perspective on trauma and the womb validated my experience and led me to dig into the topic, rounding out the book. To Peter, God knew what He was doing when he brought us together. Your experience in the acting world with your seminary academics has proven a surprise bonus for this book and its message. At my darkest hours of questioning whether I should finish the book or not, you always blessed me with a text message or facebook message cheerleading me onward. How can I say thank you enough to all of you?

My Trauma Expert Team

I thank Millie McCarty, M.A., LPCC, a trauma expert who has pioneered a Biblical Christian counseling response to those traumatized by abuse, addictions, loss, and events in their lives. What a privilege it has been to study under you in your 30-hour class Pathway to Healing, your *Why We Just Can't Get Over It* workbook, and then your 10-hour certification coaching class to lead others to freedom from their past trauma, addictions, and abuse. It is not every day that someone has the ability to learn from a seasoned, mature Christian leader who carries the peace of God and His wisdom to all she meets. You provided the expert advice needed to understand why I just could not get over it when my bottled-up emotions erupted. Using your forty years of experience in the trenches counseling thousands through trauma and abuse recovery, you confirmed that I indeed had been affected by mother's own trauma and grief while in her womb, and that the recall of my pre-birth memories was highly possible. Thank you so much for your interest in my story, taking the time to review the manuscript, for mentoring me, and our friendship.

My Editing Team

I thank everyone whom God brought to me to tediously review every single sentence, paragraph, and chapter. I especially thank Shirley Sartori and Mary Clark—my longtime friends and core editing team: When I asked you to venture with this project, you quickly said yes and coordinated your schedules. When we began, the scenes (chapters) were separate documents and quite rudimentary. You two helped "glue" the story line together and your insights enriched its message. You sacrificed hundreds of hours working through the manuscript. We drank coffee, prayed, laughed, cried, and ate many lunches together. Your spiritual support and vision for this project kept me focused. Words are not enough to show you my appreciation and love. I greatly appreciate Judah Hout, Sean Patterson, and Jennifer Polk: You stepped in at different times to assist in the editing process when I needed additional input. Your professional insight and suggestions have rounded out the pages in this book, making its message clearer and stronger.

My Professional Consulting Team

I thank Lillian Zarzar: As a friend, communications coach, writer, and professor, years ago you envisioned me as an author before I could see it and have nudged me to write ever since. I am forever grateful for our friendship and your continual prodding. Thank you for lending your professional time and advice with this book. You bring the best out in me. You bring the best out in me. *Finding My Father* is book number one, with more to go, thanks to you. I thank John Finch, filmmaker and author of the book and documentary with the same title, *The Father Effect*. You have always taken time to speak with me and to read through my manuscript. Our common stories and messages on fatherhood and forgiveness linked us together, through fellow AAE author, Brian Goslee, *Changed Through Faith*.

My Support Team

I thank everyone who interceded for the book: especially to Sharon Sayfee, you supported me from day one. May all the prayers bear eternal ramifications in the lives of many reached by the message of healing, restoration, and forgiveness found in the pages of *Finding My Father*.

For the more technical support the book required, I thank my son-in-law, Matt Woods, who provided guidance towards my website design. I thank Susan Hidy, owner of Image Arts Etc, Columbus, Ohio, who scanned the old family photos. I thank Mark Thomas of Mark and Shelly Photography for enhancing my book launch. I especially thank Debbie at Jet Launch for her creativity and patience with the design of my book design.

I thank my book party launch team: Christian Selch, Shirley Sartori, Mary Clark, Gary and Susan Shipman, Emmanuel Sotondji, Leslie Lea, Dow Tippet and many more. You captured the vision for the book and its message and came alongside me to plan the best book launch party ever. There are many more whom I could not address personally, but you know who you are. Your generosity and support made the book's release happen. Thank you for all your time, enthusiasm, and assistance.

Author Academy Elite (AAE) and Igniting Soul Tribe

I thank everyone from the Author Academy Elite and the Igniting Soul Tribe: You collectively provided hundreds of coaching hours, tips, support, and friendship. Without this community of authors and leadership of Kary Oberbrunner, I know this book would not have been started, completed, or published. I give thanks to: Dow Tippett, Brian Goslee, Stacey Greene, Lonnell Johnson whom God used to provide ideas and strategies which fine-tuned my message. Dow, you made the best MC I could ever have for my book launch party. To Brian, you connected me with John Finch. To Chris, your gentle leadership encouraged me. To Stacey, thank you for the brainstorming weekend and our collaboration on future projects. We are just beginning. To Lonnell, you faithfully kept my eye on the Word of God and His promises.

Many heartfelt thanks to everyone and to those I may have forgotten to name. You will forever be a part of this ministry. May we collectively see an abundant harvest from all our efforts to bring lasting freedom to thousands.

Lastly, but most importantly, I thank God, my Real Father. You saved me in every way—for eternal life with You and from my destructive self—emotionally, physically, and spiritually. You brought me out of the pit of darkness into Your glorious light and freedom. You loved me when I acted the most unlovable. Without Your guidance, provision, and divine inspiration, I could not have written the story You wrote upon my heart. You do, indeed, turn everything around for Your glory and purposes. May this message reach many of those with orphan spirits who wander in this life not knowing who they truly belong to and draw them to You as You drew me.

May God bless everyone richly in every way with the Father's heart,
Marian Hobgood Poeppelmeyer

Notes

Act I—Beyond Tragedy

Scene 1: Where Were You on 9/11?

1. It does not matter how few or how many persons are killed or injured in any sabotage or explosion, death is final and eternally separates the victims and their families. I could not list all the mass killings that have occurred, such as Columbine, Sandy Hook, the Boston Marathon, the Las Vegas shooting, and more recent ones. With thanks to the FBI, Homeland Security, and all the agencies involved in keeping America safe, many attempts against the US have been thwarted. Unfortunately, shootings and mass killings continue. One day, may peace come to the hearts of Americans and outrage cease—including the many murders occurring each day.

Scenes 2-3, and 5-9

1. These Scenes could not have been written without direct conversations with my mother, Marty McNeer Hobgood Weber, over the span of twenty years, culminating with an interview she granted the Suburban Newspaper in January/1997. At this interview, I heard her complete story for the first time in my 42 years. With the additional family photos, letters she had written, letters from the Philco Corporation, and the letter signed by six of Hobby's and Marty's closest friends regarding the Marion Pierce Hobgood Memorial Fund, I was able to piece a reasonably accurate rendition of events, her feelings, and the acts of love shown by her friends. My older Hobgood cousins who remembered him contributed biographical and childhood stories to round out how my real dad, Marion Pierce Hobgood lived as a man, his nature, and his character.

Scene 2: Leaving on a DC-6B

1. "A Decade of Post War Service: Air Transport Facts and Figures," *Air Transport of America Annual Report*, 17th Edition, (1956), (2019), 2, (accessed 2019), http://airlines.org/wp-content/uploads/2014/08/1956.pdf.

Scene 4: Meanwhile Back in Denver

1. This scene was compiled from various sources:

   —"A Case of 44 Mid-Air Murders," *Life Magazine,* Vol. 39, No. 22, (November 28, 1955), 35-40.

   —Don Whitehead, *The FBI Story,* (New York, NY, Random House, 1956), 1-10.

   —Andrew Field, *Mainliner Denver—the Bombing of Flight 629,* (Boulder, Colorado, Johnson Books, 2005).

   —Marty M. Hobgood Weber, conversation with author, Marian Poeppelmeyer, 1997.

   —Federal Bureau of Investigation, US Government, Wash., DC, "A Byte Out of History—The Case of the Mysterious Mid-Air Explosion," 12/09/05. https://archives.fbi.gov/archives/news/stories/2005/december/midair_explosion120905.

   —Federal Bureau of Investigation, US Government, Wash., DC, "Famous Cases—Jack Gilbert Graham," accessed March 19, 2019, https://www.fbi.gov/history/famous-cases/jack-gilbert-graham.

   —John Finn J.D., "PDX-Bound Airline was Blown Out of Sky for Mom's Insurance," Accessed June 23, 2019. https://offbeatoregon.com/1711d.united-629-dynamited-on-flight-to-pdx-471/.

   —Curtin, Dave. "Victims En Route to Varied Locations." *The Denver Post* (Denver, Colo.), Oct. 30, 2005. https://www.denverpost.com/2005/10/30/victims-en-route-to-varied-locations/.

   —Curtin, Dave. "Blast was 1st U.S. Air Sabotage. "*The Denver Post* (Denver, Colo.), Oct. 30, 2005. https://denverpost.com/2005/10/30/blast-was-1st-u-s-air-sabotage/.

   —Civic Aeronautics Board, File No. 1-0143, *Accident Investigation Report,* Released May 14, 1956.

Special thanks to Andrew Field, author of *Mainliner Denver*, who gave direct permission to reference his findings. Every attempt has been made to note specific and direct quotes. His meticulous research provides the most detailed and accurate account available. To connect with him: www.andrewfield.com.

Various online sources provide additional information when you search for November 1, 1955, or United Air Lines Flight #629. Direct quotations are cited below.

1. Andrew Field, *Mainliner Denver—the Bombing of Flight 629*, (Boulder, Colorado, Johnson Books, 2005), 15.

2. Ibid, 14.

3. Ibid, 26, 233.

4. Ibid, 19.

5. Ibid, 28.

6. Ibid, 10.

7. *"A Case of 44 Mid-Air Murders,"* Life Magazine, Vol. 39, No. 22, November 28, 1955, 40.

8. Federal Bureau of Investigation, US Government, Wash., DC, "Famous Cases—Jack Gilbert Graham," accessed March 19, 2019, https://www. fbi.gov/history/famous-cases/jack-gilbert-graham.

Act II—Through Trauma

Scene 11: Fast Forward Forty Years

1. God, the Creator of the Universe—God in the Bible and in the Christian faith—relates to man as Three Persons in One God. The Christian faith calls this mystery the Holy Trinity: God the Father, God the Son, and God the Holy Spirt. All three interact with humankind and serve various roles, yet remain one God, seated on high in heaven. Throughout the pages of my search to find my father, I took the liberty to interchange all God's titles—God, the Father, Jesus, Jesus Christ, the Holy Spirit—and including Lord, the Almighty Counselor, and other Biblical names for the one true God. Since this is not a theological dissertation, my intent is not to spur debate, but hope the readers will discover the character of God as they read how He chose to mend my brokenness and learn how much He loves everyone.

Scene 16: Determined Resolution

1. To ensure there is no misunderstanding, believers in Jesus Christ cannot be possessed by demons/evil spirits. Christians can be tormented, intimidated, and harassed by the demonic world, but not possessed. Once in Christ, the Holy Spirit indwells the person and they are a new creation in Christ Jesus. In this alternate realm, the demonic beings were ON me, not in me, only sent to harass and intimidate me. Thus, I was not possessed, but oppressed from the enemy of our souls. The topic of spiritual warfare within Christianity attracts many controversial beliefs, models for deliverance, and can incite needless fear in the hearts of many if not approached properly—both for the individual receiving healing and for those ministering to them. For the purposes of sharing my story, I want to establish from which viewpoint I am writing. In the Bible, the Greek word "daimonizomai" is poorly translated as "possession." According to the Thayer Bible Lexicon, daimonizomai means to be under the power of a demon, as opposed to being possessed. (https://www.biblestudytools.com/lexicons/greek/kjv/daimonizomai.html). According to the Mounce Interlinear New Testament, a more accurate translation would be "to be afflicted or vexed by a demon or evil spirit." (https://biblegateway.com/passage/?search=Matthew%204:23-25&version=MOUNCE).

   Once a person turns from doing life their own way and asks forgiveness from Jesus Christ, Jesus not only forgives their sins, but the Holy Spirit makes them a new creation in Christ and dwells within the person forever. The New Testament book of Colossians provides an in-depth look at who a believer is in Christ, what the believer possesses because of Christ's work on the cross and resurrection, and how Christ disarmed the powers and authorities [referencing demonic powers], He made them a spectacle of them, triumphing over them by the cross. (see Colossians 2:14). The demonic entities knew this, and in my encounter, they fled at just the Presence of Jesus.

2. Andy Park continues as a musician, worship leader, and songwriter, with over 120 worship songs written. *We Will Ride* was a popular worship song in the 1990s and words are used with permission. The song was inspired from the image of Jesus riding on his White Horse with the saints in Revelations 19:11-14 (MEV): *I saw heaven opened. And there was a white horse. He who sat on it is called Faithful and True, and in righteousness He judges and wages war. His eyes are like a flame of fire, and on His head are many crowns. He has a name written, that no one knows but Himself. He is clothed with a robe dipped in blood. His name is called The Word of God. The armies in heaven, clothed in fine linen, white and clean, followed Him on white horses.* Connect with Andy Park at https://www.andypark.ca.

Notes

Scene 17 – Babies, Mothers, and Trauma

1. Laura C. Schulz, "The Dutch Hunger Winter and the Developmental Origins of Health and Disease." *Proceedings of the National Academy of Sciences.* National Academy of Sciences of the United States of America, (September 28, 2010):107 (39). 1675716758. https://doi.org/10.1073/pnas.1012911107.

2. Dr. Florentine and Daniela Lebit, PhD, Obstetrics and Gynecology and Professor, and Dr. Rada Vladareanu, PhD, Obstetrics and Gynecology. "The Role of 4D Ultrasound in the Assessment of Fetal Behavior." *Maedica—Journal of Clinical Medicine* (April 6, 2011): 120-127.

3. Walsh, Geraldine. "15 Things You Had No Idea Babies Learn in the Womb." *Babygaga*, (blog). March 23, 2017. https://www.babygaga.com/15-things-you-had-no-idea-babies-learn-in-the-womb. In this article, Walsh compiled research and statements from various studies, including quotes from those in the medical and psychological fields.

4. R. Yehuda, *et al.* "Transgenerational Effects of Posttraumatic Stress Disorder in Babies of Mothers Exposed to the World Trade Center Attacks during Pregnancy," *The Journal of Clinical Endocrinology & Metabolism*, Volume 90, Issue 7 (1 July 2005): 4115-4118. https://doi.org/10.1210/jc.2005-0550.

5. Verny, Thomas R., MD, https://trvernymd.com/workshops.

6. NM Talge et al. "Antenatal Maternal Stress and Long-term Effects on Child Neurodevelopment: How and Why," *Journal of Child Psychology and Psychiatry*, (2007 Mar-Apr); 48 (3-4): 245-61; https://www.ncbi.nlm.nih.gov/pubmed/17355398/J Child Psychol Psychiatry.

7. López de Victoria, PhD, Samuel. "Emotional Trauma in the Womb," PsychCentral (blog). July 8, 2018. https://psychcentral.com/blog/emotional-trauma-in-the-womb.

8. P. Thompson, "The Impact of Trauma on the Embryo and Fetus: An Application of the Diathesis—Stress Model and the Neurovulnerability-Neurotoxicity Model," *Journal of Prenatal and Perinatal Psychology and Health*, 19 (1) (2004): 392-402.

9. David B. Chamberlain, "Parental Learning and Memory," *Birth Psychology*. https://birthpsychology.com/article/prenatal-memory-and-learning.

10. Christianne Northrup, MD, Obstetrics and Gynecology, *Mother-Daughter Wisdom: Understanding Crucial Link Between Mothers, Daughters, and Health*, (NY, NY, Bantam Dell, 2005), 66-67.

11. P. Thompson, "The Impact of Trauma on the Embryo and Fetus: An Application of the Diathesis—Stress Model and the Neuro-vulnerability-Neurotoxicity Model," *Journal of Prenatal and Perinatal Psychology and Health,* 19 (1) (2004): 392-402.

12. University of Virginia Medical School, Division of Perceptual Studies, "Prenatal Memories," accessed February 2019. https://med.virginia.edu/preceptualstudies/prenatal-memories.

13. Thomas Verny, MD, and John Kelly, *The Secret Life of the Unborn Child,* (NY, NY Dell Publishing, 1981), 187.

14. David B. Chamberlain, PhD, DHL, *Windows to the Womb—Revealing the Conscious Baby from Conception to Birth,* (Berkley, CA, North Atlantic Books, 2013), 112-114.

15. Ibid, xii.

Scene 19 – A Milestone Breakthrough

1. Connect with Desert Stream Ministries for their mission to churches and to help those who are relationally and sexually broken. https://desertstream.org/introduction/.

Scene 20 – The Fatherless

1. United States Census Bureau. *Majority of Children Live with Two Parents.* Accessed March 22, 2019. www.census.gov/library/stories/2017/08/majority-of-children-live-with-two-parents.

2. Pew Research Center, Fact Tank-News in Numbers, Gretchen Livingston, "About One-Third of U.S. Children are Living with an Unmarried parent," April 27, 2018, accessed June 18, 2019. https://pewresearch.org/fact-tank/2018/04/27/about-one-third-of-U-S-children-are-living-with-an-unmarried-parent/.

3. National Kids Data Center, project of the Annie E. Casey Foundation, "Children in Single-Parent Families by Race in the United States," https://datacenter.kidscount.org/data/tables/107-children-in-single-parent-families-by-race/.

4. Ibid.

5. National Center for Fathering, "The Consequences of Fatherless," Accessed March 22, 2019. www.fathers.com/statistics-and-research/.

6. National Public Radio, Claudio Sanchez, "Poverty, Dropouts, Pregnancy, Suicide: What the Numbers Say About Fatherless Kids," June 18, 2017, accessed June 19, 2019. https://www.npr.org/sections/ed/2017/06/18/5333062607/poverty-dropouts-pregnancy-suicide-what-the-numbers-say-about-fatherless-kids/.

7. Ibid.

8. Beth M. Erickson, PhD, *Longing for Dad—Father Loss and Its Impact,* (Deerfield Beach, Fla., Health Communications, Inc, 1998), 110.

9. Denna D. Babul, RN and Karin Luse, PhD, *The Fatherless Daughter Project—Understanding our Losses and Reclaiming our Lives,* (NY, NY, Penguin Random House, 2016), 9-10. https://fatherlessdaughterproject.com/.

10. Ibid, 10.

11. Ibid, 10-11.

12. The National Fatherhood Initiative, "Father Facts," Accessed May 1, 2019. www.fatherhood.org/father-absence-statistic.

13. John Finch with Blake Atwood, *The Father Effect—Hope and Healing from a Dad's Absence,* (NY, NY, FaithWords, Hachette Book Group, 2017), 141-153. For additional resources and to view 12-minute short documentary, *The Father Effect.* Connect at: https://www.thefathereffect.com. Full length documentary available.

14. Ronald C. Warren, *Bad Dads of the Bible,* (Grand Rapids, MI, Zondervan, 2013), 16.

    Additional Recommended Reading on the Effects of Fatherlessness:

    Rick Evans, *Healing an Orphan Heart – I will not leave you orphans, I will come to you. "—Jesus,* (Rick Evans, 2016) www.orphanheartministry.org

    The Fatherless Generation, "Statistics," https://thefatherlessgeneration.wordpress.com/statistics.

Scene 21 – A Father Surprise

1. The subjects of heaven and the glory of God have evoked centuries of discussion. My intent is not to enter theological debates, rather to share what I saw and heard to encourage others that there is nothing that compares with the glory of the Presence of God.

   Notes on the Transfiguration of Jesus, Heaven, the Glory of God: According to Matthew 17:2 and Mark 9: 2, Jesus took three of his disciples, Peter, John and James, up a high mountain and revealed His glorious body before them, called the transfiguration. Moses and Elijah then appeared with Jesus. In the Matthew account, Jesus' face shone like the sun and his clothes as white as light. In the Mark account, Jesus' clothes became dazzling white, whiter than anyone in the world could bleach them. This version says it so well, *His garments became shiny, extremely white as snow, such as no launderer on earth could whiten them.* (Mark 9:3, MEV).

When Jesus told me that I would later see more clearly (apart from the Throne Room with God the Father, everything was silhouetted—both the rest of heaven, my earthly father, and Jesus), I realized had God opened my eyes to see more fully—to behold my dad and Jesus—in their glorious bodies, I may not have ever returned to my earthly body because I simply would not have wanted to leave or perhaps because I wasn't ready to see their resurrected bodies. Instead, as in Matthew 28:18, I received a commission from God to tell others that heaven is real and that the Tree of Everlasting Life waits for them. Scripture speaks of the glory of God numerous times as being a radiant light with indescribable brightness.

Jesus also spoke of Himself as the Light of the World (John 8:12). The Apostle John wrote in 1 John 1:5 (MEV), *This then is the message we have heard from Him and declare to you: God is light, and in Him is no darkness at all.* Heaven will have no darkness or night, and those who are in Christ and with God the Father in heaven will have no need for any lamp or the light of the sun, for the Lord God will give them light, and they will reign forever with Him. (Rev. 22: 5). 2 Corinthians 3:16-18 speaks about how those who turn their lives to Jesus, with unveiled faces as in a mirror, reflect the Lord's glory and are being transformed into His likeness with ever-increasing glory, which comes from the Lord, who is the Holy Spirit. When I had been ushered into the Throne Room of God, I melted into this radiant light and was given a foretaste of what eternal life through the redemption of Jesus Christ is like with the Heavenly Father.

2. Steve Sjogren, *The Day I Died*, (Regal Books, 2006).

Scene 24 – Ripples of Trauma

1. Miller, Don, June 25, 2018. "Building a Story Brand with Donald Miller—Episode 102." Podcast audio. *Why You Need to Pay Attention to Mental Health at Work,* Accessed July 2014. www.stitcher.com/podcast/storybrand/building-a-story-brand-with-donald-miller-helping-you-clarify [note: Dr. Lee Norton, expert on trauma, interview with Don Miller].

2. 9news Web Team, "50 years later: First NBSP Commercial Plane Bombing in U.S. History," October 13, 2005, Accessed June 23, 2019. Https://

www.9news.com/article/news/local/50-years-later-firstnbspcommercial-plane-bombing-in-us-history/73-344677379.

3. Miller, Don, June 25, 2018. "Building a Story Brand with Donald Miller—Episode 102." Podcast audio. *Why You Need to Pay Attention to Mental Health at Work,* Accessed July 2014. www.stitcher.com/podcast/storybrand/building-a-story-brand-with-donald-miller-helping-you-clarify [note: Dr. Lee Norton, expert on trauma, interview with Don Miller].

4. Ibid.

5. Govt. of Virginia, https://www.ptsd.va.gov/understand/common/common_veterans.asp.

6. Miller, Don, June 25, 2018. "Building a Story Brand with Donald Miller—Episode 102." Podcast audio. *Why You Need to Pay Attention to Mental Health at Work,* Accessed July 2014. www.stitcher.com/podcast/storybrand/building-a-story-brand-with-donald-miller-helping-you-clarify [note: Dr. Lee Norton, expert on trauma, interview with Don Miller].

Additional notes and to learn more about Dr. Lee Norton, go to:

https://www.centerfortraumatherapy.com/mass-casualty-events/.

https://www.grammy.com/musicares/news/musicares-partner-profile-dr-lee-nortons-lifesaving-trauma-work.

Scene 25 – Repercussions of Sin

1. Wayne Grudem, *Systematic Theology—An Introduction to Biblical Doctrine,* (Intervarsity Press and Zondervan Publishing, 1994), 490.

2. Millie McCarty, M.A., LPCC, *Pathways to Hope & Healing—Getting to the Root of it All,* (Pickerington, Ohio, International Institute for Abuse Counseling Publication, 2002), 152.

3. Denna D. Babul, RN and Karin Luse, PhD, *The Fatherless Daughter Project—Understanding our Losses and Reclaiming our Lives,* (NY, NY, Penguin Random House, 2016), 11. https://fatherlessdaughterproject.com.

4. Ibid, 11.

Scene 26 – Well-Diggers Anonymous

1. Gendry Sebastien, "Laughter Online University," Accessed June 15, 2018. www.LaughterOnlineUniversity.com/research.

2. Mayo Clinic, "Positive Thinking," Accessed June 1, 2018. https://www.mayoclinic.org/healthy-lifestyle/stress-management/in-depth/positive-thinking/art-20043950.

3. John Hopkins University, "The Power of Positive Thinking," Accessed June 2, 2018. https://www.hopkinsmedicine.org/health/healthy_aging/healthy_mind/the-power-of-positive-thinking/.

4. Harvard University, "Optimistic Women Live Longer and Healthier," Accessed May 28, 2018. https://news.harvard.edu/gazette/story/2016/12/optimistic-women-live-longer-and-healthier/.

Scene 27 – The Hook of Anger and Hate

1. Strong, Debbie, "7 Ways Anger is Ruining Your Health," *Everyday Health*. May 29, 2015. www.everydayhealth.com/news/ways-anger-ruining-your-health.

2. Staicie ML, Cutor M., "Anger and Health Risk Behaviors," *Journal of Medicine and Life*, Carol Davila University Press (November 25, 2010).

3. Larkin KT, Zayfert C., "Anger Expression and Essential Hypertension: Behavioral Response to Confrontation," *Journal of Psychosomatic Research*, Vol. 56, Issue 1 (January 2004): 113-118.

4. Don Colbert, MD, *Deadly Emotions: Understand the Mind-Body-Spirit Connection that Can Heal or Destroy You*, (Nashville, TN, Thomas Nelson, 2003), x.

5. Caroline Leaf, PhD, *Who Switched off My Brain?* (Texas, Caroline Leaf, PhD, 2007), 74-77.

Epilogue

1. Leslie Weatherhead, *The Will of God*, (Whitmore and Stone, 1954). My mother kept their original book, costing $.52, safely in her box. Upon opening it, my father's notes in pencil remain legible.

2. Rozeman, Martin, "A Daughter's Search for her Father." Photos by Michael Barber. *Suburban Newspaper, Hilliard Northwest News* (Columbus, Ohio), February 26, 1997, 20-21.

About the Author

Marian Poeppelmeyer possesses a fervent passion to see others living fully free as God intended. As an author, speaker, and coach, she helps others connect with God, explore their gifts, dream big, and blaze new trails.

Out of her pain of trauma, loss, and brokenness, she understands not only the healing process but also the importance of making each day count to always spread the hope and joy within her wherever she goes.

Marian has devoted years to reaching out to the homeless, immigrants, and inner-city communities. Among her many hats worn through the years in public administration, non-profit, and for-profit sectors, she has also served as manager over volunteers and community liaison for hospice patients in a ten-county region.

Marian and her husband have two grown children with wonderful spouses and one grandchild. She refers to herself as being just a mother in tennis shoes and enjoys a great cup of coffee with friends.

Available for coaching, workshops, and speaking events.

Connect at:

MarianPoeppelmeyer.com

*Marian
Poeppelmeyer*

invites you to embark on your

Road to Freedom

Connect at:

MarianPoeppelmeyer.com

FREEDOM. LIFE. JOY.

Got a story inside you?

Author Academy Elite could be the perfect choice for helping you write, publish, and market your book.

Discover more at:

www.6figurebooks.com

CPSIA information can be obtained
at www.ICGtesting.com
Printed in the USA
LVHW081037311019
635534LV00016B/77/P

9 781640 856295